Changing Images of Civil Society

Civil society has become one of the key parts of the reference framework for governance, seeking to replace traditional public action in which representative democracy is combined with bureaucratic implementation. The success of the civil-society myth contrasts with and consequently manifests itself in the problems of political and social legitimacy and representation.

This book assesses the shift in the meaning and application of civil society, from citizen protests to its incorporation into public action. It examines the diversity of interpretations and uses of civil society in different political contexts and seeks to understand the reasons for its surfacing and its multiple forms in political discourse. The authors critically analyse and compare how different types of regimes in countries such as Italy, France and the UK, Poland and Czechoslovakia, South Africa, China, India and Chile have incorporated or otherwise responded to the new discourse.

Analysing the surfacing and uses of civil society, this book will be of interest to students and scholars of political science, analysts, policy-makers, non-profit think tanks and organisations interested in comparative international studies on the third sector.

Bruno Jobert is a senior researcher (emeritus) at the Centre National de la Recherche Scientifique, France. **Beate Kohler-Koch** is Professor at the International Graduate School of the Social Sciences, Bremen, and former Chair for International Relations and European Affairs at the University of Mannheim, Germany.

Routledge studies in governance and public policy

Changing Images of Civil Society

From protest to governance

**Edited by Bruno Jobert and
Beate Kohler-Koch**

Routledge
Taylor & Francis Group

LONDON AND NEW YORK

First published 2008
by Routledge
2 Park Square, Milton Park, Abingdon, Oxon, OX14 4RN

Simultaneously published in the USA and Canada
by Routledge
270 Madison Ave, New York NY 10016

Routledge is an imprint of the Taylor & Francis Group, an informa business

Transferred to Digital Printing 2010

Typeset in Times by Wearset Ltd, Boldon, Tyne and Wear

British Library Cataloguing in Publication Data
A catalogue record for this book is available from the British Library

Library of Congress Cataloging in Publication Data
Changing images of civil society: from protest to government/edited by Bruno Jobert and Beate Kohler-Koch.
p. cm. – (Routledge studies in governance and public policy; 11)
Includes bibliographical references and index.
1. Civil society. 2. Civil society–Case studies. I. Jobert, Bruno. II. Kohler-Koch, Beate, 1941–
JC337.C527 2008
300–dc22   2007052259

ISBN 10: 0-415-46614-8 (hbk)
ISBN 10: 0-415-58666-6 (pbk)
ISBN 10: 0-203-89475-8 (ebk)

ISBN 13: 978-0-415-46614-1 (hbk)
ISBN 13: 978-0-415-58666-5 (pbk)
ISBN 13: 978-0-203-89475-0 (ebk)

Contents

Illustrations

Figures

Tables

Contributors

Jacques de Maillard is Professor of Political Science at the University of Rouen and researcher at PACTE (Grenoble). His main research interests are crime prevention policies at the local level and justice and home affairs policies at the European Union level. He recently published *Réformer l'action publique*, 2004, and co-edited (with A. Smith) 'Union européenne et sécurité intérieure: institutionnalisation et fragmentation', *Politique européenne*, 23, 2007.

Stefanie Edler-Wollstein has studied Political Science at The University of Mannheim and The Johns Hopkins University, Baltimore. She has worked on questions of ethnicity and nationalism.

John K. Glenn is Director of Foreign Policy at the German Marshall Fund of the United States, and a visiting scholar at the Paul H. Nitze School of Advanced International Studies of The Johns Hopkins University. He is the author of *Framing Democracy: Civil Society and Civic Movements in Eastern Europe*, 2001, and co-editor of *The Power and Limits of NGOs: A Critical Look at Building Democracy in Eastern Europe and Eurasia*, 2002, as well as numerous articles in scholarly journals and publications.

Thomas Heberer is Professor of Political Science/East Asian Politics at the University of Duisburg-Essen, Germany with long-term experience in China. Among his recent publications in English are: *Doing Business in Rural China. Liangshan's New Ethnic Entrepreneurs*, 2007; *Rural China, Economic and Social Change in the Late Twentieth Century*, 2006 (with Jie Fan and Wolfgang Taubmann); *The Power of Ideas. Intellectual Input and Political Change in East and Southeast Asia*, 2006 (with Claudia Derichs, ed.); and *Private Entrepreneurs in China and Vietnam. Social and Political Functioning of Strategic Groups*, 2003.

Bruno Jobert is senior researcher at the CNRS. He works in PACTE, a research centre attached to the Institut d'Études Politiques of Grenoble. He has worked on the role of discourses and ideas in public policies. See *Létat en action*, 1987 (with Pierre Muller); *Le tournant neo libéral en Europe*, 1994 (with Jacques Commaille, eds); *Les métamorphoses de la régulation politique*, 1998.

Beate Kohler-Koch is Professor at the International Graduate School of the Social Sciences, Bremen, and former Chair for International Relations and European Affairs at The University of Mannheim. She is coordinator of the Network of Excellence 'CONNEX' on Efficient and Democratic Governance in a Multi-level Europe. She has published widely on European integration and EU governance. Her most recent publications include *The 'Governance Turn' in EU Studies*, 2006 (with B. Rittberger); *The Institutional Shaping of EU-Society Relations: A Contribution to Democracy via Participation*, 2007 (with B. Finke); *Debating the Democratic Legitimacy of the European Union*, 2007 (edited with B. Rittberger); *A Decade of Research on EU Multi-level Governance*, forthcoming 2008 (edited with F. Larat).

Alfio Mastropaolo is Professor at the University of Turin and Director of the Department of Political Studies. He published extensively on the crisis of Italian democracy, on populism and antipolitics. See *Antipolica, L'Ancora*, 2000; *La mucca pazza della democrazia. Nuove destre, populismo, antipolitica*, 2004; *Il Parlamento. Le assemble legislative nelle democrazie contemporanee*, 2005 (with L. Verzichelli).

Hélène Michel is maître de conferences in political science at the University of Lille II and researcher at the Groupe de Sociologie Politique Européenne (GSPE-PRISME), laboratory of Sciences Po Strasbourg. Her main research deals with interest groups and the policy of European institutions toward civil society. She recently published *Lobbyistes et lobbying de l'Union européenne*, 2005. She also contributed to *Déloye, Dictionnaire des élections européennes/Encyclopaedia of European Elections*, 2006.

Konstantinos Papadakis is a researcher at the International Institute for Labour Studies (IILS) of the International Labour Organisation (ILO, Geneva). His recent publications include: *Civil Society, Participatory Governance and Decent Work Objectives: the Case of South Africa*, 2006, and 'Socially sustainable development and participatory governance: legal and political aspects' (Discussion Paper), 2006.

Yannis Papadopoulos is Professor of Public Policy at the University of Lausanne. He recently co-edited with Arthur Benz, *Governance and Democracy: National, European and International Perspectives*, 2006. He is also co-editor with Philippe Warin of a special issue of the *European Journal of Political Research* on 'Innovative, participatory, and deliberative procedures in policy-making: democratic and effective?', and with Arthur Benz and Carol Harlow of a special issue of the *European Law Journal* on 'Accountability in the EU multi-level system', 2007.

Per Selle is Professor of Comparative Politics at the University of Bergen in Norway. Among his publications are 'Limits of civil society voluntary organizations, and the Norwegian welfare state: from mutual trust to contracting?' 2003 (with Magne Eikås); 'Participation and social capital formation:

Norway in comparative perspective?', 2003 (with Dag Wollebæk) and 'Age and generation: patterns of associational fertility and survival', 2007 (with Sigrid Roßteutscher and Lucia Medina).

Raúl Urzúa is Professor of Sociology of the University of Chile and director of the Centre for Public Policies. He is the author of *Fault-lines in Democratic Governance*, 1998 (with F. Aguero); *Urban Poverty and Decentralization*, 1997 (with D. Palma), and *Social Change and Public Policies*, 1997. His current main research area is the impact of economic globalisation on the state, society and public policies at the local level.

Dag Wollebæk is a PhD student of comparative politics at the University of Bergen in Norway. He has previously published two books (in Norwegian) and numerous articles on voluntary organisations, social capital and civil society. Among his recent publications are: 'The origins of social capital: socialisation and institutionalisation approaches compared' (with Per Selle, *Journal of Civil Society*, 2007) and 'Voluntary associations, trust and civic engagement: a multi-level approach' (with Kristin Strømsnes, forthcoming in *Nonprofit and Voluntary Sector Quarterly*).

Preface

This book analyses the rise and metamorphosis of civil society, a subject which has in recent years taken its place in political discourse internationally, as reported by many observers. In Spain, for example, the return of civil society was celebrated by Victor Perez Diaz (1993) who showed how the development of the market, contracts and associations had paved the way for a return to democracy. Cohen and Arato (1992), combining the experiences of the new left in the West with those of dissidents in the East, heralded the advent of civil society as a third sector alongside the market and the state. For John Keane (1998), the return of civil society corresponds not only to the failures of state-centred models but also to a breach in the very foundations of social order. Keane's work, which presents a synthesis of the diffusion of the civil-society theme throughout the world, views civil society as embodying a pacific pluralism, constituting the end of society based on a single principle.

Leading thinkers have incorporated the idea: Michel Foucault pleaded for the need to 'listen to civil society'. Others (e.g. Rosanvallon 2004) have announced 'the age of self-management', a socialism freed from vested bureaucratic interests. In Germany, Jürgen Habermas (1997) and Ulrich Beck (1996), each in his own way, have called for a civil society that transcends the frame of traditional dialogue between states, parties and social partners. Robert Putnam (Putnam 2000; Pharr and Putnam 1992) has analysed civic disengagement in the United States, associating it with the concept of social capital, a minimalist version of civil society.

The proliferation of academic writings on civil society should not cause us to forget that it is to political and social militants that we owe the resurrection of this term. Polish dissidents inspired by Gramsci claimed to undermine state power through the conquest of hegemony. Grassroots communities in Latin America made self-organisation and solidarity the driving force of their opposition to dictatorship. Elsewhere in the Western world, the self-management myth sustained the hopes of a left that had lost its faith in the virtues of a planned economy.

The alter-globalisation and radical left speaks tenderly of civil society, as the following excerpt from a letter by Mexican Zapatistas attests: 'initially this letter was supposed to be a communiqué but we have chosen this option because, for better or for worse, every time we have spoken to you, dear civil society, we have done so in a personal tone' (letter from the Zapatista Army of National Liberation to civil society, 21 June 2005). But this darling of the guerrillas must surely have other charms, for elsewhere municipalities and governments hardly suspected of leftist leanings also invoke and recruit personalities from civil society, new heroes in suits from diverse backgrounds, ranging from entrepreneurs to activists in non-profit associations or humanitarian organisations. The World Bank and IMF likewise share the same devotion to civil society as the radical left in the World Social Forums.

In the name of good governance civil society is becoming an expanding industry that guarantees the prosperity of various consultants and collaborators: civil-society organisation officers, engineers in social capital, artisans of participative budgets and assisted deliberation, experts in social development, promoters of democracy and multicultural participation, instruments of empowerment. New institutions are appearing, including various forums and specialised agencies in international institutions. Others, such as NGOs and think tanks, are flourishing throughout the world.

Few critiques of civil society are as direct as those expressed by European sovereignist MPs 'Brussels talks to Brussels': 'The convention is supposed to listen to civil society, but here civil society consists above all of lobbyists paid by European institutions themselves' (press conference of the Forum for Democracy, 27 June 2002, www.autre-europe.org). Witness the neo-conservative movements which, despite their extreme scepticism regarding organised interest groups, rely just as much on a strong network of think tanks and foundations to spread their new gospel. Indeed, most ideological currents have their own connection to civil society, which inhibits the expression of a global critique on the subject. Therefore, the subject of our research is precisely that diversity of approaches and their use in different political contexts.

In current discourse civil society seems to be what sociologists of science call a boundary object, that is, one of:

> those objects that both inhabit several communities of practice and satisfy the informational requirements of each of them. Boundary objects are thus both plastic enough to adapt to the local needs and constraints of the several parties employing them, yet robust enough to maintain a common identity across sites. They are weakly structured in common use and become strongly structured in individual-site use. The objects may be abstract or concrete ... Such objects have different meanings in different social worlds but their structure is common enough to more than one world to make them recognisable, a means of translation. The creation and management of boundary objects is a key process in developing and maintaining coherence across intersecting communities.
>
> (Bowker and Star 1999)

The choice of this metaphor reflects the purpose of our book, which is to account for the diversity of interpretations and uses of civil society. We therefore distinguish our approach from the three main currents of research on the subject. Our intention is not to add yet another volume to the many books on political theory, written to determine the real nature of civil society since its invention during the Enlightenment. Nor is our objective one of social engineering, like those who aim to promote as well as to evaluate deliberation and the participation of civil-society organisations in public action (Blondiaux and Sintomer 2002; Callon *et al.* 2001; Fung and Wright 2001).

Instead of analysing the meanings of civil society per se, as many authors do, we endeavour to understand how it is articulated in political and policy discourses. The starting point of the book is that the success of the civil society myth contrasts with and consequently manifests itself in the problems of political and social legitimacy and representation. In totalitarian states which claimed to shape society to suit their ideology, civil society embodied citizens' ability to articulate values and to organise themselves outside of the state. Later, it was the wide disenchantment with existing forms of democracy that fuelled the emergence of civil society. We show, however, that in this respect we cannot settle for generalisations. Processes of de-legitimisation of existing institutions in the name of civil society need to be analysed in detail. For instance, the processes that characterise the Italian political party crisis are not the same as those associated with the democratic deficit of European institutions. The prophets of civil society promise 'a deepening of democracy', one that is more dialogical (Giddens 1998), more deliberative (Callon *et al.* 2001) and more open (Fung and Wright 2001). We posit that these developments should be understood above all as a response to unresolved problems of legitimacy. Moreover, the definitions of these problems themselves differ, depending on political orientations: civil society takes the form of a number of different reference frameworks in widely diverse contexts.

The project was initiated by Bruno Jobert, but the book is the result of a collaborate effort. Scholars gathered in a working group organised within the European Network of Excellence CONNEX (Connecting Excellence on European Governance), directed by Beate Kohler-Koch. In two sessions in Paris, in April 2005 and March 2006, a common framework of analysis was elaborated to compare systems as different as Norway, Italy, France, the UK, China, India, South Africa and Chile. It was not difficult to persuade colleagues, who were both country experts and well-versed with the more theoretical debate on civil society and framing, to contribute to the project. But, as usual, time constraints impeded some of our colleagues to supply a chapter to the book. We are, nevertheless, very grateful for their participation. In close cooperation we as editors selected the final contributors and with the invaluable support of Stefanie Edler-Wollstein, we engaged in close communication with all our authors to produce a coherent volume.

In our meetings, when we discussed our research in depth, our observation was confirmed that these interpretations of civil society are the subject of debates transcending national borders. The chapters are structured around the leading hypothesis that the return to civil society might be interpreted as a response to unresolved problems of political legitimacy. The introductory chapter of the book, by Bruno Jobert, develops this framework in its analytical and ideological dimensions. The case studies elaborate the central theme in detail. The concluding chapter by Stefanie Edler-Wollstein and Beate Kohler-Koch presents an analytical evaluation scheme to assess similarities and differences when comparing the distinct cases.

We would like to thank all participants of the two workshops for their useful insights and, above all, the authors for providing valuable and interesting contributions. Moreover, we want to thank Stefanie Edler-Wollstein who greatly contributed to the successful completion of this book. She did not just act as a language editor but also contributed considerably to the improvement of the manuscripts. Last, but not least, we want to acknowledge that without the support of CONNEX this research cooperation would not have been possible.

Bruno Jobert and Beate Kohler-Koch
Grenoble and Mannheim, 2008

References

Beck, U. (1996) *The Reinvention of Politics. Rethinking Modernity in the Global Social Order*, Cambridge: Polity Press, 216.
Beck, U. and Giddens, A. (1994) *Reflexive Modernization*, Stanford: Stanford University Press.
Blondiaux, L. and Sintomer, Y. (2002) 'L'impératif délibératif', *Politix* 15 (57).
Bowker, G.C. and Star, S.L. (1999) *Sorting Things Out: Classification and its Consequences*, Cambridge: MIT Press.
Callon, M., Lascoumes, P. and Barthes, Y. (2001) *Agir dans un monde incertain. Essai sur la démocratie technique*, Paris: Seuil.
Cohen, J.L. and Arato, A. (1992) *Civil Society and Political Theory*, Cambridge: MIT Press.
Fung, A. and Wright, E.O. (2001) 'Deepening democracy: innovations in empowered participation governance', *Politics and Society*, 29 (1).
Giddens, A. (1998) *The Third Way and the Renewal of Social Democracy*, Cambridge: Polity Press.
Habermas, J. (1997) *Droit et démocratie*, Paris: Gallimard.
Keane, J. (1998) *Civil Society, Old Images, New Visions*, Stanford: Stanford University Press.
Perez Diaz, V. (1993) *The Return of Civil Society*, Cambridge: Harvard University Press.
Pharr, S.J. and Putnam, R.D. (1992) *Disaffected Democracies*, Princeton: Princeton University Press.
Putnam, R.D. (2000) *Bowling Alone: The Collapse and Revival of American Community*, New York: Simon and Schuster.
Rosanvallon, P. (2004) *Le modèle politique français: la société civile contre le jacobinisme de 1789 à nos jours*, vol. 1 (L'Univers historique), Paris: Seuil.

Part I
Civil society and politics
Contending frameworks and democratic deficits

1 Contending civil-society frameworks

Beyond the tutelary model

Bruno Jobert

Porto Allegre, the beacon city of alter-globalization, pioneer in the establishment of a participatory budget, has entered the World Bank's catalogue of good practices designed to increase the influence of the poor. This encounter has consecrated the unexpected alliance between macroeconomic orthodoxy and social radicalism – provided that the latter is confined to local management. It is based on civic discourses in which the civil society theme is both predominant and entirely ambiguous. This chapter proposes some references for understanding the variety of representations of civil society in civic discourses. After a short introduction in which the key concepts are presented, we propose four ideal types of civil frame.

Civil frame

Discourse on civil society relates to vast philosophical or ideological controversies, from Locke, Fergusson, Hegel or Tocqueville to the current debate on deliberation, initiated by Habermas. In this respect, research on civil society relates to the conditions of the formation and practice of a political community, based not on tradition but on the free association of individuals. From this point of view, it furthers reflection on the horizontal relations allowing such free association. These relations are based on contracts. The rule of law is not imposed by an outside sovereign, it is produced on the basis of agreement between people. This agreement derives its legitimacy from the fact that it is the outcome of deliberation, free of the constraints and influences of particular interests. Through debates between peers, civil society can produce a vision of the common welfare, grounded in agreement on the principles of justice.

Discourse on civil society aims to transcend an approach to politics focused on the adjustment between interests through negotiation and compromise. The idea is to produce an image of a political community based on rational communication between equals. The utopian nature of this discourse explains why the civil society theme has often been mobilized as opposition discourse. Civil society provides a normative frame that can serve to denounce governmental practices based on unilateral action by policy-makers. It suggests a potential for self-organization by citizens, that is independent of the state and political representations. This supposed ability to transcend existing institutional barriers explains the appeal of civil society rhetoric to various social and political movements.

The return of civil society has been announced and promoted as a key topic by opponents to authoritarian regimes, from Latin America to Eastern Europe and beyond. The new social movements have also used it extensively in their demands for a space for public debate that is no longer limited to the state's usual partners (Perez Diaz 1993). The civil-society theme is particularly attractive in so far as it serves to conceal conflicts and differences between the diverse components of 'civil society'. The mythical unity created thus serves as a powerful tool for criticizing opponents in the struggle to open the public sphere.

However, when it comes to government action, it proves to be far more difficult to maintain. Government action requires trade-offs between the claims of groups and sectors that have been federated for the accession to power. The political rhetoric that prepares the conquest of power is characterized by ambiguity and *soft* ideas. By contrast, the actual conduct of public policies involves processes of selection and ranking that necessarily undermine some of the ambiguity of political debate. Discourse on civil society is no exception to the rule. On the public scene it is a powerful myth with multiple actions, a symbol of citizens' resistance. In the public-policy sphere, mobilization of civil society is embodied in various frames put to the service of opposing global strategies.

The purpose of this chapter is to present several references and hypotheses for the study of these frames of civil involvement. We propose four types of frame, corresponding to separate answers to the three basic questions that pertain to the understanding of contending concepts of civil society:

1   the role of politics in the constitution of civil society;
2   the modalities of involvement of civil-society organizations in government action;
3   the conditions of rehabilitation of civil society when it has been disrupted.

Before considering the four ideal types, a few comments on the questions are called for. Civil society derives its legitimacy from its self-organization. Citizens unite ad hoc to deliberate and put forward their views of the public interest. Yet, even the most symbolic examples of a spontaneous appearance of civil society suggest that its birth cannot be conceived independently of politics and socializing institutions. Can the rise of Solidarnosc be explained without reference to the Catholic Church's support? Can the Orange Revolution be explained independently of policies to export democracy that provided protest organizations with resources and know-how?

Political authority has a wide range of instruments to act on the constitution of civil-society organizations. Access to public policy forums is often contingent on the organization's recognition, which is also the first step in a process of incorporation into public action. This ranges from subsidies to consultation and, finally, direct involvement in policy implementation. Through a handling of these public-policy instruments, the state can influence the selection, reinforcement or weakening of currents running through civil society. The criteria applied to this channelling are a discriminatory element of the typology of frames established below.

Civil involvement policies – the second key question to differentiate the four models of civil-society concepts – can be analysed in terms of three dimensions: the policy sector, the relation to knowledge, and the relation to interests. The definition of public-policy arenas, which by their nature defy any civil involvement, is a key element in the understanding of these policies. When an independent central bank opens forums to civil society, the idea is certainly more to convey transparency on its functioning to the public, than to open channels of influence on its monetary policy. Likewise, introducing neighbourhood participatory practices may well be combined with the closure of macroeconomic policy-making arenas. That is why civil involvement policies must be understood in context, or in other words, the significance of individual civil-society involvement emerges only when looking at the process as a whole.

The relationship to knowledge is the second dimension of civil involvement policies. Here, the proposition is twofold, either to mobilize the ordinary citizen's wisdom, or to draw on the original experience of the concerned citizen. Citizen's wisdom is systematized by procedures of assisted deliberation, such as citizen juries. In situations in which negotiation between interests leads to stalemate, where controversies are exhausted in mutual misunderstanding, these procedures call on ordinary, non-militant citizens in the hope that, once informed, they will be able to outline some form of agreement. An emblematic example relying on the experience of the concerned citizen are patient organizations. What is at issue in involvement policy is the taking into account of a unique experience that is sometimes difficult to communicate to the ordinary citizen. Moreover, patients' participation is a basic dimension of their cure and of the control of epidemics. It implies extensive reshuffling of relations between the medical profession and patients/citizens.

The relationship with organized interests is the third dimension to differentiate between the types of civil involvement policies. The question of civil-society involvement generally comes into play when existing forms of mediation – by political representatives or social partners – are weakened or threatened. Depending on the strategy, civil involvement policies will aim either at replacing former modes of mediation or at supporting them by incorporating new partners in the public arena. In the former situation, the promotion of proximity management by NGOs may go hand-in-hand with the decline of trade unions. In the latter, an organized civil society embracing churches and non-profit organizations along with the trade unions is mobilized in social dialogue.

The question of reparation or of rehabilitation of a disintegrating civil fabric is the third question guiding our typology of civil society. It is crucial if we are to understand the emergence of civil frames. A programme is not imposed as a frame simply on the basis of its arguments. First the former frame, undermined by its incapacity to provide the tools and symbols likely to respond to a new situation, has to be delegitimized. We will see that there is a direct link between the proposed diagnosis of the crisis and the civil frames set up. This diagnosis of crisis often refers to dysfunctions in the political realm but it might relate also to failures in the social fabric itself, as elaborated in the social capital literature from Putnam to Van Deth.

As we will show, the neo-conservative model is fed by dysfunctions of the tutelary modernization model. The various 'Third Ways' are themselves answers to the ills spawned by neo-conservatism. The integrative model emerges from transformations to the neo-corporatist/social democratic model.

The tutelary modernization model

Up to a few decades ago, a model of tutelary modernization prevailed in Western Europe, where the governments relied on professional elites and bureaucratic corporations for the conduct of policies. This hegemony of professional elites strictly defined the game of civil society. It corresponds to the phase of economic growth and the spread of the welfare state in the post-Second World War years.

The wage standard in the constitution of civil society

In the tutelary modernization model, a strong belief in the progress of growth promotes the structuring of civil society around producers. Social democracy, for example, is organized around the protagonists of *wage* relations, which extend to all spheres of social life (Castell 1995). All public resources go into the organization of this wage society: the recognition of representatives of civil-society organizations paving the way for a monopoly of representation, and systems of social negotiations and co-management, especially in the field of social welfare systems. This allows the exchange of substantial resources between the social partners. In this model, one of the main functions of civil-society organizations is to socialize and recruit the activists to a neo-corporatist system of interest intermediation. In post-Second World War France, for example, the Communist and Catholic Action movements both recruited many of the managers of the social negotiation system.

Civil involvement policies

Despite the inclusion of both sides of industry, this wage-earner democracy is under the control of the state and the professional elite. The social partners are invited, at best, to find global compromises on the production of national wealth, but more often to participate in the processes of social redistribution. In sectoral policies their role is second to the professional experts. The social partners in the national health systems, for instance, are not supposed to question the quality and organization of healthcare.

The emergence of users' associations is also characteristic. A vast array of organizations pioneered in establishing new services (as described aptly by

Pinell and Zafiropoulos (1983) in relation to the care for handicapped children in France). Nevertheless, it is still predominantly the professional elites who define services and needs. Recipients' demands are legitimate and audible only in so far as they can match these administrative and professional definitions of needs. The knowledge required by social representatives, whether they are partners or recipients, is therefore necessarily limited by the tutelary authority of both the state and the professions.

The question of the representation of interests is a point of differentiation between several versions of the tutelary model. In the pluralistic, elitist version of the model, the incorporation of interests in public political forums is conditioned by a complex process of recognition and institutionalization that transforms these particular interests into social partners. In the neo-corporatist version of the model the starting point is a highly centralized and disciplined representation of both sides of industry. The authority of these social organizations is based on their capacity to represent and discipline their membership, which makes them equal partners to government. This tripartite system constrains autonomous activities of civil society.

Problems and crises of the tutelary model

The tutelary model comes into crisis when it becomes obvious that its performance does not live up to expectations and violates the very principles on which it is based. Growth does not solve social problems. Poverty is rediscovered in rich countries. Science and technology are no guarantee of continuous progress. Furthermore, neo-corporatism is always in danger of turning into a closed system. This provokes opposition and fuels the emergence of autonomous actions and social movements. This is especially the case when new issues come up and the variety of concerns is not taken into account. This opposition will be voiced by social movements operating outside the system, who are neither capable nor willing to become incorporated.

The first response to the challenge of underperformance is usually a quest for the completion or the expansion of the welfare state. The 'new society' of Chaban-Delmas in France in the early 1970s, for instance, as well as the 'great society' of L.B. Johnson in the United States in the late 1960s, were supposed to respond to left-wing protest by further developing the welfare state. The incorporation of the socially underprivileged was sought through their mobilization. They were encouraged to voice their demands and to become active in the improvement of their living environment. However, the protests not only concerned social rights but highlighted the absurdities of urban planning and housing policies that were decided by experts behind closed doors.

Challenging professional experts has become even more radical in the struggle against nuclear energy and for the ecological cause in general. The tutelary model wavers when doubts arise concerning the universal virtues of productivism and when the large socializing institutions – the church and the parties – lose their aura and their grip on the people.

The neo-conservative model

The neo-conservative model tries to evade the problems of the tutelary model. From a neo-conservative perspective, the state, its representative system and its interest groups are causing the decline of the institutions that form the backbone of society: the family, religion and the fatherland. Under pressure to act in favour of the most underprivileged, the welfare state is said to increase the dependence on welfare, resulting in the demoralizing passivity of the beneficiaries.

In the United States in 1965, the Moynihan report on the African-American family was a turning point in the government's approach to the dynamics of a sustainable civil society. The report claimed that the crisis of African-American ghettos could be associated 'with the breakdown in family structures and the rise of welfare dependency' (Moynihan 1996: 178). This was seen as enforcing social decline which 'among Negro youth had the predictable outcome in a disastrous delinquency and crime rate as well as narcotic offences' (ibid.).

This analysis has often fed the neo-conservatives' argument. To them, the causal relation is obvious: 'If the Irish immigrants in nineteenth century America had something comparable to our present welfare system, there would have been a "welfare explosion" then and a sharp increase in Irish family disorganization too' (Kristol 1999: 49). An additional neo-conservative argument is that the expansion of the welfare state cannot even be attributed to the demands of the beneficiaries themselves: 'This explosion was created by public officials and public employees who were executing public policies as part of the 'war on poverty' (ibid.: 47). According to Kristol, it was these actors, relayed by non-profit organizations, which weakened the reluctance of the poor to accept welfare.

Civil society under control

This explains why the neo-conservative revolution has adopted a very reserved position regarding policies for the promotion of civil society. Turning the theories of collective action into iron laws, they advocate the withdrawal of the state, as well as the decline of the trade unions and of those non-profit organizations that are clients of the state.

The neo-conservatives often undertake strong efforts to convert the public opinion to their ideas, thus making direct and indirect use of public resources, although they generally denounce the perverse effect of public spending for educating people. The willingness to use public money for civic education is most pronounced when the aim is to promote the linked cause of market and democracy. It is paradoxical to see the development of active policies of civil society constitution by the same people who denounce its pitfalls.

Neo-conservative involvement policies: depolitization and client discourse

In the neo-conservative model, the role of civil society is strictly circumscribed. The key strategy consists of breaking up the expansionist coalition formed by the administration, elected officials and interest groups. Rather, three main functions are attributed to civil society in the neo-conservative strategy: the struggle for transparency and against corruption, the controlled management of services, and the promotion of quasi markets in the public sector.

With the agencyfication of public policy, supported by the neo-conservatives, comes the problem of political control. If control is not exercised from above by the government, it must be exerted by stakeholders. An active communication policy is needed to create a public forum. Such fora are not meant to reorient the objectives of the agencies, but rather to ensure administrative accountability. Transparency and publicity are seen as a safeguard against deviant and inefficient behaviour. Shifting the responsibility for the management of certain services to NGOs is often used by neo-conservatives as a means for circumventing public bureaucracies. But these NGO's action capacity is strictly controlled by an elaborate system of evaluation and the strings attached to project and programme funding that limit their leeway, thus facilitating their instrumentalization.

The shift from voice to exit is the third neo-conservative focus of civil society's involvement in public action. Through the establishment of quasi-market mechanisms in the public sector, users are supposed to behave like customers.

Disciplining civil society

The main concern of the conservative revolution is to eradicate the ever growing dependence of individuals on the state because those who are dependent are seen to neglect their duties as citizens and parents. The market fundamentalism (Giddens 1994) developed by neo-conservatives has a moralizing impetus, intending to revive the value of work – 'you will earn your bread by the sweat of your brow' – and the honour of the head of the family by restoring his primary role as a breadwinner.

The civil society envisaged by neo-conservatives is a society embedded in traditional institutions. It is supposed to restore the family as the mainstay of social life and to open a wider field to religious organizations than in more secular times. Family and religion are supposed to retain citizens in a state of deference to the authorities which, in turn, will readily use constraint to obtain respect and obedience.

In this frame, those who have difficulties are requested to be responsible and to manage on their own, rather than asking for aid. The neo-conservatives confine civil society to the struggle against corruption and for transparency and promote strong supervision of individuals by traditional authorities.

The transatlantic Third Way

According to the most eminent theoretician of the Third Way, Anthony Giddens, neo-conservatives are prisoners of an insurmountable contradiction. Through their 'market fundamentalism', they release forces in society that undermine the very same traditional institutions on which they rely to guarantee a viable social order: the nation, religion and the patriarchal family (Giddens 2000). The result is the erosion of civil society by a twofold phenomenon of exit: voluntary exit of the mobile top segment of society who withdraw from a deteriorated public domain, and bottom-up exclusion of those who have neither voice nor exit. In their fight against democracy overload, neo-conservatives are said to produce a large-scale loss of interest in democracy (Pharr and Putnam 2000), which cannot be compensated by a return to paternalism. What is needed is, as Tony Blair put it, 'the construction of a strong civil society in which rights and responsibilities go hand in hand' (in *Le Monde*, 14 November 2002).

Constituting civil society beyond the established social partners

This project to activate civil society is not intended to revive the pillars of the old social democratic order. Tripartite social negotiation is not put on the agenda again. Rather, the aim of activating civil society is to give space to 'social entre-preneurs' who are likely to emerge in societies that are well-endowed with social capital. The Third Way builds its strategy on the potential of civil engagement in post-modern societies. However, there are areas of exclusion in which uncivil behaviour prevails. For these areas, the Third Way claims to create the conditions for the reconstruction of good citizenship. Elsewhere it proposes to channel social movements towards beneficial partnerships.

Activation or instrumentalization of civil society?

The field opened to civil society in the Third Way is broad and narrow at the same time. The field of macroeconomic strategies is not the domain of civil involvement. Recognizing the merits of the economic policies of their neo-liberal predecessors, the advocates of the Third Way, especially in Britain, grant no priority to social dialogue and negotiation between social partners. The domain reserved for civil society is proximity management and implementation, rather than setting policy objectives. The task assigned to civil society is to mobilize detailed knowledge on the social fabric and thanks to its strong capac-ity for adaptation to differentiated demands, to boost 'the excluded', to make the community aware of uncivil abuses, and to revive a widened public sphere. Hence, civil society engagement becomes a substitute for the bureaucratic implementation of public action. Civil society and its avatar, the NGOs, are, thus, a tool for circumventing public administrations and their professional bodies. It remains to be established whether these organizations, so strongly involved in public management, can retain their own mobilizing power and their ability to make an autochthonous message heard – one that is distinct from that of their public tutor.

The Third Way appeals for a reconciliation between social entrepreneurs and economic entrepreneurs and for an activation of society. It has less to say about the role of non-profit organizations in the conduct of policy-making. As to trade unions, its position is one of mistrust, especially in the public sector. The idea of a social pact and negotiated reform among the social partners is not part of the rhetoric in the Third Way's arsenal.

Moral appeal and accountability

In contrast to the downgrading of the social partners, the Third Way puts the empowerment of the disadvantaged at the core of its mission. By doing so, it accentuates a contradiction between insiders and outsiders, between employees who selfishly defend their status and their social welfare, and those who are consequently left with nothing. But the idea of empowerment should not conceal that in this concept rights come with duties. Beneficiaries are made aware that the door is not just open to claims in terms of social rights based on democratic citizenship or in terms of a social debt. Underlying the idea of empowerment is the suspicion of fraud and moral risk. Beneficiaries of social benefits have to prove that they use them responsibly and serve the community in return (Giddens 2000: 52). Hence, the Third Way introduces a system of constraints obliging the socially dependent to become self-supporting again, to return to work and to become involved in the community. The question here is whether the NGOs that are expected to accomplish this task are not caught in the contradictory injunctions between the moralizing tutelary authority and the call for autonomy.

The Third Way concepts, thus, lead to a particular encounter between the precepts of economic orthodoxy and the assertion of a moral imperative to struggle against poverty, all of which pushes the social partners to the margins.

The integrative model

The main focus of our last model is on civil society's role in shaping public interests, rather than on the direct incorporation of civil-society organizations in the policy process or their contribution to public services. The integrative model aims at changing the overall context of the policy-making process through civil-society involvement. It envisages two major transformations: the employment of strategies of empowerment in order to foster the inclusion of weak interests, and the embedding of bargaining and decision-making processes in broader deliberative settings. To this aim, the integrative model invites new interlocutors to the public debate, beyond the usual lobbying networks and the established social partners, and it modifies the rules of interactions in the public sphere. The projected result of public debate is not supposed to be a compromise between particularistic interests, but a negotiated agreement on the public good. The introduction of deliberative procedures in an open public sphere is expected to modify power relations by developing a mutual understanding and reciprocity and, thus, facilitating an autonomous civil society that gives expression to the autochthonous voices of citizens (Habermas 1992; Walzer 1995).

Civil society and the state

The role of the state in relation to civil society comprises two functions: the state intervenes in the constitution of civil-society organizations and it ensures that the public sphere is open to weakly institutionalized movements. Regarding the first function, we can distinguish between various ways of state interference. For instance, as has been documented by Henry Milner (2002), the integration of citizens into the public debate necessitates the state to reinforce the civic competences of the people. In that respect, the high level of what Milner calls 'civic literacy' in social democratic Scandinavian countries is associated with a strong public support of state-supported institutions promoting civic competences, e.g. adult education programmes. In other cases, political agents play an eminent role in the empowerment of underprivileged groups.

Regarding the second function, the state's task to keep the public sphere open to the voices of less institutionalized or less consensual groupings and movements, the state has to ensure a balance between interests that are highly focused and easy to organize, and those that are equally important but less pronounced and more diffuse. This implies a particular dilemma for the integrative model. The predicament is that, quite obviously, the quality of deliberation depends on competent and experienced citizens and, therefore, often tends to be put into practice through established organizations. This entails the danger that the public sphere becomes monopolized by the institutionalized partners while the door remains closed to the bearers of new or different public interests.

Contrasting approaches to the involvement of organized interests in the deliberation process

Proponents of the integrative model have suggested various solutions to resolve the dilemma described above. Some recommend a reform of the deliberation process by incorporating independent voices, which are not bound to entrenched interests, in public debates. This position is adopted by Habermas (1992) who considers the new social movements as major protagonists of the deliberative process.

Other advocates of the integrative model rather stress the importance of the search for new forms of deliberative and bargaining processes. Here we can see some parallels to the social pacts and cooperative governance approach. The integrative model does not share the Third Way model's reluctance toward the social partners, however, and civil dialogue is not thought of as an alternative to social dialogue. The similarity rather applies to procedures and objectives. In procedural terms, there is a shift from a tripartite to a pluripartite social concertation, in which civil-society organizations are incorporated in the socioeconomic strategic debates. An illustrative example of competitive corporatism (Rhodes 1998) is the inclusion of a third pillar consisting of farmers' associations and community and voluntary sector organizations in the Irish concertation (Hardiman 2006), where a balance between economic adjustment goals and social development has been sought. A more radical shift in political preferences is documented in Papadakis' contribution on South Africa in this volume (Chapter 10). As he describes, in its first year of government the ANC put priority on 'growth through redistribution' and this was to be achieved by including civil society into government.

Hybrid fora

The broader involvement of social interests is reflected in the diversity of the knowledge that is mobilized in the public debate. The integrative model aims at setting up 'hybrid fora' (Callon *et al.* 2001: 29 and 59), which gather experts, professionals and the public, the latter consisting of either activists and mobilized citizens, or ordinary citizens. Patients' associations in the field of public health are an example of mobilized citizens' participation. In cases like this, the hybrid forum seeks to include the knowledge accumulated in social movements and through the particular experiences of those concerned (cf. Rabeharisoa and Callon 2002). In contrast, hybrid fora incorporating ordinary citizens aim at fostering an enlightened public by conveying expert knowledge to unconcerned individuals. Citizen' juries or consensus conferences, for example, are hybrid fora that do not consist of stakeholders or representatives of social interests, but of individuals of the wider public, the aim being to develop a deliberation that is detached from contending interests and values. In practice, the organizers of these new deliberative procedures try to combine different forms of civil involvement in the public debates, putting the (sometimes extreme) demands of the activists into perspective by confronting them with the down-to-earth judgement of ordinary citizens (Brugidou and Jobert 2007).

The transformation of the public sphere

The integrative model intends to improve the policy process by transforming the public sphere, suggesting that the emergence of an informed civil society can influence the orientation of public policies. The definition of public interest is to be derived as the result of deliberative procedures. For theoreticians like Habermas, the deliberative process consists of a debate among equals, in which the well-reasoned argument prevails over particularistic interests. Walzer (1995) points to the importance of deliberation processes in reaching a modus vivendi, rather than a rational consensus, between different groups by recognizing each other's different convictions, understanding differences and searching for an agreement based on the respect of the other's position. The hypothesis here is that a compromise elaborated under the conditions of reciprocity has a different quality from a solution which has been reached through negotiations behind closed doors, where rival particular interests come to an agreement through bargaining.

This promotion of the communicative power in the public sphere (Habermas) is not limited to the policy formulation process, however. From the point of view of the integrative model, civil-society organizations should also be involved in the implementation and evaluation process.

Civil and social dialogue

The answer of the integrative model to failures of social mediation, for instance when irreconcilable interests and values lead to a situation of stalemate, is to aim for a better recognition of weaker voices and the establishment of new rules of debates. To that end, countries with a strong social democratic tradition have been the initiators of many experiments with assisted consultations or civil participation. However, cases of civil-society organizations becoming incorporated into national social negotiations – as in Ireland – are rare and the results of these experiments are uncertain (see Baccaro 2002). Most often, the relation between the various procedures of deliberation and the bargaining and decision-making processes remain unsystematic.

In general, civil-society organizations are usually invited to participate in 'forums', while organized interests and social partners are invited to negotiations. This imbalance is problematic because the difference in effects on public policy are striking. The question remains whether a model of activation of the social-democratic type can limit these tendencies towards 'dualization' (Barbier 2004). Above all, the reconstruction of forums of social dialogue which are likely to bring spokespersons of the marginalized segments of the population to the negotiation table appears a matter of urgency.

Conclusion

The literature on the role of ideas and discourses in politics and policy is abundant. This contribution aims at filling a gap by proposing an analytical framework for the study of those representations, images, symbols and strategies that delineate the relation between governments and non-political actors. These civil frames have been defined by four variables: by the role of politics in the constitution of civil-society organizations; by its relation to organized interests by its approach to knowledge and, finally; by the field open to these organizations. Based on these four dimensions, we have proposed a typology of civil frames. The key hypothesis was that the emergence of new frames is a tentative answer to problems of legitimacy.

The crisis of a tutelary model explains the emergence of the three other contending frames that have been described. Each of them delineates a particular potential shift in the citizenship regime, understood here as the institutional arrangements, rules and meanings organizing the configuration of the public sphere (Jenson and Phillips 1996). It remains open to debate if the four different types are mutually exclusive or, as has been argued by Raul Urzúa in his chapter on Chile in this book (Chapter 8), if the hypothesis of their coexistence in different sectors of a state holds true.

References

Baccaro, L. (2002) 'Civil society meets the state', Geneva: ILO Discussion Paper.

Barbier, J.-C. (2004) 'Activation policies: a comparative perspective', in A. Serrano Pascual (ed.) *Are Activation Policies Converging in Europe, The European Employment Strategy for Young People*, Brussels: ETUI, 47–84.

Brugidou, M. and Jobert, A. (2007) 'Quels critères d'évaluation du débat public?', in M. Revel and C. Blatrix (eds) *Le Débat public: une experience française de démocratie participative*, Paris: La Découverte.

Callon, M., Lascoumes, P. and Barthes, Y. (2001) *Agir dans un monde incertain – Essai sur la démocratie technique*, Paris: Seuil, 358.

Castell, R. (1995) *Les métamorphoses de la question sociale*, Paris: Fayard.

Giddens, A. (1994) *Beyond Left and Right – the Future of Radical Politics*, Cambridge: Polity Press.

—— (2000) *The Third Way and its Critics*, Cambridge: Polity Press.

Habermas, J. (1992) *Between Facts and Norms: Contribution to a Discourse Theory of Law and Democracy*, Cambridge: MIT Press.

Hardiman, N. (2006) 'Politics and social partnership: flexible network governance', *The Economic and Social Review*, 37: 343–374.

Jenson, J. and Phillips, S. (1996) 'Regime shift: new citizenship practices in Canada', *Revue Internationale d'Études Canadiennes*, 14: 111–136.

Kristol, I. (1999) *Neoconservatism, The Autobiography of an Idea*, Chicago: Elephant Paperbacks.

Milner, H. (2002) *Civic Literacy: How Informed Citizens Make Democracy Work*, Lebanon: University Press of New England.

Moynihan, D.P. (1996) *Miles to Go – A Personal History of Social Policy*, Cambridge: Harvard University Press.

Perez Diaz, V. (1993) *The Return of Civil Society*, Cambridge: Harvard University Press.

Pharr S.J. and Putnam, R.D. (2000) *Disaffected Democracies*, Princeton: Princeton University Press.

Pinell, P. and Zafiropoulos, M. (1983) *Un siècle d'échecs scolaires (1882–1982)*, Paris: Editions Ouvrières.

Rabeharisoa, V. and Callon, M. (2002) 'L'engagement des associations de malades dans la recherche', *Revue Internationale des Sciences Sociales*, 171: 65–73.

Rhodes, M. (1998) 'Globalization, labour markets and welfare states: a future of "competitive corporatism?"', in M. Rhodes and Y. Meny (eds) *The Future of European Welfare: A New Social Contract?*, London: Macmillan.

Walzer, M. (1995) 'The concept of civil society', in M. Walzer (ed.) *Toward a Global Civil Society*, Providence: Berghahn Books.

2 Framing civil society
Lessons from Eastern Europe

John K. Glenn

This chapter looks at the concept of 'civil society' as it emerged in debates in Eastern Europe in the 1970s and evolved after the fall of communism. It reviews explanations for the fall of communism based on the rise of civil society and draws on the literature on contentious politics to redefine the concept as a 'collective action frame' with which movement activists sought to mobilize popular support against Leninist regimes. This grounds the concept in the actions of political actors seeking to influence change and allows comparison across countries. By contrasting Solidarity in Poland and Civic Forum and Public Against Violence in Czechoslovakia with the efforts by other alternatives, such as smaller movements and the old regimes, the chapter grounds the concept of civil society within a political explanation for transformation. Finally, this chapter will look at the 'fate' of the concept of civil society once new democracies had emerged. While critical for the successful mobilization of movements against the old regime, the concept had negative consequences for the development of democratic politics, rendering both countries vulnerable to populist and nationalist challenges.

Redefining 'civil society'

Media images of crowds surrounding and toppling the Berlin Wall in November 1989 have led many to think of the fall of communism in Eastern Europe as an inevitable revolution driven by 'people power' often described as 'civil society' that rose up to overthrow communist regimes. This popular view, I will argue below, is limited by conceptual imprecision about the meaning of civil society and its failure to integrate the concept within a political explanation for change. It has led to misunderstandings about the power of civil society under communism and its apparent failure after the revolutions of 1989 with the success of populists and nationalists across the region. Drawing on the literature on contentious politics, I argue in this chapter that the concept of 'civil society' should be reconceptualized as a collective action frame with which civic movements across Eastern Europe sought to mobilize public support in light of changing political opportunities.

Collective action frames are defined as strategically oriented interpretations of events by which movement activists seek to mobilize a previously quiescent group in pursuit of their aims (Snow and Benford 1988, 1992; Snow *et al.* 1986). Master frames are broader models that specific movements draw upon in their struggle. They explain why and how movements frame their claims in particular ways, attempting to draw upon resonant symbols and the collective memory of previous struggle. Movement activists seek to motivate people to act by shaping what they perceive they are capable of doing as well as what they should do in particular circumstances. Framing strategies link action to cognitive 'schema', or shared, internalized patterns of thought and feeling that mediate between individual drives and the external environment in which those drives are pursued (D'Andrade and Strauss 1992). Their influence, therefore, is partly informational, signalling changes in the potential for action, but also motivational, appealing for individuals to act in particular ways. Thus, framing by movement leaders operates within the latitude between their strategic aims and their moral commitments to principled beliefs as well as those whose support they seek.

Civil society should be analysed, like the anthropologist Katherine Verdery (1996: 105) suggests, as 'key symbolic operators, elements in ideological fields, rather than organizational realities'. Framing must be operationalized clearly, so that competing claims can be compared against those of other challengers and analysed in light of their alignment with potential social networks of support. I follow Gamson (1992), analysing framing strategies as three sets of inter-related claims: injustice, identity and agency. Injustice refers to moral indignation about a situation that is laden with emotion. Although Gamson acknowledges the criticism in the literature on social movements that injustice may be too widespread to account for particular instances of collective action, he argues that the transformation of injustice into a shared grievance with a target of collective action must be explained rather than taken for granted. The failure by movement activists to do so may explain the absence of movements even when conditions otherwise seem ripe (such as opportunities created by state breakdown). A sense of injustice must be combined with identity, which defines 'us vs. them' and a sense of agency, or awareness that change is possible and that individual action can be effective. It is this last claim, agency, which bears most directly on the question of competing visions of what should be done.

Framing, however, must be linked to the broader political environment and to organizational resources. Mobilization rarely succeeds without sufficient institutional resources that shape the ability of the movements both to use framing strategies and to form strategic alliances among social groups. Framing, no matter how resonant, cannot mobilize popular support faced with overwhelming state repression, for example. Although social movement research has emphasized the influence of political opportunities on successful framing (Diani 1996; Gamson and Meyer 1996; Koopmans and Duyvendak 1995; Noonan 1995; Oberschall 1996; Zuo and Benford 1995), insufficient attention has been paid to the potential links between framing and existing social networks that provide organizational advantages to challengers. This entails bargaining between social movement entrepreneurs and leaders of networks, beliefs about what is right and what is possible, and the need to maintain the conditional support of network members.

Framing plays an essential role not merely by persuading individuals to join movements under favourable opportunities but also by aligning the claims of movements with the identities of pre-existing networks (McAdam *et al.* 2001). As Friedman and McAdam (1992: 163) note, framing typically does not create entirely new collective identities but rather 'redefine[s] existing roles within established organizations as the basis of an emerging activist identity'. Such organizations may link previously isolated groups by fostering 'the creation of social ties that encourage the recognition of commonalities on a scale considerably broader than could be expected on the basis of informal social networks alone' (Gould 1995: 22). Thus, the mechanism by which framing links its claims to pre-existing networks is making more likely the 'attribution of similarity' between the identities of members of networks and mobilizing claims by challengers (Strang and Meyer 1993).

Framing effects are not equally probable for every person or every issue. Broadly speaking, Popkin (1994: 82) argues that framing effects occur 'whenever altering the formulation of a problem, or shifting the point of view of an observer, changes the information and ideas the observer will use when making a decision'. Thus, framing is unlikely to motivate people to act if the same information or metaphors always arise around a given subject, if there is a single, dominant attitude about a subject, or if people's attitudes about a subject are integrated into a single measure.

Finally, mobilization must be linked to bargaining among political actors that determines new institutions and forms of participation. Mobilization influences such bargaining among elites by introducing new actors into political arenas, by altering the bargaining power of representatives of movements, and by articulating new demands that shape the range of outcomes considered. Bargaining influences mobilization by shaping the aims and the scope of political competition, as well as the definition of who is permitted to participate in the political sphere. Outcomes can be evaluated through comparison of the interaction between challengers and regimes under uncertainty and conditional popular support. This chapter will evaluate evidence for claims made by competing groups with organizational efforts to mobilize support, as well as the congruency between appeals to supporters and demands made at the bargaining table. It specifies the mechanisms by which movement leaders can be held accountable to their members and broader constituencies. Even if direct public involvement may be low, elite choices may be constrained by public attention to their actions and the perception of conditional support.

This approach grounds the concept of civil society in its use by political actors seeking to influence change and enables comparison of its impact across countries. To explain the success of civic movements, I analyse competing attempts to mobilize public support by examining the congruency between claims of what should be done and potential networks of organizational resources. Because outcomes can rarely be attributed to the actions of any single movement, I analyse competition among challengers by highlighting failed alternatives and counterfactuals representing other potential outcomes (Fearon 1991). Although not all alternatives have an equal probability of success, comparison provides analytic leverage in explaining the contestation that shapes outcomes. By focusing on the claims challengers make, I do not make any assumptions that such claims represent comprehensive ideologies or rational blueprints for the future. Rather, I analyse how movements offer competing claims about injustice, identity and agency in their attempts to mobilize networks of support.

The fall of communism in Eastern Europe

The fall of communism and rise of new democratic governments in Eastern Europe offers a valuable opportunity to reconceptualize civil society within a political explanation for change.[1] The scholarly literature on the fall of communism has widely argued that 'civil society played a key role in the overthrow of communist regimes in 1989' (Bernhard 1996: 308). Bernhard (1993: 309) defines civil society as composed of four components: a 'public space ... located between official public and private life', composed of a range of 'autonomous organizations' that are 'separated from the state by law' and guarantee those within civil society 'personal and group liberties' that enable them to 'pursue their broadly conceived interests'. Thus, Weigle and Butterfield (1992: 1–2) argue that 'expanding independent activism increasingly contradicted the legitimacy and power base of the single ruling party, leading to the end of Communist rule'. Drawing on Habermas' conception of the public sphere, Cohen and Arato (1992: 64) argue that the 'groups, associations, and indeed movements outside the official institutions would have the primary tasks of pushing the reforms through'. Similarly, Tismaneanu (1992: x, xiii) argues that these 'nuclei of autonomous social and cultural initiative' in each country explain how 'the breakthrough could result in a smooth, nonviolent change' in 1989.

Such explanations are limited by their mono-causal logic and conceptual imprecision. They obscure the impact of the Leninist regimes as media agents and negotiating partners in the reconstruction of states. These regimes were not simply overcome by political protest led by independent groups but shaped the patterns of change independently of the efforts of these movements. Civil-society explanations cannot explain the emergence of democracy because it they lack a model to explain the interaction between states and movements that created the new political institutions. Further, these explanations fail to distinguish among a wide array of independent activity under Leninist regimes (from rock music to underground publishing to religious pilgrimages) with an opposition strategy of self-organization adopted in Eastern Europe in the 1970s. They misunderstand the strategic nature of the discourse of civil society and the conditional nature of public support for the civic movements. Cohen and Arato, for example, do not answer Jadwiga Staniszkis' critique that the self-limiting strategy 'was ... always a purely defensive one and is not suited for real social change' (quoted in Cohen and Arato 1992: 59).

Rather, civil society should be understood as a 'master frame' for protest that emerged across Eastern Europe in the 1970s. Master frames are broader models for mobilizing support that particular movements draw on in their struggle. They are not unified cultural systems, nor universally accepted, but are contested, emerging through struggles with adversaries and within movements. The civil-society master frame defined injustice as the persecution of human rights protected by international agreements and national constitutions. This claim, although not new in history, was given international legitimacy with the signing of the Helsinki accords in 1975 by 35 governments in Europe (including all the communist governments of Eastern Europe except for Albania). The notion of human rights was embodied in the collective identity as 'citizens'. In the context of Eastern Europe, the notion of citizens stood in opposition to that of membership in parties, classes or nations whose voice the regime claimed to represent. Finally, the agency claim was legal, non-violent protest seeking to pressure the regime to reform itself, rather than seeking political power. The rejection of political aims may have been an attempt to avoid repression by the communist regimes, but it clearly did not do so, as movements including Solidarity in Poland and Charter 77 in Czechoslovakia faced threats, harassment and imprisonment throughout their existence.

As is widely recognized, the political opportunities for opposition shifted in Eastern Europe in the 1980s as a confluence of new international opportunities created by the rise of Mikhail Gorbachev in the Soviet Union, changing capacities and propensities for repression by communist regimes, and a growing sense of economic crisis. Yet in no country were there organized political factions simply waiting to seize power. Even in Poland, years of martial law had weakened Solidarity, which failed to rouse the country for a national strike in April 1988. By analysing competing attempts to mobilize popular support in conditions of state breakdown below, I explain the outcomes in each country in light of multiple possible equilibria. This is not an argument to explain how revolutionaries result from the intentions of leaders nor a cultural explanation focused on the elaboration of symbolic discourses by movement leaders. Rather it integrates civil society as a framing strategy into a political explanation for how competing challengers mobilize popular support given the constellation of political opportunities.

Comparison of Poland and Czechoslovakia demonstrates the application of this approach in two different paths of democratization: 'from above' whereby democratic institutions are secured by political elites through negotiated pacts, and 'from below' whereby challengers outside the political sphere arise to overthrow old regimes. In each case, I review the historical context and present competing challengers which used different framing strategies in their efforts to mobilize popular support, as well as to link their claims to social networks that could offer institutional resources at a time of uncertainty.

Poland

Despite the long history of political struggle in Poland after the Second World War, the negotiated agreement for partially free elections in early 1989 has widely been perceived in the scholarly literature as an instance of a pacted transition whereby elite negotiations led to an agreement in which the old regime retained significant positions of power (Linz and Stepan 1996; Staniszkis 1991; Stark and Bruszt 1998). The outcome whereby Solidarity formed a 'grand coalition' with the former satellite parties that were part of the old regime, however, cannot be explained by bargaining alone. The result, unforeseen by regime and opposition bargainers, resulted from the interaction between bargaining that determined the rules of competition and successful mobilization of voters by Solidarity, employing collective action frames stressing the 'honourable compromise' that drew on pre-existing networks of the Catholic Church. In this manner, Solidarity transformed what was to have been their co-optation into parliament into a competition for votes in which they could demonstrate their trustworthiness to the Polish public.

The historical context can be summarized as follows. In the late 1980s, in light of a failed referendum proposed by the state in 1987 and failed strikes by Solidarity in April 1988, a political impasse had been reached whereby neither the state nor Solidarity could unilaterally mobilize sufficient popular support to resolve Poland's increasing economic problems. In the public statements of both sides, the notion of an 'anti-crisis pact' emerged in which the impasse would be resolved by a limited opening: the Solidarity trade union would be legalized in exchange for support for the government's proposed economic reforms and limited participation in the government. This idea was developed through bargaining at so-called 'round-table' negotiations between Solidarity leaders and the old regime. These negotiations culminated in an agreement for partially free elections in which Solidarity would compete for a limited number of seats in parliament. To the surprise of observers and participants, Solidarity won all of the seats that it contested in June 1989 and formed a new government with the unforeseen defection of the smaller, former-satellite parties that were part of the government coalition.

Although in retrospect it may seem inevitable that Solidarity would form a new government, the nature and extent of public support for Solidarity in the autumn of 1988 was unclear. Solidarity's failure to mobilize a national strike in April 1988 had demonstrated its weakness in Polish society, as well as the emergence of a new generation of activists, and increasing popular unrest did not necessarily translate into support for negotiations with the old regime. By comparing Solidarity's 'honourable compromise' framing strategy with which it sought to mobilize support against attempts by the regime and nationalist groups, the agreement for partially free elections can be explained as the outcome of bargaining in light of perceived support from the public. Because Solidarity's support was perceived by its leaders to be conditional, its framing efforts in turn constrained the choices that they were willing to accept. Notably,

Table 2.1 Competing framing strategies and networks, Poland

Challenger	Injustice	Identity	Agency	Networks
Leninist regime: 'Polish patriotism'	External crisis	Polish nation united against danger	Co-optation	Party structures and media
Solidarity: 'honorable compromise'	Crisis due to party and martial law	'Society' as citizens	Compromise, legal change	Underground structures, Catholic Church
Nationalist groups	Foreign domination	Poles as ethnicity	War against the state	Small groups

each of the three groups – Solidarity, the regime and Polish nationalists – sought to construct an identity of the Polish nation which they represented.

How did the Solidarity movement, which had previously urged workers to strike in factories or protest on the street, organize and run a successful election campaign against an opponent with a national network of known candidates and local administrative offices? Solidarity perceived itself to be at a disadvantage given the constraints of the round-table agreement for non-confrontational elections, the very brief period between the announcement of the agreement and the actual elections, the absence of pre-existing organizational structures, and the international political context (since neighbouring communist regimes had not fallen). As one analyst observed, 'Solidarity ... cannot count on mass enthusiasm to make up for its organizational disadvantages' (quoted in Stokes 1993: 126).

In these circumstances, the key to Solidarity's success was the transformation of the network of local Catholic parishes and Clubs of Catholic Intelligentsia into Citizens' Committees on the basis of the congruency between the claims of what I will refer to as Solidarity's 'honourable compromise' framing strategy and the identity of the Polish Catholic Church as the bearer of national tradition. The Warsaw headquarters of the Citizens' Committees began by establishing a Group for Aid to the Regions and preparing a map of Poland that identified dioceses of the Catholic Church in all the voting districts. Kosela (1990: 128) found that 'most of the [citizens'] committees began their activities in church halls ... [and] at least half of all committees were ... using church premises from the beginning of the campaign'. This claim is corroborated by archival data for the Citizens' Committee, including the records of a survey sent to the Warsaw headquarters by each of the Citizens' Committees in the 49 voting districts of Poland. Analysis of these records indicates that 23 out of 49 voting districts identified their organizational base in local parishes or Clubs of Catholic Intelligentsia, which also provided electoral assistance in 35 out of 49 voting districts.[2]

Solidarity's electoral efforts were not only based in churches, but actively supported by church clergy. For example, Kosela (1990: 128–130) details 18 'organizational solutions' by the church during the pre-election campaign, including schooling of many activists, assistance by priests to initiate and organize some local committees, use of church halls for meetings, use of pulpits to inform people about the establishment of local committees, nomination of candidates, and gathering of signatures to place candidates on the official voting list. Transcripts of Central Committee meetings from the time indicate that these activities were noted by the regime. At a 2 May 1989 meeting, General Kiszczak expressed concern that the Church was offering support for the registration of candidates, since the neutral position of the Church was considered 'essential' to the party's election campaign.[3] Solidarity candidates competed against those nominated by the regime, whose electoral strategy might be characterized as one of emphasizing Polish patriotism. The regime attempted to redefine the political and economic situation as an external threat to the Polish nation so large that the nation had to unite or be destroyed. By identifying itself as the 'government coalition', the regime sought to obscure its identity as the communist party whose leading role was guaranteed by the constitution. Finally, for the party this was not a path to revolution but an attempt to create a 'Polish humane and democratic model of socialism'.[4] This approach was based on the assumption that the party was strong enough to maintain control over limited democratization. The election results were to be controlled by the regime, which would maintain the authority to implement reforms in exchange for granting a minority voice to the opposition.

From an organizational perspective, some have observed that 'in theory, the government should have been far better prepared to wage a political campaign than were the ad hoc civic committees set up by Solidarity, even with the organizational assistance provided by local parishes' (Heyns and Bialecki 1991: 354). Although the regime had never had to organize an election campaign against an opponent before, it had a network of party structures and control over the national media at its disposal. Yet by all accounts its campaign was lacklustre in contrast to the flurry of energy and symbolic action of its opponent (Castle 1995). For example, whereas Solidarity chose its candidates by internal nomination and ran a centralized campaign stressing a unified message, the government coalition nominated its candidates at the local level, ran a decentralized campaign, and highlighted the diversity of beliefs of its candidates, apparently motivated by the desire to appear more democratic. As a result, voters were presented with an unexpectedly clear choice at the polls between candidates representing a single national message from Solidarity and a messy range of beliefs and candidates from the regime.

Czechoslovakia

The fall of communism in Czechoslovakia has been characterized as an instance of 'democratization from below', whereby mass protest led to the collapse of the regime and formation of a new democratic government (Linz and Stepan 1996; Stark and Bruszt 1998; Wheaton and Kavan 1992). In contrast to Poland, where the regime agreed to negotiations with Solidarity that led to partially free elections, a national general strike in Czechoslovakia following the repression of a student demonstration on 17 November 1989 provoked the resignation of the Central Committee and agreement for a new 'government of national understanding'. While the strike was the turning point that demonstrated that the regime had lost control over the population, the new government in which communists unexpectedly retained positions of authority can only be explained in light of bargaining on conditions of uncertainty. The historical context can be summarized as follows. After years of repression of all independent activity, the regime in Czechoslovakia became vulnerable in the late 1980s in light of international changes in the Soviet Union and the fall of regimes in Poland and Hungary. Routine repression of a student demonstration in November 1989 sparked an unprecedented and widespread protest against the regime. New movements, calling themselves Civic Forum in the Czech Republic and Public Against Violence in Slovakia, emerged calling initially for the regime to redress the repression of the student demonstration and past human rights abuses. In a matter of days, these moderate demands escalated to calls for a new government, provoked the unexpectedly swift resignation of the communist prime minister and Central Committee, and resulted in the formation of a new government led by the civic movements in which representatives of the old regime continued to hold positions of power, such as that of the prime minister.

To explain the outcome in Czechoslovakia, as suggested earlier, we must reconstruct the uncertainty seen by political actors in 1989 and introduce the failed attempts by smaller, lesser-known groups to influence the outcome. Because none of the challengers existed before the repression of the student demonstration in November 1989, they had to locate or create the resources needed to mobilize public support. Mobilization was neither inevitable nor effortless, but rather the result of competing challengers seeking to influence events. Table 2.2 contrasts the successful challenge by Civic Forum in the Czech Republic and Public Against Violence in Slovakia with the failed attempts of two competing challengers – socialism with a human face by reform communists in the 'Obroda' movement and rapid democracy by the Democratic Initiative – and a counter-factual challenge, one that plausibly might have but did not emerge during the revolution in 1989 – Slovak nationalism.

Table 2.2 suggests that while the injustice claim is largely similar among challengers (with the exception of the counter-factual Slovak nationalists), identity and, more importantly, agency differ. Attention to pre-existing networks makes possible comparison of potential organizational advantages. Prior to the repression of the student demonstration, no group had overwhelming resources, although reform communists might have mobilized those purged after 1968. Attention to framing and networks suggests that the failure of the competing groups was not simply the result of the superior resonance of the civil society framing strategy, but of their inability to link their claims to the dynamic political environment in November 1989 and, critically, to the striking theatres that could provide the network to mobilize the population for the general strike. Once the theatre strike had begun, the group able to link its claims to this

Table 2.2 Competing framing strategies and networks, Czechoslovakia

Challenger	Injustice	Identity	Agency	Networks
Reform communists: 'socialism with a human face'	Stalinism, 1968	Ex-party members, working-class	Reform, social democracy	Obroda, ties to current party
Democratic initiative: 'rapid democracy'	'Massacre' of students, 1968	New political elites	Immediate elections	Small, national network
Slovak nationalism (counter-factual)	Czech centralism	Slovak ethnicity	Constitutional change	Non-existent
Civic Forum/ Public Against Violence: 'civil society'	'Massacre' of students, 1968	Citizens with human rights	Strike, pressure state to make changes	Isolate dissidents, striking theatres

network would have a formidable advantage that would prove impossible to overcome.

Competing attempts to mobilize public support are perhaps most clearly evident in the demonstration on behalf of the strike on Sunday 26 November, which an estimated 750,000 people attended. This demonstration, broadcast on national television, provides an opportunity to analyse the efforts by competing groups to frame the general strike and the direct response from the public. The speeches by Civic Forum spokesperson Vaclav Havel, Czechoslovak Prime Minister Adamec, and leader of the Prague Spring Alexander Dubcek provide three contrasting framing strategies. However primitive, the crowd's responses to the speakers provide a glimpse into the failure of the state to contest the authority of the civic movements. They demonstrate the potential support for Dubcek and his attempt to frame events as an opportunity for Gorbachev-like reform. Above all, they demonstrate Civic Forum's successful linking of its claims with the theatres and artists. This would be crucial for the next day's decisive demonstration of Civic Forum's support in the general strike.

Hypothetically, Czechoslovak Prime Minister Adamec's speech could have been a turning point for the regime whereby the communist party would cooperate with Civic Forum with Adamec as the leader of this joint effort. Although greeted with applause as he approached the microphone, he ended his speech interrupted by boos and calls for his resignation audible to the entire country watching on television. After thanking Civic Forum for inviting him, Adamec described his meeting with Civic Forum as an attempt to 'calm the situation'.[5] He argued that the strike should only last several minutes rather than two hours. 'What is the meaning of dialogue?' he asked rhetorically. 'That which joins us, to resolve the situation by political means.' At this point, boos broke out. Cries of 'demise!' are recorded. Adamec appeared unable to break out of the language of the communist party, calling for a perestroika-style 'improvement of the economic situation'. 'It's already too late!' voices called out. He concluded his speech which called for further meeting amid cries of 'It's already too late! Demise! That's already been done!' Others on the platform attribute the catcalls his speech received to the 'apparatchik-like' style in which he spoke (Otahal and Sladek 1990: 609).

Dubcek was greeted with applause. In contrast to Adamec, he declared: 'This is not a calm time and so there can not be calm which would halt the great people's movement ... Calm would mean the end of this process'. The crowd roared its support, calling, 'Dubcek to the castle!' meaning, Dubcek for president, whose office is in Prague Castle. Yet, he differed from Civic Forum by framing the situation as an opportunity for socialism with a human face: 'Twenty one years ago we went out on the path of linking socialism and democracy. It was expressed by the slogan Socialism with a human face' (Otahal and Sladek 1990: 516–517). He referred to Gorbachev's declaration in the previous day's Pravda that 'The main aim of the politics of perestroika is to build socialism with a human face.' Despite his conclusion, 'we are united with youth!' Dubcek's references to socialism allied himself with the past rather than the future. As noted earlier, he retained personal prestige as a symbol of the suffering by Czechs and Slovaks under communism but his call for reform socialism would fall on deaf ears and would be unable to mobilize the potential support of the networks of reform communists from 1968.

Civic Forum, as the organizer of the event, continued to portray itself as the representative of the nation by presenting speakers from all parts of society. Havel declared: 'after forty years, *citizens* are beginning to meet freely. It has happened after what we all called for – dialogue with the powers that be!' (Wheaton and Kavan 1992: 89, emphasis added). He called for participation in the strike the next day, stressing the non-violent and legal agency claims of the civil society framing strategy: 'We do not want to destroy, on the contrary, we want everything to work better.' He called upon those at the rally to form local branches of Civic Forum and 'self-administering and independent representatives of the common will throughout the republic'. Consistent with its identity as the embodiment of the nation represented by the striking theatres, actors from the National Theatre and the Vinohrady Theatre in Prague spoke. The speakers at the demonstration also included representatives of the students, of the Romany movement, as well as of soccer players. The peaceful aims of Civic Forum were emphasized by its concluding invocation of forgiveness of the old regime.

The key to the successful mobilization for the general strike that established their authority to speak for the 'nation', however, was the ability to garner popular support throughout the country. Lacking prior history or organizational resources, the new movements had to create a national network within days to organize the strike as a demonstration of their popular support. Like Solidarity's alliance with the Catholic Church, Civic Forum and Public Against Violence sought to transform pre-existing cultural networks outside the political sphere, in this case the network of theatres which had gone on strike in support of the students after the repression of the demonstration. While this may seem curious, theatres in Czechoslovakia, like the Catholic Church in Poland, could draw on the association with the birth of the nation, as it was in theatres where the Czech language could be spoken in the nineteenth century under the Habsburg Empire. More recently, theatres were a relatively independent space in many communist states where people could gather to hear subtle criticism of the regime in the subtext and staging of plays. Rather than closing their doors on strike, actors in the theatres across the country opened their stages to public discussion every evening, in what amounted to daily appeals for participation in the general strike and support for the civic movements. Analysis of archival data indicates that branches of Civic Forum and Public Against Violence were formed in theatres in 18 cities and towns in Czechoslovakia and that actors helped to mobilize support for the general strike in 45 cities, 23 universities and high schools and seven enterprises.[6]

'Civil society' in post-communist Eastern Europe

At the close of the twentieth century, democracy appeared to have overcome the Cold War division of the world, and the fall of authoritarian regimes across the world in the latter part of the twentieth century prompted some to declare the end of history in which a global consensus on liberal-democratic governance had emerged. The reconceptualization of civil society as a master frame proposed in this chapter provides insight into the puzzle for many of the apparent weakness of civil society in post-communist Eastern Europe. Bernhard (1996: 310; see also Howard 2003) asked, 'how a civil society strong enough to precipitate the collapse of a communist regime could now become weak?' The focus on master frames and competing movements suggests that civil society itself was not suddenly weak, but the mobilizing power of the frame of civil society had drastically diminished.

If we analyse framing as inter-related claims of injustice, identity and agency, we may see how the civil society master frame failed to foster democratic governance. It left new governments vulnerable to populism or the rejection of representative rule in favour of plebiscitarian solutions. After 1989, injustice claims concerning the violation of human rights by illegitimate regimes no longer made sense with new governments that renounced the use of force against citizens and declared their commitments to abide by international treaties concerning human rights. In contrast to the emphasis on 'truth' in the writings of Havel, post-communist politicians grappled with disagreements over complicated political, economic and legal reforms that were difficult to make sense out of in such terms. Identity claims to represent a united 'society' offered little guidance for resolving disagreements within democratic institutions. In parliamentary democracies, the 'nation' is not represented (in all but extreme circumstances) by a united 'society' but by a range of groups representing different interests.

After 1989, attempts by post-communist governments to govern in the name of a united society, rather than revitalizing democratic politics, actually obstructed the development of competing political interests within democratic institutions. The similarity between claims to represent a united society by both civic movements and populists highlights the incompatibility with democratic governance. As Hirst (1991: 234, italics in original) observes, ' "Civil society" as a homogenous political force is an idea at variance with modern pluralist democracy, which relies on the *divisions* of civil society expressed in political competition contained within the party system to ensure social and political order.' Lastly, after the distaste with which Solidarity viewed its 'compromise' in 1989, Polish politicians would have to explain that compromise is the basis for nearly all agreements within democratic institutions. Agency claims rejecting politics (combined with the mistrust of political parties that was one of the legacies of communism) turned social groups away from their potential role as watchdogs of the state, a vital function often attributed to civil society. As Walzer (1992: 105) observes, the state 'can never be what it appears in liberal theory, a mere framework for civil society'.

After 1989 the diminished potential for mobilization meant that political actors could no longer rely on the support of the networks associated with the birth of the nation so crucial earlier, namely the Catholic Church in Poland and theatres in Czechoslovakia. Contrary to the media images of thousands of supporters in the streets, the civic movements actually found themselves institutionally weaker than one might have predicted. This was especially true when the communist parties and the parties that emerged from them largely retained their national institutional networks. Without the cultural institutions that served as their founding networks, the civic movements had to recreate again new organizational structures for elections. In Poland, one saw the legendary unity of Solidarity destroyed almost immediately, followed by a fragmentary parliament and years of unstable governments. Walesa's war on the top represented a populist challenge to the gradualist approach of the new government. This legacy was not confined to the short term. It can be seen in the recent rise of the Law and Justice Party whereby former-Solidarity activists Lech and Jaroslaw Kaczynski successfully mobilized support for their populist challenge to the legitimacy of the 1989 Round Table agreement in Poland. By contrast, in Czechoslovakia, while the first post-communist government appeared stable, it was unable to resolve the constitutional challenges of a federal state and led to the dissolution of the state in 1993. Populism has been a recurrent theme in Slovak politics, from governments led by Vladimir Meciar after 1993 to the current government of Robert Fico which governs with the support of Meciar.

Given its strategic nature deriving from opposition to communism, civil society could not be a programme for the future because 'it had not yet developed into a new consensus in which a new political system could be built. It was actually the other way around: the new political system had to develop step by step the new democratic consensus and civil society in a rather conventional way' (Von Beyme 1996: 41). Indeed, for some, the fall of communism offered not a new vision of the future but 'a restatement of the value of what we already have, of old truths and tested models, of the three essentials of liberal democracy and the European Community as the one and only real existing Common European Home' (Ash 1991: 122).

Notes

1 The arguments and data in this chapter draw upon their fuller exposition in Glenn (2001).
2 Citizens' Committee Surveys, in Citizens' Committee Archives, Polish Senate.
3 In Perzkowski (1994: 356). This translation and all subsequent from Polish are my own.
4 Czyrek in *Uncensored Poland News Bulletin*, No. 15/88, 18 August 1988: 18.
5 This and subsequent information come from a document in the private papers of Ivan Havel which describes the contents of the Czechoslovak television broadcast of the demonstration. Informacni Komise, Monitor 2. The translation and all subsequent from Czech are my own.
6 'Diskusni vecery na scanach Rokoka a ABC [Discussion evenings on the stages of Theater Rokoko and ABC]' and Memorandum, 26 November 1989, Theater Institute Archive, Prague, Xeroxed documents.

References

Ash, T. (1991) 'Tell me your Europe and I will tell you where you stand', in M. Kaldor (ed.) *Europe From Below*, London: Verso, 122–221.

Bernhard, M. (1993) *The Origins of Democratization in Poland: Workers, Intellectuals, and Oppositional Politics, 1979–1980*, New York: Columbia University Press.

—— (1996) 'Civil society after the first transition', *Communist and Post-Communist Studies*, 29 (3): 309–330.

Castle, M. (1995) 'A successfully failed pact: the Polish political transition of 1989', unpublished dissertation, Stanford University.

Cohen, J. and Arato, A. (1992) *Civil Society and Political Theory*, Cambridge: MIT Press.

D'Andrade, R.G. and Strauss, C. (1992) *Human Motives and Cultural Models*, Cambridge: Cambridge University Press.

Diani, M. (1996) 'Linking mobilization frames and political opportunities: insights from regional populism in Italy', *American Sociological Review*, 61: 1053–1069.

Fearon, J.D. (1991) 'Counterfactuals and hypothesis testing in political science', *World Politics*, 43 (1): 169–195.

Friedman, D. and McAdam, D. (1992) 'Collective identity and activism', in A. Morris and C. Mueller (eds) *Frontiers in Social Movement Theory*, New Haven: Yale University Press, 156–173.

Gamson, W. (1992) *Talking Politics*, Cambridge: Cambridge University Press.

Gamson, W. and Meyer, D. (1996) 'Framing political opportunity', in D. McAdam, J. McCarthy and M. Zald (eds) *Comparative Perspectives on Social Movements. Political Opportunities, Mobilizing Structures and Cultural Framing*, Cambridge: Cambridge University Press, 275–290.

Glenn, J. (2001) *Framing Democracy: Civil Society and Civic Movements in Eastern Europe*, Stanford: Stanford University Press.

Gould, R. (1995) *Insurgent Identities: Class, Community, and Protest in Paris from 1848 to the Commune*, Chicago: University of Chicago Press.

Heyns, B. and Bialecki, I. (1991) 'Solidarnosc: reluctant vanguard or makeshift coalition?', *American Political Science Review*, 85 (2): 351–370.

Hirst, P. (1991) 'The state, civil society and the collapse of Soviet communism', *Economy and Society*, 20 (2): 217–242.

Howard, M. (2003) *The Weakness of Civil Society in Post-communist Europe*, Cambridge: Cambridge University Press.

Koopmans, R. and Duyvendak, J. (1995) 'The political construction of the nuclear energy issue and its impact on the mobilization of anti-nuclear movements in Western Europe', *Social Problems*, 42 (2): 235–251.

Kosela, K. (1990) 'The Polish Catholic Church and the elections of 1989', *Religion in Communist Lands*, 18 (2), 124–137.

Linz, J. and Stepan, A. (1996) *Problems of Democratic Transition and Consolidation: Southern Europe, South America and Post-Communist Europe*, Baltimore: Johns Hopkins University Press.

McAdam, D., Tarrow, S. and Tilly, C. (2001) *Dynamics of Contention*, Cambridge: Cambridge University Press.

Noonan, R. (1995) 'Women against the state: political opportunities and collective action frames in Chile's transition to democracy', *Sociological Forum* 10: 81–111.

Oberschall, A. (1996) 'Opportunities and framing in the Eastern European revolts of 1989', in D. McAdam, J. McCarthy and M. Zald (eds) *Comparative Perspectives on Social Movements: Political Opportunities, Mobilizing Structures and Cultural Framings*, Cambridge: Cambridge University Press, 93–121.

Otahal, M. and Sladek, Z. (eds) (1990) Deset prazskych dnu (17.-27. listopad 1989) Dokumentace (Ten Prague days, 17–27 November 1989, Documentation), Prague: Academia Praha.

Perzkowski, S. (ed.) (1994) *Tajne Dokumenty Biura Politycznego i Sekretariatu KC Ostatni Rok wladzy 1988–1989* (Secret Documents of the Politbureau of the Polish Communist Party, the Last Year in Power 1988–1989), London: Aneks.

Popkin, S. (1994) *The Reasoning Voter: Communication and Persuasion in Presidential Campaigns*, 2nd edn, Chicago: University of Chicago Press.

Snow, D.A. and Benford, R.D. (1988) 'Ideology, frame resonance, and participant mobilization', in B. Klandermans, H. Kriese and S. Tarrow (eds) *International Social Movement Research I*, Greenwich: JAI Press, 197–217.

—— (1992) 'Master frames and cycles of protest', in A.D. Morris and C.M. Mueller (eds) *Frontiers in Social Movement Theory*, New Haven: Yale University Press, 133–155.

Snow, D.A., Rochford, E.B., Worden, S.K. and Benford, R.D. (1986) 'Frame alignment processes, micromobilization, and movement participation', *American Sociological Review*, 51 (4): 464–481.

Staniszkis, J. (1991) *The Dynamics of the Breakthrough in Eastern Europe: the Polish Experience*, Berkeley: University of California Press.

Stark, D. and Bruszt, L. (1998) *Postsocialist Pathways: Transforming Politics and Property in East Central Europe*, Cambridge: Cambridge University Press.

Stokes, G. (1993) *The Walls Came Tumbling Down: the Collapse of Communism in Eastern Europe*, Oxford: Oxford University Press.

Strang, D. and Meyer, J. (1993) 'Institutional conditions for diffusion', *Theory and Society*, 22 (4): 487–511.

Tismaneanu, V. (1992) *Reinventing Politics. Eastern Europe from Stalin to Havel*, New York: Free Press.

Verdery, K, (1996) *What was Socialism, and What Comes Next?*, Princeton: Princeton University Press.

Von Beyme, K. (1996) *Transition to Democracy in Eastern Europe*, New York: St. Martin's Press.

Walzer, M. (1992) 'The civil society argument', in C. Mouffe (ed.) *Dimensions of Radical Democracy: Pluralism, Citizenship, Community*, London: Verso, 89–107.

Weigle, M. and Butterfield, J. (1992) 'Civil society in reforming communist regimes: the logic of emergence', *Comparative Politics*, 25 (1): 1–23.

Wheaton, B. and Kavan, Z. (1992) *The Velvet Revolution: Czechoslovakia, 1988–91*, Boulder: Westview.

Zuo, J. and Benford, R. (1995) 'Mobilization processes and the 1989 Chinese Democracy Movement', *Sociological Quarterly*, 36 (1): 131–156.

3 A democracy bereft of parties

Anti-political uses of civil society in Italy

Alfio Mastropaolo

If once there were mass political parties with whom democracy identified, today they have been replaced by agencies of political marketing which strive to get candidates elected. Within this context, civil society has adopted a new role that shall be examined in this chapter. We will show how civil society first of all constituted a legitimate political space that competed with parties in the 1970s and 1980s, before then – in tandem with the transformation of political parties – becoming a complementary link between politics and the state. Over time, civil society's role as a substitute for politics has become extremely ambiguous. On the one hand, the rise in popularity of governance has meant that civil society and its organizations have been accorded an enhanced role in dialogue and negotiation processes. However, on the other hand, political parties have long sought to stifle competition from civil society whether by using it as a buzzword designed to rejuvenate their own jaded and discredited images or by exploiting it as a source of political recruitment. While the parties have not been entirely successful in this, it is clear nonetheless that civil society has become a key battleground of political competition and is open to a series of uses and misuses.

The rise and fall of political parties

In the period between the economic crisis of 1929 and the post-Second World War era, the state subjected the market economy to systematic regulation, covering the welfare state and, since the late 1960s, unions and business associations. This has been defined as 'organized capitalism' (Lash and Urry 1988). At more or less the same time 'organized democracy' emerged. It was founded on three basic elements:

1 the institution of democratic pluralism, along with the recognition of political and civil rights;
2 party government;
3 the advancement of welfare benefits to 'social' rights, which provided the basic link between organized democracy and organized capitalism by complementing 'civil' and 'political' rights.

Organized democracy and organized capitalism sustained each other. From the point of view of organized capitalism, the state provided the basic remedy for market failures and, if universal suffrage had at first been interpreted as a serious threat to political stability and social order, organized democracy enabled political parties to turn this threat into a means of rallying electoral and non-electoral consensus, as well as to establish a counterweight to the influence of key economic centres of power.

Most likely, this was the secret behind the success of three glorious decades between 1945 and 1975 that made Western Europeans forget the terrible three decades that had preceded them, marked by one-party fascist regimes (such as in Italy, Germany, Spain and Portugal) and by serious challenges to the remaining democratic regimes from a variety of reactionary right-wing movements. In contrast to the interwar period, when parties were looked upon distrustfully and some countries preferred an authoritarian one-party state to a competitive multi-party system, parties gained extraordinary cultural and constitutional recognition in the post-Second World War period. This was reflected both in the Italian Constitution and the German *Grundgesetz*, in which parties were institutionalized in order to complement the state. Indeed, their very presence seemed to offer not only a chance for democratization, but a guarantee of it. Moreover, parties played a fundamental role as instruments of social and political integration (Neumann 1956).

Even though the parties may not have entirely coincided with society, they were able to coordinate many other forms of social organizations, such as unions, cooperatives, sports clubs, women's-, youth- or retired people's organizations. Their reach was extremely broad, except for the realm of the church and religious organizations, which nevertheless often established solid ties with religiously oriented parties, and business organizations, whose ties with parties were significantly weaker and less steady (in the case of Italy, see Manoukian 1968). Thus, despite the parties' omnipresence, their authority was not universally accepted and the favourable climate towards them was not to be taken as a given. Towards the end of the 1960s, a legitimacy crisis of political parties was triggered by a combination of factors, including socioeconomic transformations (in particular the decline of class conflicts and the expansion of the middle class), as well as the emergence of new communication strategies and campaign technologies which had begun to affect party competition (Kirchheimer 1966).

From the mid-1970s onwards, the parties' loss of legitimacy was associated with yet another dynamic: Democracy was held to be overloaded with expectations it could not meet and this reduced its potential for governing and led to flagrant waste and inefficiencies. Market failure, however, was translated into government failure. The economic crisis that had afflicted advanced capitalism became a political and democratic crisis in which every problem was attributed to the interference of democratic institutions, the welfare state and the parties themselves. Therefore, what had to be reformed now was democracy itself. Those who had been sceptical or downright hostile towards democracy turned into its most committed supporters overnight. They posited themselves as the protectors of democracy from the alleged intrusiveness of professional politicians and parties and even former conservatives reinvented themselves as innovators and reformers.

Meanwhile, the state was incrementally reduced to make room for the market, and parties increasingly lost ground as membership numbers declined and activist participation decreased. Little attention has been paid to this development, even though it was one of the cornerstones of the neo-liberal blueprint. Parties can be thought of at the same time as being responsible for this process and as its target. Established democracies had been shaken by cultural upheavals. The masses had become better educated, average income had increased, a culture strongly influenced by individualistic and post-materialistic values had spread, society was no longer based on the Fordist model and the media had taken on a new role. However, political parties did not simply adapt to these changes, but rather ended up making themselves redundant, as they abandoned their potential for mass mobilization.

In 1975, the 'Trilateral Commission', an influential transatlantic think-tank, published a report on 'The crisis of democracy' (Crozier *et al.* 1975). The Commission's report, which became well known in Italy,[1] took issue with the governability of democracies and, among other remedies, considered it paramount that parties channel political demands and keep control of participatory elements. The reason why party leaders adhered to those prescriptions might be quite simple. As legitimate potential members of government, it was more cost-effective for them to compete among themselves, rather than to cultivate mass followings, and to rely on public resources for survival.[2]

From a broader perspective, one might say that while at the level of policies neo-liberal orthodoxy had won the day, at the level of politics what can be termed 'post-democratic' orthodoxy had prevailed. Encouraging and legitimizing the reorganization of the parties' operating rules and regulations, these orthodoxies led to a profound transformation of the democratic regimes.[3] Characteristically, executive branches were strengthened and legislative assemblies weakened. Parties reinvented themselves as associations of citizens and developed into coalitions of elected officials and electoral marketing agencies. Finally, elected officials became less and less responsive, as voters increasingly failed to articulate and communicate their preferences.

This process of change was particularly pronounced in Italy. During the first two post-war decades, Italy had been conditioned by the presence of parties more than any other Western European country. This was due to the weakness of the Italian state, the lack of a homogeneous national identity, as well as the delayed modernization of the economy, massive migrations and movement of labour. Hence, Italian society was influenced more deeply than other countries by the new cultural climate. Nonetheless, political change appeared as a long period of decline and rejection of all the crucial institutions governing society, i.e. schools, universities, the military and the judiciary, as well as the Catholic Church, which despite the cultural changes had preserved its strong role, and most important in the context of the present discussion, it affected the parties.

Important developments highlighted this process. First, the unions' 'monopoly' of labour protests was broken in the early 1960s at the headquarters of the car industry in Turin. Only by the end of the 1960s did the unions regain the initiative, however they had to distance themselves from the parties to do so (for instance, by giving up their established practice of sending their highest-level leaders to parliament). Second, Catholic dissent mobilized and received further impetus after the Second Vatican Council. Third, as in most Western European countries in the period around 1968, students mobilized against the establishment – however, in Italy the resulting unrest lasted for almost ten years and student protests blended in with an equally long period of worker struggles, which often bypassed the unions altogether.

The early 1970s saw further struggles in several big cities for the right to housing, the emergence of ecological and pacifist movements, as well as a civil rights and women's rights movement, which was primarily sparked by the demand to legalize divorce and culminated in the mobilization on the issue of the legalization of abortion. However, the political parties were in fact the main targets of this widespread mobilization. Even the Communist Party, which traditionally had been very strong at the organizational and ideological levels, was challenged by new left movements. The parties found it difficult to read the signs of change. The confessional party, the Christian Democrats (DC) failed to come to terms with the fact that society had become more secularized. It stubbornly fought against the introduction of divorce legislation, which was nevertheless eventually introduced by parliament and backed by a large majority of voters in a national referendum.

The continuing alienation of the parties from society was reflected at the normative level as the term 'party' no longer evoked stability, continuity and professionalism, or the ability to promote and achieve social change. Rather, it stood for heaviness, slowness, bureaucratic opaqueness, ideological dullness and obstinate resistance to innovation. Thus, a new discourse started to prevail, celebrating movements, both at the descriptive and the normative levels, because the notion evoked the absence of solidified hierarchies and suggested lightness, flexibility, subjectivity and creativity. More and more people became convinced that movements were 'democratic', while parties had simply never been so (Melucci 1977). In an attempt to make use of the positive connotations attached to the term, every organization became a 'movement'. Even the unions, which were among the strongest, best equipped and also most bureaucratized organizations, jumped on the bandwagon and turned into 'the Union's movement'.

The parties' instinctive reaction was to label social movements as causes of disorder. For example, the Communist Party was at the forefront in condemning the student movement and expelled a group of dissidents who had published a radical newspaper, *Il Manifesto*.

Uses and misuses of civil society

It was in this period of searching for interpretations for the processes of change, when the notion of civil society entered political discourse. Civil society stood out among other conceptual categories because, like the term movement, it incorporated positive values such as morality, spontaneity and freedom. The word civil evokes civis and civitas – i.e. the idea of democratic citizenship. The most characteristic definition of civil society was put forward by Norberto Bobbio in a dictionary of politics (Bobbio 1976). Bobbio reviewed the genealogy of the concept from Hobbes to Gramsci and explained the contemporary use of the term:

> The contrast between civil society and the state is often made out of polemical motives. This contrast can bring out many affirmations. For example, civil society is moving more quickly than the state. The state is incapable of taking in all the ferment that is coming out of civil society. Processes of delegitimization take shape within civil society that the state is not always capable of stopping. At moments of social rupture people predict a return to civil society, just as natural law theorists had predicted the return to the state of nature.
>
> (Bobbio 1976)

While the term *civil society* was becoming widespread, even among neo-Marxists (Stame 1977), another concept which would become common currency for both left and right was *partitocrazia* (partyocracy). This denoted an illegitimate distortion of the democratic regime, in which parties had adopted the spoils-system, sharing out top positions in public administration, in state agencies and within that vast part of the country's economy under the control of the state. Due to this distortion, criteria such as merit, competence or efficiency were systematically ignored.

Party government affected Italy to an extraordinary degree and in a manner which was unique among Western European democracies. The party system was extremely uncompetitive: for almost half a century, the same parties controlled and occupied central government. Indeed, it is worth noting here that even the dramatic crisis of the party system in the early 1990s has not brought an end to party government in Italy as the parties have remained fundamental conduits for the selection of national and local ruling classes. The parties also continue to dictate the orientation of public policies and control the public administration, as well as several key resources, especially public broadcasting. Already, back in the 1950s, both the liberal and fascist right had accused all parties of having established a regime of partyocracy (Lupo 2005). However, by the end of the 1960s the left (that had never taken on government positions until then) also adopted the term, as did the Radical Party, an organization focused on fighting for civil rights. At the same time, various intellectuals close to the Communist Party showed a preference for the term *clientelism* – that is political patronage – accusing the ruling Christian Democrats of identifying their party with the state.[4] Strange as it may seem, this is how a century-old set of critiques of political parties, i.e. the anti-parliamentary ideology of Gaetano Mosca and Vilfredo Pareto that had flourished between 1870 and the First World War and had been banished from the political sphere during the Fascist era, was rediscovered and put to use, albeit in a significantly different form. The anti-parliamentary ideology that had spread before the First World War – and which would peak with the advent of fascism – had indeed backed the idea of the 'strong state', envisioning the existence of a regime of notables who would be flanked by a strong and competent bureaucracy and should not be conditioned by political struggles. After the Second World War, anti-party factions (including those harking back to elements of fascism) continued to exist within Italian society. These advocated a strong state and, after 1958, looked to France under De Gaulle as a model. The novelty of the 1970s was the fact that an anti-party current of the left emerged. Unlike its counterparts on the right, this discourse contrasted the parties not with the state, but with civil society. The most interesting aspect of these developments for our discussion is that the parties did not seek to respond to the challenge posed by civil society through dialogue, but by seizing on and appropriating for themselves the very critique of the parties which had been put forward. It is true, of course, that the mobilization of civil society helped bring about important changes such as the introduction of divorce in 1973. However, the main point to be noted here is that, by the mid-1970s, the critique of Italian party government had become widespread within the party system itself and was often accompanied by praise for civil society. The first party to embark on this path was the Communist Party, followed swiftly by the Socialist and then several internal Christian Democratic factions. Thus, over a period of years, a significant part of 'official politics' came to support the claims of civil society, extol its merits and declare its desire to open up to it by co-opting its key figures and promising to introduce a radical reform of the Constitution in order to combat the oligarchic elitism of the parties.

Let us look at events one by one (Mastropaolo 2001). In 1968, collective protest movements and a new, 'ultra-democratic' left emerged, advocating direct democracy and the utopian vision of rule by committee. Similarly, by the mid-1970s the critique of partyocracy had already spread very widely. Interestingly, although the *Corriere della Sera* – one of Italy's oldest and most prestigious newspapers – had long hosted anti-party critiques by liberals and conservatives, it also began to support the civil rights movement in the mid-1970s. In 1976, La *Repubblica*, a new newspaper that was close to the non-communist left, was founded and enjoyed immediate success. Both newspapers became mouthpieces of a new kind of politics, propagating renewal through a new set of professionally competent leaders who would be sensitive to the views of common citizens, free of party loyalties and unencumbered by 'orthodox ideologies' and the ties of political patronage.

Above all, the basic factor contributing to the success of the concept of civil society were the radical changes mentioned above, which had revolutionized democratic regimes (both in Italy and elsewhere) from the mid-1970s onwards. Over a period of years, Italy thus developed a new understanding of democracy that hinged on a critique of the parties. In the mid-1970s, the Christian Democrats and the Communists struggled hard to build a 'grand coalition' government, which was not popular among ideologically pure militants and did not attract much support among party voters either. The idea of working towards an eventual coalition between the Christian Democrats and the Communist Party was immediately dismissed by many commentators and political figures as an opportunist, consociative manoeuvre.[5] Critics from the left feared the decline of the Communists once in government, while critics on the right accused the Christian Democrats of seeking to relinquish its role as the guarantor of Italy's pro-Western stance and as the representative of moderates in Italian society. Others claimed that the move would lead to the removal of political opposition, a development exacerbated by the fact that, in their view, the democratic cultures of both the Communists and the Christian Democrats already left much to be desired. Finally, the Socialist Party, positioned between the two main parties, feared that it would be marginalized by a grand coalition. This scenario therefore offered an excellent opportunity to further denounce the power of the parties and their connivance with one another (which, it was held, would lead to the silencing of the opposition), while at the same time acclaiming the upcoming actor of civil society.

Public debate was no longer concerned with social conflict, or the possibility of managing conflict through integrative strategies similar to those adopted in other countries. No-one regarded communism as an actual threat anymore, and even communists themselves no longer believed in the transition from a capitalist to a socialist economy. On the other hand, 'democracy' and 'the economy' were still seen as highly dependent on the political parties. Their power, coupled with their reluctance to change, generated a strong counter-movement. The supposed virtues of civil society were at the core of the rhetoric, somewhat similar to the discourses in Eastern Europe and Latin America, with their frequent references to the decline of Soviet hegemony and the fall of South American dictatorships. Nevertheless, it would be misleading to claim that Italian 'society' at some point spontaneously rebelled against 'the state'.

The civil-society rhetoric was used again as a label by new (but in fact often highly institutionalized) political entrepreneurs towards the end of the 1970s, by this time the same parties (first and foremost the Christian Democrats) had been in office for four decades and the call for a change of political leadership had become widespread.

At the same time, sections of the political and economic establishment began to promote the virtues of civil society as well. However, they not only tried to reduce the role of political parties and thus to limit corruption and patronage, but also attempted to break the social-democratic pacts and to abolish welfare policies. These political and economic actors were supported by the media, which in the meantime had become the long arm of politics.

From the late 1970s to the early 1990s the most incisive role in charting the future of Italian politics was played by actors with consummate experience, who had been active in social movements for many years and had hence become skilled political organizers. They helped to bring about the political earthquake that struck the party system and plotted out what Arendt Lijphart termed the transformation from a 'consensual' into a 'majoritarian' democracy (Lijphart 1984). Others who spoke out against official politics included eminent second-rank party leaders and well-known intellectuals, who were not totally free of party ties. They were joined by members of the political establishment from leading and supporting ranks, and by members of the highly institutionalized circles of Catholic associations.

Initially, the Socialist Party, which towards the end of the 1970s sought to exploit the advantages of its position in between the Christian Democrats and the Communists, played a fundamental role in the process, by launching a campaign in favour of new electoral rules and by advocating constitutional reform. Its main objective, however, was to create favourable conditions which would pave the way for its own leadership.

In addition to the Socialist Party's attempt to reform official politics from within, several self-proclaimed members of 'civil society' challenged official politics to restore the morality of the political system. One illustrative example is Società civile (Civil Society), a combative cultural association that also published a journal of the same name. It was founded in Milan, in order to promote the morality of politics. One of its initiators was Nando Dalla Chiesa, the son of a prefect who had been killed by the Mafia in Sicily. As a university professor who had already been active in the social movements, Dalla Chiesa eventually embarked on a successful political career. Another example is the well-articulated array of anti-Mafia associations in the South. Southern political leaders were often accused of colluding with the Mafia at local level. Following each assassination of public figures (from politicians to high government officials, prosecutors and journalists), the number of new members of anti-Mafia associations increased. They were strongly supported by a network of Catholic associations, parishes, and even Jesuit priests. For a long time they were led by Leoluca Orlando, another university professor who had been active in the ranks of the Christian Democratic Party. Thanks partly to these associations, Orlando was elected mayor of Palermo in 1985. A third example is that of Catholic-inspired movements. Some of these were long established and strong in terms of membership. Furthermore, the Jesuits founded a school for political training in Palermo in the mid-1980s aimed at developing a new class of local and national leaders, motivating citizens and fostering moral values. In the following years, their example was followed by bishops, priests, as well as religious and lay organizations all over the country.

At the end of the 1980s, the Lega Nord (Northern League), an ethno-populist party in Italy's northern regions, presented a new political element. The Lega translated the opposition between official politics and civil society into a clash between North and South, tainted by racist, anti-Southern overtones. The Lega idealized 'honest and hard-working people of the productive North', who had allegedly turned Italy into a modern industrial economy, in contrast to the South, said to be living off the North (Albertazzi and McDonnell 2005).

Nevertheless, the most relevant and paradoxical phenomenon was the mobilization of civil society by official politics itself, with politicians making fiery anti-political speeches. By the end of the decade, almost all parties had joined the Socialists in denouncing the pitiable conditions of Italian public life and praising 'civil society'. Some of the better-known civil-society activists were even fielded as candidates in elections.

The Communist Party at the end of the 1980s had become a key force in the mobilization against official politics. Indeed, although civil society had initially challenged traditional politics, many from within the political class had proved able to turn that very same rhetoric to their own advantage and to infiltrate civil society structures. In the case of the Communist Party, in the wake of the fall of the Berlin Wall in 1989, it decided to change its name, rejecting Marxism and the Communist tradition, and reinvented itself as the representatives of civil society through which civil society was supposed to achieve full recognition as a political actor.

At the beginning of the 1990s, the nature of the increasing interest shown by politicians in civil society changed. Various secondary figures in the traditional parties and several leaders of the smallest parties sought to promote themselves as civil-society leaders. They called on the media for support as they referred to the existence of a reforming faction that was supposed to be 'outside' of politics. In effect, however, this reforming faction was for the most part only virtual, a rhetorical invention that appeared as the driving force of a combating campaign against official politics. One illustrious example of a political U-turn was that of Mario Segni who, as the son of a former President of the Republic, had once nurtured great political ambitions. Segni – the Christian Democrat, university professor and former Undersecretary of State – who had been a member of parliament several times, now became the leader of a referendum movement, which successfully promoted a new electoral law, aimed at introducing a majoritarian voting system that (according to the movement's leadership) would reduce corruption in politics.

The final collapse of the party system was sparked by the government parties' modest loss of votes in the 1992 general election. At the same time the media, along with various politicians and economic actors, raised alarm at the fact that public debt had apparently reached dangerous levels. Shortly afterwards, state prosecutors began investigating and then charging a series of members of the governing political class. This heralded the famous *Tangentopoli* period and the crisis of the party system. Two emergency governments were formed and, once the electoral law had been changed, new elections were held, which dealt a death blow to the former governing parties, in particular the Christian Democrats and the Socialists. The 1994 elections finally introduced bipolarism to Italian politics – a development which was acclaimed by the moralizers of public life and brought yet another new factor into the Italian political world – Silvio Berlusconi.

Berlusconi did not present himself as a member of 'civil society', but as someone belonging to the 'common people', which nonetheless allowed him to claim he was an outsider, a businessman who loved his country. According to Berlusconi, as he said in a speech given on 24 January 1994 on all his television channels (see: www.forza-italia.it/notizie/mov_2801.htm), he had decided to 'take to the field and put his professional experience at his crisis-stricken nation's disposal'. In reality, like many Italian businessmen, he had always benefited from strong political connections, and this had facilitated his construction of a media empire, for instance by allowing him to introduce nationwide commercial television. Nevertheless, to a certain extent he was in fact a *homo novus*, the new man who ended up promoting an extensive turnover of political personnel by drawing from among the ranks of his companies to recruit the leadership of the new party he had created overnight, *Forza Italia*.

Berlusconi's electoral victory came about at a time when the rise of Italian civil society had reached its peak (at least in the rhetoric of those claiming to represent it). The main political leitmotif in the years to follow was the parties' repossession of control over politics. While between 1996 and 1998, right-wing parties were busy institutionalizing themselves (including the Northern League, Berlusconi's own Forza Italia, and the ex-fascists of the National Alliance), centre-left parties (including many of the heirs of the traditional parties of the so-called 'First Republic') were still praising 'civil society'. One example of this was their support for people who did not have any previous political experience as mayoral candidates. However, this situation changed at the end of the 1990s. First of all, Forza Italia strengthened its structure and provided a home for some of the middle-ranking former leaders of traditional parties, who had been divested of office during Tangentopoli. In the meantime, activists who had become involved with politics with the centre-left as members of 'civil society', had either abandoned political life or had by now become professional politicians themselves.

This does not mean that civil society no longer played a significant role. On the contrary, the myth of civil society gained more and more credit each time the government suffered another crisis or underwent yet another reorganization. When, in the aftermath of the 2001 general election, centre-left parties seemed unable to respond to the success of Berlusconi and the centre-right, civil society came forward to invigorate the opposition. For instance, a very large non-governmental pacifist movement mobilized against the war in Iraq – which the Berlusconi government had decided to take part in. Moreover, the anti-globalization movement gained further momentum in reaction to the violent repression of demonstrations in Genoa in the summer of 2001 (Andretta *et al.* 2002). Civil society – in this case the unions – also mobilized against the harsh measures taken by Berlusconi's government against employees and the prospect of pension cuts. Finally, in 2002, civil society – or rather, the intellectuals – gave rise to the *girotondi* (literally, the ring-around-the-roses) movement, that demonstrated primarily against Berlusconi's enduring conflict of interests. In particular, protests focused on his grip over the media in Italy, given that not only did his family retain control of the three main private television stations but, as prime minister, he was able to wage massive influence over the public RAI network. A more recent example of the use of civil society demonstrates the continuous amalgamation of civil society and official politics. In 2006, the inhabitants of a valley near the French border rose up against the building of a high-speed rail tunnel through the Alps. The project had been planned by a centre-left government and was finalized under a centre-right government, but the mayors of many affected towns were among the leaders of the anti-high-speed-railway movement, calling once again upon the moral and political authority of civil society.

The 'other' civil society

According to Michel Foucault, the concept of the nation was invented in the seventeenth century as a useful means of delineating a social and political body in opposition to the absolutist state. As Foucault also observed, however, the concept was swiftly taken over by the state, which deployed it for its own purposes (Foucault 1997). The destiny of civil society has not been so different. The notion of civil society originated in Italy at the end of the 1960s as a form of mobilization against the interference of the parties and against official politics. Within a decade it had turned into its opposite. Secondary segments and dissidents of official politics, along with government representatives, claimed to represent 'civil society' and gave vigorous anti-political speeches that exacerbated the legitimacy crisis of the party system. Of course, they did this in order to cultivate their own ambitions, even though they sometimes blended in with parts of society that were genuinely mobilizing in order to renew politics.

As described above, this widespread mobilization had substantial effects including the collapse of the old party system, the establishment of a majoritarian democracy, the emergence of several new parties, and the marginalization of the unions. While official politics had stifled the parties' function as channels of participation, the government invented substitute forms of civil-society empowerment.

In this context 'civil society' refers to its function in the so-called third sector. In other advanced democracies, the term mainly denotes the array of actors reacting to the deficiencies of the state, following its shift towards neoliberalism. Often the traditional associations are revitalized. Therefore, 'civil society' includes a set of agencies outside both the state and the market, which have developed into major suppliers of public services. The state often stimulates and financially supports such forms of collective self-start organizations and self-help groups and even delegates areas of public services to them. Thus, the state is consolidating a new form of entrepreneurship that is neither directly economic nor directly political, and the success of which cannot be measured in profit but in 'social usefulness'.

This meaning of 'civil society' has long been overshadowed by the strictly political concept. Yet, recently it has thrived in Italy, where the resistance of the parties and the unions along with the political mobilization of civil society prevented the type of radical neo-conservative depoliticization described by Bruno Jobert in Chapter 1 of this volume. This different definition of civil society has inspired some noteworthy theoretical interest, too. Inspired by Giddens' 'Third

Way', public discourse has taken up the classical argument that the state and party politics are obsolete and should be substituted by associations and other pre-political mobilizations. Catholic intellectuals and social scientists in Italy have been particularly receptive to these ideas (Garelli and Simone 2000; Magatti 2005). In terms of ethics, the Catholic world had to recede due to secularization, although it continues to wield considerable influence over Italian political life. Its recent reinvigoration is linked with the long and charismatic reign of Pope John Paul II and the disappearance of other competing agencies, such as the parties. In particular, it has profited from the decline of the welfare state, to which it has offered an alternative in the name of civil society, as we can see from the large number of Catholic associations that have steered towards volunteerism.

As a charity, Caritas originated in the Conferenza episcopale italiana (Italian Episcopal Conference) and has spread all over Italy. The organization coordinates voluntary work in a variety of fields (for instance by providing assistance to immigrants, prison inmates, minors, the homeless and those with psychiatric disabilities) often with the economic support of public administrations (Dorangricchia and Itçaina 2005). Another such organization is the Compagnia delle Opere (Companionship of Deeds) which is an 'association of businesses' originating from Comunione e liberazione (Communion and Liberation), a traditionalist church movement. According to its website, the Compagnia links together 15,000 businesses and 200,000 members. Like Caritas, it enjoys considerable support from public administrations for the services it offers through 'non-profit' cooperatives. That said, the organization also turns a profit in many others areas, for instance it has taken on a leading role in providing healthcare in Lombardy, where its president comes from.

Over the last 20 years, 'non-profit' organizations have grown considerably, and not only within the Catholic world. Both centre-left and centre-right governments have encouraged non-profit associations to become involved in delivering public services. Hence, anti-racket associations protect shopkeepers and small businessmen, while other organizations administrate the resources seized from the Mafia, or are engaged in environmental protection. An ethical bank has been established and several foundations operate to serve the common good in the areas of social assistance, health and sports. Finally, thanks to some (mainly Catholic) pacifist associations, civil society has even taken on a number of foreign-relations tasks (Donati and Colozzi 2001). 'Social cooperatives' also claim to form part of civil society. These organizations often act like private businesses, and are entrusted with a great variety of tasks by public administrations, such as looking after the elderly, providing cleaning services for schools, running university libraries, etc.

The third sector as a whole currently encompasses 221,000 organizations, 630,000 employees and 3,200,000 volunteers, with a turnover of 38 million euros (Barbetta *et al.* 2003; Marcon 2005). These figures in mind, it might be argued that this sector should be regulated by the state, although it is open to discussion whether parliament, which has recently introduced new legislation, has simply been inactive in this area or whether it has furthered the development by transferring increasing numbers of tasks to the third sector. Two parliamentary initiatives are particularly worthy of note. First, an independent authority was set up in 2000 to oversee 'non-profit, socially useful organizations' and oversee the 'uniform and correct observance of legislative and regulatory discipline'. The authority's first president was the current chancellor of the Catholic University of Milan, while his successor was a Catholic economist. Second, the principle of subsidiarity was incorporated into the Italian Constitution in 2001.

Civil society has cut its own peculiar path in Italy's democracy. By the last decade of the twentieth century, the call for a 'majoritarian' democracy was widespread because consensual democracy was blamed for the amount of negotiations and horse-trading required in order to reach decisions in parliament, between political parties, interest groups and the trade unions. Thus, public discourse had discredited negotiation and mediation related to official politics, while at the same time acclaiming decision-making processes associated with 'civil society'. As a consequence, the deliberation processes seen in other Western democracies were delayed in Italy. However, many local administrations have now initiated deliberative consultations in order to help resolve complex and politically sensitive issues concerning public services (Pellizzoni 2005; Ravazzi 2007).

It remains to be seen if and to what degree civil society will further contribute to easing the democratic malaise which is constantly highlighted by public opinion polls. Will there be a similar level of disappointment with civil society in the long run as part of what we might call a 'deliberation fatigue'? In the media, the growing involvement of citizens in non-profit organizations is portrayed as the other side of the coin of declining political participation and is interpreted as a positive sign of the state of the democratic institutions.[6] The non-profit sector itself also markets a very positive self-image (Marcon 2005). In any case, while there is no evidence of an actual relationship between the increasing involvement of citizens in civil society and the decline of conventional political participation – after all, there is nothing stopping citizens from participating both in civil-society organizations and in political life – it is worth considering two final points. The first is that if civil society is portrayed as a virtuous alternative to conventional political participation, then the legitimacy of both the latter and traditional political institutions is inevitably weakened. The second point is that civil society and associations constitute a highly selective area of political participation. For example, while NIMBY movements have included citizens from diverse social and educational backgrounds, the majority of civil-society groups tend to attract those who are well-informed, highly-educated and already familiar with how politics works. By contrast, one of the key traditional roles of mass organizations such as parties and trade unions has been to draw in people from all sectors of society, irrespective of class or educational qualifications. It seems legitimate therefore to ask: to what extent are those outside the middle classes involved in environmental groups, third-sector initiatives or protests such as those staged by the 'girotondi'?

Of course, this aspect of civil society does not only relate to Italy. What is particular to Italy, however, is the fact that, having previously avoided the neo-conservative reduction of civil society to the family seen elsewhere (as part of an attempt to change the social order), this phenomenon has now emerged in Italy at a time when it appears to have failed in other countries. Its main promoters are the hierarchy of the Vatican, the bishops and the parties of the right. As in other post-industrial societies, levels of religious worship in Italy have long been in decline. Nonetheless, the Catholic vote continues to be a key battleground for the two main centre-right and centre-left coalitions. This competition has offered new opportunities to Catholic groups (strongly influenced by the post-Vatican II revisionism of the last two papacies) not only to secure significant benefits for their organizations, but also to promote their values and policies, particularly as regards the family. This renewed strength was reflected by the 'Family Day' rally in May 2007 when a million people gathered in Rome to defend the sanctity of the traditional family model. Only later did it emerge that not all those present were in fact Catholic – several hundred thousand came from Protestant congregations. Either way, however, once again the holy spirit of civil society had been summoned.

This shows how an idea which, in principle, appears democratically positive can be subject to political manipulation. Indeed, we might say that this is the main lesson to be drawn from the Italian case. Born as a constellation of political actors that wished to escape from the bureaucracy of official politics, civil society in Italy has been primarily a parallel form of politics. It has served as a substitute for official politics and, later, as a substitute for the welfare state. Thus, it has not only lent itself to dubious political manoeuvres, but also to those whose democratic stance is questionable.

Notes

1 Giovanni Agnelli, the most prestigious Italian businessman at the time, wrote a preface to the Italian version.
2 This was explained by the theory of the 'cartel party' (Katz and Mair 1995) later on.
3 The provisional outcome of this transformation has recently been described as the 'presidentialisation of politics' (Poguntke and Webb 2005).
4 It was Tarrow (1967) who introduced the concept of clientalism in a book translated into Italian in 1972, which generated widespread political discussion.
5 Incidentally, the term *consociative* was not attributed its appropriate meaning (see Lijphart 1977).
6 A research project was promoted by ARCI (a federation of leftist associations) on the occasion of its 50th anniversary. It found that in 2006 the percentage of Italians participating in activities promoted by cultural, recreational, social-assistance and religious organizations varied from 24.1 per cent to 28.8 per cent. More specifically, cultural and recreational organizations attracted 28.8 per cent of citizens, social-assistance 26.7 per cent, religious organizations 24.1 per cent and sporting associations 21.8 per cent. This research project, conducted on a sample of 1,000 individuals, prompted the influential centre-left daily newspaper *Il Riformista* (4 April 2007) to run an article entitled 'Volunteer organizations beat politics 3 to 1'.

References

Albertazzi, D. and McDonnell D. (2005) 'The Lega Nord in the second Berlusconi government: in a league of its own', *West European Politics*, 28 (5): 952–972.

Andretta, M., della Porta, D., Mosca, L. and Reiter H. (2002) *Global, Noglobal, New Global. La protesta contro il G8 a Genova*, Roma-Bari: Laterza.

Barbetta G., Cima, S. and Zamaro, N. (eds) (2003) *Le istituzioni nonprofit in Italia. Dimensioni organizzative, economiche e sociali*, Bologna: Il Mulino.

Bobbio, N. (1976) 'Società civile', in N. Bobbio and N. Matteucci (eds) *Dizionario di politica*, Torino: Utet.

Crozier, M., Huntington, S.P. and Watanuki, J. (1975) *The Crisis of Democracy. Report on the Governability of Democracies to the Trilateral Commission*, New York: New York University Press.

Donati, P. and Colozzi, I. (eds) (2001) *Generare 'il civile': nuove esperienze nella società italiana*, Bologna: Il Mulino.

Dorangricchia, A. and Itçaina, X. (2005) 'Les mobilisations catholiques face à la politisation de l'immigration', in E. Ritaine (ed.) *Politiques de l'étranger: l'Europe du Sud face à l'immigration*, Paris: Presses Universitaires de France.

Foucault, M. (1997) *'Il faut défendre la société'. Cours au Collège de France, 1976*, Paris: Gallimard-Seuil.

Garelli, F. and Simone, M. (eds) (2000) *Quale società civile per l'Italia di domani? Atti della 43. Settimana sociale dei cattolici italiani*, Bologna: Il Mulino.

Katz, R.S. and Mair, P. (1995) 'Changing models of party organization and party democracy', *Party Politics*, 1: 5–28.

Kirchheimer, O. (1966) 'The transformation of the Western European party systems', in J. LaPalombara and M. Weiner (eds) *Political Parties and Political Development*, Princeton: Princeton University Press.

Lash, S. and Urry, J. (1988) *The End of Organized Capitalism*, Cambridge: Polity Press.

Lijphart, A. (1977) *Democracy in Plural Societies*, New Haven: Yale University Press.

—— (1984) *Democracies. Patterns of Majoritarian and Consensus Government in Twenty-One Countries*, New Haven: Yale University Press.

Lupo, S. (2005) *Partito e antipartito. Una storia politica delle prima Repubblica (1946–78)*, Roma: Donzelli.

Magatti, M. (2005) *Il potere istituente della società civile*, Bari: Laterza.

Manoukian, A. (ed.) (1968) *La presenza sociale del PCI e della DC*, Bologna: Il Mulino.

Marcon, G. (2005) *Come fare politica senza entrare in un partito*, Milano: Feltrinelli.

Mastropaolo, A. (2001) 'Italie: quand la politique invente la société civile', *Revue française de science politique*, 4: 621–636.

Melucci, A. (1977) *Sistema politico, partiti e movimenti sociali*, Milano: Feltrinelli.

Neumann, S. (1956) 'Towards a comparative study of political parties', in S. Neumann (ed.) *Modern Political Parties. Approaches to Comparative Politics*, Chicago: University of Chicago Press, 395–421.

Pellizzoni L. (ed.) (2005) *La deliberazione pubblica*, Roma: Meltemi.

Poguntke, T. and Webb, P. (2005) *The Presidentialization of Politics. A Comparative Study of Modern Democracies*, Oxford: Oxford University Press.

Ravazzi, S. (2007) *Civicrazia. Quando i cittadini decidono*, Roma: Aracne.

Stame, F. (1977) *Società civile e critica delle istituzioni*, Milano: Feltrinelli.

Tarrow, S.G. (1967) *Peasant Communism in Southern Italy*, New Haven: Yale University Press.

4 A social democratic model of civil society?

Dag Wollebæk and Per Selle

Introduction

In the literature on civil society the Scandinavian voluntary sectors are often labelled as 'social democratic' (Janoski 1998; Salamon and Anheier 1998). Does this help us to make sense of their main characteristics and evolution? And what type of civil society are we talking about?

A lot of energy has gone into debating who 'owns' the civil-society concept (e.g. Cohen 2007). We leave this academic exercise aside, and acknowledge with Edwards (2004) the coexistence of several legitimate understandings of the concept. However, this does not preclude clarity. In this chapter, we develop a typology of perspectives on civil society, based on the two dimensions *individualism* vs. *collectivism* and *consensus* vs. *conflict orientation*. We focus on the one part of civil society that is invariably included in any definition, namely voluntary organizations. We refer to them as 'organized civil society'.

The four approaches, which are elaborated in detail below, comprise different expectations towards voluntary organizations in civil society and democracy. Within each paradigm, prototypical organizations can be identified. In the empirical section, we demonstrate that organized civil society in Norway has evolved within this scheme – from conflict and society orientation towards consensus and individual orientation. This shift calls for a revision of the expectations from voluntary organizations in civil society and democracy.

For a long time, social democracy and civil society have been regarded as a contradiction in terms, as formulated in early non-profit theory, the 'crowding-out' hypothesis and the 'colonization' argument (e.g. Berger and Neuhaus 1996; Etzioni 1995; Fukuyama 1995; Weisbrod 1977; Wolfe 1989). However, the idea that a strong welfare state and an extensive, vital and rather autonomous voluntary sector cannot coexist has been refuted by comparative data to such an extent that it must be considered falsified (e.g. Baer 2007; Lundström and Svedberg 2003; Schofer and Fourcade-Gourinchas 2001; Wollebæk and Selle 2007).

Salamon and Anheier's (1998) *social origins* theory represents a more empirical and refined conceptualization of a social democratic model of civil society. They build on Esping-Andersen's (1990) well-known welfare regime theory in order to construct a typology of third-sector regimes based on the two dimensions government welfare spending and scope of non-profit sector. Social democracy emerges as one category, characterized by a small voluntary welfare sector measured by the number of employees, and a strong 'expressive' role, referring to culture, leisure and advocacy (i.e. non-welfare).[1]

In this chapter, we argue that the characterization of the Norwegian model of organized civil society as social democratic is misleading. The conflict and collectivist-oriented movements which made a lasting imprint on the sector, *predate* social democracy. Their contribution includes the introduction of a hierarchical local–national organizational structure, which perhaps more than anything else unites the Nordic countries but is not discussed in any of the regime theories. Second, in the heyday of social democracy, it was not 'expressive' organizations that expanded, but organizations within the welfare field. Finally, in the current period, social democracy has lost its hegemony. The sector is increasingly characterized by individualist and consensus-oriented organizations. The current growth in 'expressive' organizations cannot reasonably be seen as a product of social democracy, but rather of globalization and neo-liberal ideas.

The empirical section is structured into three parts, labelled background, snapshot and trends. The first section outlines the emergence of organized civil society in Norway. The second part places the most typical traits of the Norwegian voluntary sector in comparative perspective. Finally, we analyse the development over the past decades in order to indicate the direction in which organized civil society is moving.

A typology of approaches to civil society

The contemporary literature is saturated with wildly different definitions of civil society. A typology helps to untangle some of the rather unproductive arguments concerning what is the 'right' definition and whether civil society has been weakened or strengthened. If we acknowledge the existence of several conceptions of civil society, we may rather speak of transitions between types of civil societies. This, in our view, enhances the analytic power of the concept.

In the following, we introduce two dimensions on which civil society perspectives differ fundamentally; first, between conflict and consensus-orientation and second, between individual and collective-orientation (Wollebæk and Selle 2002a). These perspectives have their corollaries in the literature on voluntary organizations and civil society. The difference between a conflict perspective in which politicized elements of civil society are regarded as positive and natural and a consensus perspective which sees disruption and destruction in the same elements – represents the most important schism in the contemporary literature (Edwards 2004). The conflict perspective emphasizes the role of voluntary organizations as provider of a democratic infrastructure, as mediators of interests and guarantors of plurality of values and preferences. The consensus perspective represents a social rather than political interpretation of the role of voluntary organizations. In this context, their most important contribution to society is to create interpersonal ties and social integration in local communities.

The two perspectives can also be classified along an individual–collective dimension. Is civil society primarily an arena for individual fulfilment or for developing larger, collective projects? Smith (1993) makes a useful distinction between public-benefit and private-benefit organizations. Public-benefit groups serve the public rather than members, while member-benefit groups work exclusively for those affiliated. Advocates of the value of member-benefit groups either accentuate the positive externalities of the group's activities (i.e. the social capital perspective), or the legitimate representation of interests vis-à-vis powerful institutions (i.e. pluralism, corporatism).

By combining the two dimensions, we arrive at four groups of perspectives. The typology is presented in Table 4.1, where the main societal role the perspective ascribes to organizations is stated and examples are given of typical organizations within each type.

In the perspective of *social capital* (Putnam 2000), civil society is primarily an arena of social interaction and socialization. The contribution of voluntary organizations is a by-product of their activity, namely social networks and inter-personal trust. Non-political leisure associations are often acclaimed as more productive sources of social capital than conflict-oriented groups, as the networks of the former type tend to be more 'horizontal' (i.e. power-free) and cross-cutting with regard to established patterns of loyalty in society. We have labelled these groups as service organizations, since their main purpose is to supply members with benefits, usually in the form of leisure activities.

Pluralism represents an individual and conflict-oriented approach. In this perspective, the collective is merely the sum of individual preferences and values. Thus, individual, not societal needs constitute the point of departure. The pluralist approach emphasizes that in an ideal situation, interest organizations are in continual competition, that they represent real interests and values among

Table 4.1 Approaches to civil society

	Individual	*Collective*
Conflict	Pluralism	Public sphere theory, comparative associationalism, social movement literature
	Civil society as competition between interests	Civil society as competition between ideas and values
	Most valued organizations: *interest organizations* (e.g. unions, advocacy groups)	Most valued organizations: *critical organizations* (e.g. 'old' and 'new' social movements)
Consensus	Social capital	Communitarianism
	Civil society as socialization	Civil society as social cohesion
	Most valued organizations: *service organizations* (e.g. culture and leisure groups, cooperatives)	Most valued organizations: *community organizations* (e.g. neighbourhood associations, social and humanitarian organizations)

people, and that everyone has the same opportunity to influence political decisions. At the same time, cross-pressures resulting from overlapping organizational memberships moderate views and counter factionalism (e.g. Dahl 1961; Rokkan 1967).

Communitarianism emphasizes the value of the collective over the individual. Thus, it represents a reaction against perspectives (such as pluralism) which place utility maximation and self-interest at the core of how we understand human action. The communitarian perspective on voluntary organizations downplays local conflict (Bellah *et al.* 1985; Etzioni 1988). The responsibility of local associations is to build good local communities, solve social problems and secure a sense of belonging. Organizations which do not only work for the interests of members, but also take considerable responsibility for the benefit of the public are necessary to fulfil these aims. In the real world, neighbourhood and community associations and humanitarian organizations are the closest approximations of these ideals.[2]

Finally, in the upper-right quadrant, we find perspectives that see conflict as an integral part of civil society. These include the *public sphere theory* (Cohen 2007; Cohen and Arato 1992), and the *social movement* literature (Della Porta and Diani 2005) along with what Edwards (2004) labels *comparative associationalism* (such as Skocpol 2003; Wollebæk and Selle 2003, 2004). Public-sphere theorists see the development of a sense of the 'common' or 'public' interest as the main function of civil society (Edwards 2004). Civil society is an arena for deliberation, association and collaboration. It is crucial that this sphere is open and that alternative viewpoints are represented. Thus, consensus-oriented voluntary associations are dismissed by some authors as not representing 'real' civil society, but merely 'civil society talk' (Cohen 2007). However, a polarization of politics that is too strong and the factionalism of special interests represent just as big a threat as the de-politicization of the public sphere. This is a main difference to pluralism, in which the institutionalization of conflict is seen as a positive element of the political system. The public-sphere perspective presupposes a willingness to see oneself through the eyes of others, and a desire to reach compromises.

Comparative associationalism emphasizes in particular the role of representation and institutions. While the deliberative direction states that a common or public interest can and should be reached, comparative associationalism stresses that this cannot be done without aggregation of interests in a democratic structure. Thus, the *structure* of voluntary organizations is crucial. Historically, a hierarchical–federated structure, linking the local and national level, has enabled organizations to take policy initiatives. This role is not limited to the most explicit political organizations, such as unions or parties. Social policies in the post-war era developed through symbiotic relationships between government and associations (Selle and Kuhnle 1992; Skocpol 1999).

Thus, the principle of representation is a very important theme in comparative associationalism. The linkage between citizen and political system is maintained through institutional ties, the emphasis being on the importance of mass-membership organizations with great numerical strength. The local–national structure enables citizens to raise concerns at higher political levels, using the local chapter of their organization. In this perspective, the revival of the local, non-political associations celebrated by social capital and communitarianism is insufficient or even harmful as they represent a withdrawal from politics.

These four broad visions of civil society are reflected in different types of voluntary organizations. In the social capital approach, importance is attached to service organizations (e.g. leisure groups, cooperatives) that benefit democracy indirectly by means of generating social networks and values that enhance cooperation and collective action. Communitarians value groups that improve local social integration and welfare (e.g. neighbourhood associations, cultural heritage groups). Pluralists emphasize effective interest mediators (e.g. unions and advocacy organizations). Finally, public-sphere theorists and comparative associationalists approve of organizations that are conflict-oriented and not merely representatives of narrow interests (e.g. social movements). We have labelled these groups critical organizations.

Where does organized civil society in Norway stand within this scheme? As we shall see, there is a clear historical movement from conflict towards consensus, and from collectivism towards individualism. This development can be interpreted in very different ways, depending on the observer's vision of civil society. In a public sphere or comparative-associationalist perspective, the development represents a weakening of organizations as intermediary institutions, and as such a democratic problem. On the other hand, social capital theorists and to some extent communitarianists would see the development as partly positive because of the increase in locally based and consensus-oriented organizations, some of which also have a collective orientation. Thus, rather than speaking of a decline or a revitalization of civil society, it is more adequate to speak of a transition from one type of civil society to another.

Background: historical origins of organized civil society in Norway

Pre-social democracy, in the era of democratization and mass mobilization, the focal point of the sector was within *critical* organizations. In this period, two crucial characteristics were established: first, a culture of mass participation emerged; second, the hierarchical structures that were necessary in order to link local community with national politics evolved. These structures remained unchallenged until the 1960s.

Between 1837 and 1845, the freedom of organizations was improved by a series of laws.[3] This early liberalization laid the foundations for mobilization for a number of causes, which gained pace in the second half of the nineteenth century. The organizations were linked in broader movements – the labour movement, for instance, consisted of unions, the political wing (the Labour Party), and, primarily in the cities, a variety of voluntary groups for sports, leisure and educational activities. Similar tripartite functions (professional, political and cultural/leisure) were found in the farmers' movement. The other mass movements (anti-alcohol movements, the liberal *Venstre* movement (which was linked to language organizations and humanitarian organizations), and the Christian mission movement) fulfilled both political and cultural ends. They established hierarchical structures and decision-making channels linking the geographical levels.

The movements differed on many issues, but the struggle for more political freedoms and national independence were common causes for most of them. They were conflict-oriented, represented alternatives to the establishment and wanted to influence society. Rather than advocating the interests of members, they worked for collective purposes. Obviously, the movements in the economic field clearly had an agenda on behalf of their members, but the struggle for worker's rights was also part of a general struggle for social equality, which transcended interest politics.

The peak of social democracy (from the mid-1930s until after the first two post-war decades) was characterized by the strong increase of consensus and society-oriented (*communitarian*) associations, in a climate of post-war reconstruction and expansion of the welfare state. In general, these organizations advocated increased government responsibility within welfare services, and were more concerned with providing the population with the best available services than to carve out a separate ideological niche for themselves. This does not mean that they were docile servants of the state. The most critical among the organizations, *Norske Kvinners Sanitetsforening* (Women's Public Health Association), emerged in overt conflict with political authorities and has always aimed as a main objective at exerting political influence. The other main organization in the field, *Nasjonalforeningen for folkehelsen* (Norwegian National Health Association), has been more establishment-oriented (Selle and Berven 2001).

Towards the end of the social democratic peak time, the first of signs of weakness among the early movements became apparent. The counter-cultures (language, Christian mission and alcohol abstention) deteriorated; hardly any new associations were founded, while existing groups disbanded at an accelerating rate. Finally, the 1960s represent a watershed in Norwegian politics, as well as in the history of voluntary associations in Norway. In 1963, the Labour Party was briefly ousted from government in a vote of no confidence, signifying the beginning of the end of the social democratic hegemony.[4]

The voluntary sector continued to expand after 1960, but within new activities. The main field of growth was now what we have labelled *service* organizations – organizations that cater to the interest of their members with little societal or political ambition. The new social movements, which were quite visible in the cities in the 1970s, never penetrated the rural communities. The growth in social and humanitarian associations stopped. Thus, society-oriented organizations, whether critical or communitarian, lost ground.

In the 1980s and afterwards, this trend has continued: all critical organizational types are now in decline, while most member and/or consensus-oriented purposes proliferate. However, even in these fields, some types are struggling now, such as associations for children and youth, indicating that organizational society has reached a point of saturation in Norway. The main areas of growth are now organizations for the disabled, culture and leisure groups, and not least neighbourhood and area associations. The development in this most recent phase is detailed in the third empirical section of this chapter.

Snapshot: characteristics of organized civil society in Norway

The organizational expansion that had taken place over more than a century produced a voluntary sector of considerable volume. The timing of the emergence of mass movements in a period in which numerical strength was crucial to organizational success, produced an organizational society that is highly participatory with a broad membership base. The impact of these movements and their emergence through concurrent bottom-up and top-down processes also left Norwegian organizations with an integrated, democratic and hierarchical structure. In the following we place the Norwegian sector in comparative perspective along the three dimensions: volume, structure and type.

Volume

Several cross-national surveys have established that the individual participation rates in Nordic voluntary organizations are among the highest in the world. Figure 4.1, based on the European Social Survey (2002), confirms this finding. The Nordic countries, alongside the Netherlands, rank highest whether organizational activity is measured by nominal affiliation or by active participation. The West European countries follow, while Eastern and Southern Europe display the lowest participation rates. There is a North–South, as well as an East–West dimension: countries in the North and in the West generally show higher participation rates than countries in the South and in the East.

The extensive voluntary work also reflects a low degree of professionalization in the Nordic voluntary sectors. Data from the Johns Hopkins Comparative Non-profit Sector Project (CNP) show that if measured in terms of paid employees, the Norwegian and Swedish sectors are quite small, but the amount of volunteering is higher than in any other country (except the Netherlands). When both measures are combined (giving economic value to voluntary work), the economic size of the Nordic non-profit sectors is close to the European average (Salamon *et al.* 1999; Sivesind *et al.* 2002).

A third measure of the size of organized civil society is the strength and composition of local organizational activity. This has been known as the 'dark matter' of the non-profit sector, due to the lack of significant data and interest from the research community (Smith 1997). Recently, however, more comparative data has been collected. Local organizations in Norway have been mapped three times (in 1980, 1990 and 2000) in one county (Hordaland, population of *c.* 400,000) (Wollebæk and Selle 2002a). Other recent publications with data from several European cities (Maloney and Rossteutscher 2007) and Danish regions

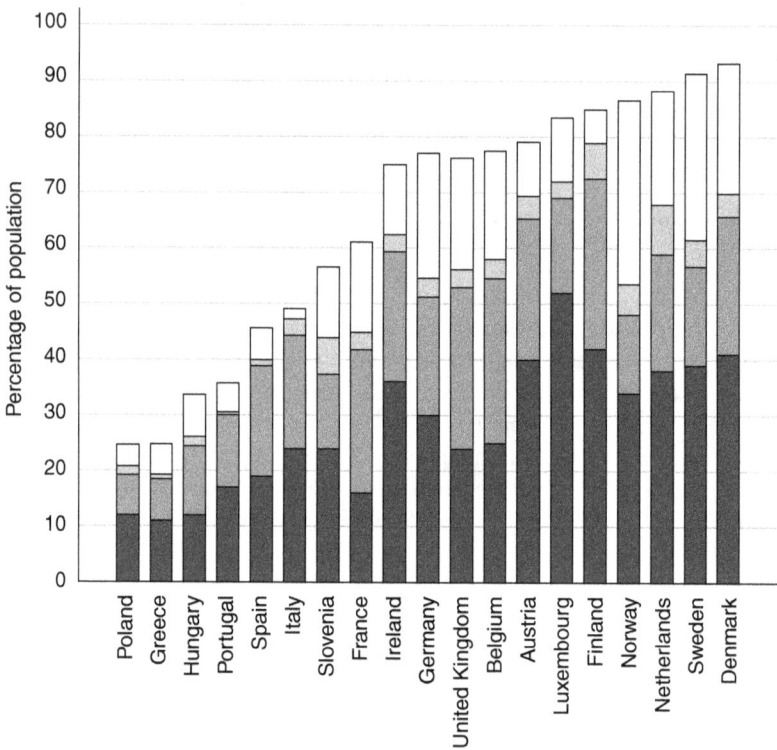

Figure 4.1 Organizational participation in European countries.

(Ibsen 2006) allow us to directly compare the proliferation of local voluntary organizations in Norway and elsewhere. The Norwegian city of Bergen (population of 250,000) has a higher organizational density than any of the cities covered by the aforementioned projects. Furthermore, the 28 *rural* municipalities in Hordaland outrank by far any of the towns that were surveyed in the other projects.

In Norway, in contrast to elsewhere in Europe, we find much higher organizational density in the periphery than in the centre, which indicates the strong integration of the periphery into the overall political and organizational society.[5] Geographical obstacles and long distances between villages necessitated a highly decentralized organizational structure. Most of the nineteenth-century movements emerged from the rural communities and surrounding towns and cities, coupled with central efforts to build national federations.

In summary, regarding all indicators, save the number of employees, the Norwegian voluntary sector is very large in comparative terms. Unsurprisingly, we find no evidence of 'crowding out'. The high participation rates and high number of organizations has arguably been maintained and nurtured by social-democratic policies of welfare and equality, but a culture of mass participation had been present long before the Labour Party came into power.[6]

Structure

The voluntary sector in Norway functions simultaneously on local, regional and national levels of activity. Originally, local associations were organized around the *bygd*, the village, and institutionally tied to national and/or regional mother organizations. This structure allowed discussions and decisions at the local level to reach the national level, rendering the local branches a pillar in the internal organizational democracy. Almost without exception, organizations imitated the levels of the political system and chose the same structure as the parties. Often they were directly affiliated to them. However, even for the associations without an explicit political purpose, the linkages from the local to the national sphere implied that the participants in the *bygd* were part of a larger movement, the importance of which reached beyond their everyday lives. The above-documented extensive volume of the sector underlines the great significance of this structure in order to link the individual to the political system.[7]

This characteristic is not unique to the Norwegian case. Torpe and Ferrer-Fons (2007) refer to it as the 'classical secondary association model'. Skocpol (2003) emphasizes that even in the United States, where grassroots activism is often imagined as a purely local phenomenon, most local associations were chapters of national federations. Yet, in a comparative perspective, the position of the hierarchical model is unusually strong in Norway, and it has been a dominant factor for a longer period of time. As a consequence of the move-ments' impact on organizational life in general, the hierarchical model held a near hegemonic position for a very long time. It was adopted by most new organizations even without a political or national purpose until well into the 1960s.

Thus, the Norwegian organizational society has traditionally been *integrated*, in the sense that the same organizations can be found at the local and national level, and not *two-part*, as in many European countries and the United States. Almost three-quarters of contemporary voluntary associations are organized along these lines – a much higher percentage than Torpe and Ferrer-Fons' (2007, p. 101) report from five other countries. As we will see in the following section, this proportion was even higher some decades ago.[8]

The hierarchical model is also a democratic one, with the *membership* institu-tion at its core. Being a member guarantees those affiliated democratic rights within and co-ownership of the organization.[9] Thus, volunteering by non-members has a very weak tradition in Norway (cf. Figure 4.1; Wollebæk *et al.* 2000). This phenomenon can also be observed in Sweden, whereas in other parts of Europe only slightly more than half of the people doing unpaid work are members (Gaskin and Davis Smith 1995: 33). Furthermore, Norwegian volun-teers attach substantial value to this affiliation: in a 1998 survey, 43 per cent state it is very important to be a member of the organization for which they vol-unteer; and altogether almost 80 per cent say it is very important or somewhat important (Wollebæk *et al.* 2000).

Thus, volunteering in Norway is inextricably linked to the membership institution. Organizational memberships provide the individual adherent with democratic rights within a trans-local, hierarchical structure and function as the main link between the individual and the political system. It is inconceivable that voluntary organizations could play the same expressive role (cf. Salamon and Anheier 1998) in organized civil society and politics, or achieve the same results, without the structures outlined above. These structures constitute the most characteristic trait of the countries commonly classified as 'social democratic'. These traits are crucial for our understanding of the role of the voluntary sector in these countries and, more general, even of the political culture. Yet, they are consistently overlooked in regime theories. As the structures are unrelated to social democracy both in timing and in content, the use of the label 'social democratic' further understates their significance.[10]

Type

Salamon and Anheier (1998) asserted that there was a social democratic pattern of organizational participation. In contrast to the welfare-dominated sectors in the liberal and Continental models, social democratic countries produced strong *expressive* organizations, i.e. interest and advocacy groups alongside hobby and recreational organizations.

Figure 4.2 shows the types of organizations that Norwegians join, compared to the rest of Western Europe and other 'social democratic' countries. On the surface, Salamon and Anheier's assertions of a strong 'expressive' sector appears to be correct: unions and professional organizations, sports, hobby and youth clubs, as well as advocacy groups for consumers, automobile owners and patients, mobilize more members in Norway than elsewhere. In terms of the typology presented above, we find the clearest overrepresentation in the organization types focusing on the individual, i.e. interest and service associations.

Contrary to the expectations of the above-cited regime theories, however, welfare-oriented social and humanitarian organizations are stronger in Norway than elsewhere. Although one could say that many of the memberships are passive in nature, the proportion of the population who has volunteered for a social and humanitarian organization is higher in Norway than in any other European country, followed by Sweden and Denmark.[11] Thus, the hypothesis of a weak voluntary sector in the welfare field holds up only if one disregards the input of active members.

The high participation in social and humanitarian groups more than compensates for the lower percentage involved in 'charity'. This concept has negative connotations in Norway, partly because of the egalitarianism and the very weak bourgeoisie/middle class predating social democracy (Tranvik and Selle 2007). The non-symmetrical relationship between charitable volunteer/donor and recipient is also at odds with the reciprocal nature of the membership institution. The comprehensiveness of this structure is in itself an important reason why typical charity-based organizations have historically been so weak.

We would also expect from social origins theory that newer 'expressive'

Percentage of Norwegian population who
are members, deviation from Western
European and 'social democratic' average

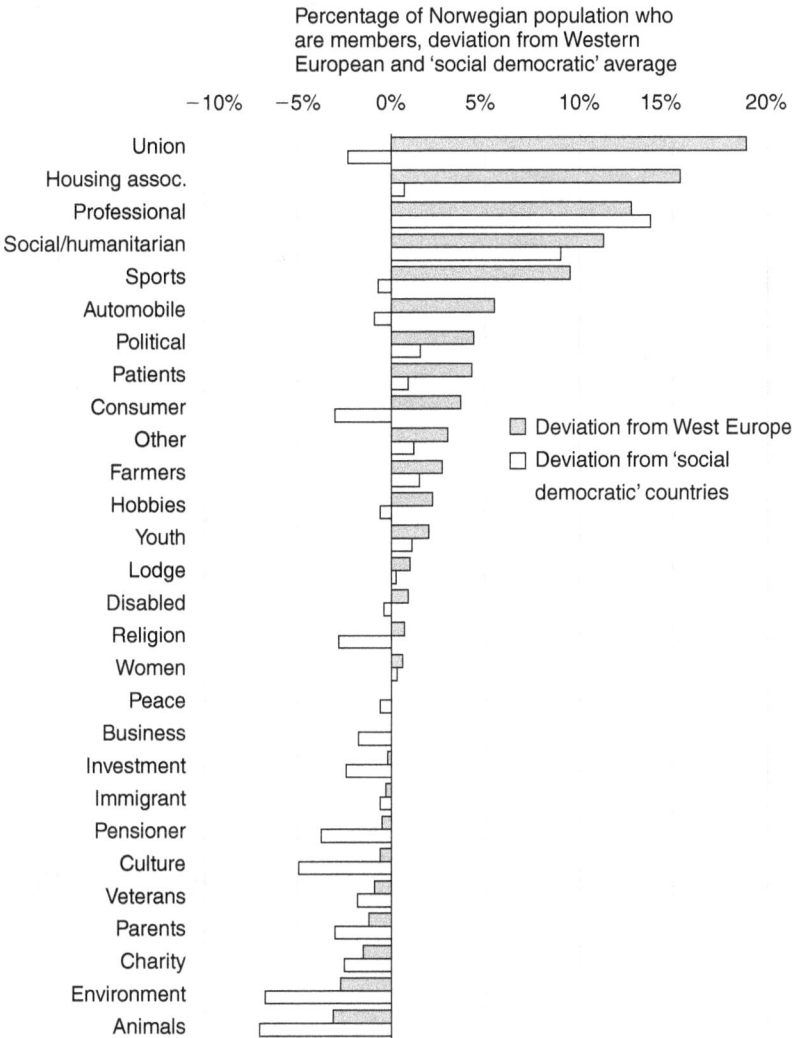

Figure 4.2 Proportion of population affiliated with different types of associations.

Data from the CID-survey (van Deth and Montero 2007). Western European average: Great Britain, Germany, Sweden, Denmark, Spain, Portugal, Switzerland, the Netherlands. 'Social democratic' average: Sweden, Denmark, the Netherlands.

organizations, i.e. the New Social Movements (NSM), are stronger in the social-democratic states than elsewhere. In Norway, this is clearly not the case. The environmental and animal protection movements are comparatively weak, and participation in women's rights and peace organizations is at the European average. The Norwegian anti-globalization movement is also weak in terms of number of adherents.[12]

The development over time of the dominant organizations in Norway presents another challenge to the social democratic label. Most of today's dominant organizations had established a mass membership long before the advent of social democracy. This applies to the unions, the sports movement, and the (by now weakened) counter-cultures. All major social and humanitarian organizations were also established before the first lasting social democratic government was formed in 1935. Moreover, their main period of growth coincides with the most rapid expansion phase of the welfare state (1945–1960). Even though they have shrunk and lost political importance as the state has assumed increased responsibility within the health and social field, they have by no means disappeared.

In summary, organized civil society in Norway is not uniformly 'expressive'. There is widespread participation within welfare-oriented organizations which have expanded alongside the welfare state. Expressive organization types that have been successful elsewhere (NSM) have had less impact in Norway. Furthermore, the fact that most participation today takes place in structures that were in place before the breakthrough of social democracy, or in structures that have developed after its peak, indicates that this label offers an incomplete account of the layout of the current sector.

Recent developments: convergence

We have seen that in terms of *volume*, measured by the number of entities and individual participation, organized civil society in Norway is large. In terms of *structure*, it is still largely based on a model linking local, regional and national levels. In terms of *type*, while the early mass movements were mainly critical in orientation, the snapshot revealed most of all extensive participation within the other three types, i.e. service-, communitarian-, and interest organizations.

However, organized civil society is unlikely to remain unaffected by global trends such as individualization, marketization and improved communication. One likely consequence is that the difference between 'regimes' decreases. Specifically, the Norwegian model of organized civil society is becoming more aligned with what we find elsewhere in Europe and the US.

Volume

With regard to *volume*, the rise of individualism and changing conceptions of time clearly represents a challenge for the organizations depending on loyal members and long-term commitment. Voluntary organizations, especially those with intricate vertical structures and tedious decision-making processes, appear inert compared to Internet petitions or local citizen initiatives. Thus, at the beginning of the twenty-first century, we see the first symptoms of an overall decline in organizational participation.

Figure 4.3 presents data from the *Survey on Level of Living*, which is a periodic face-to-face survey carried out by the Norwegian Central Bureau of Statistics. The results show a marked decline in the organizational participation of

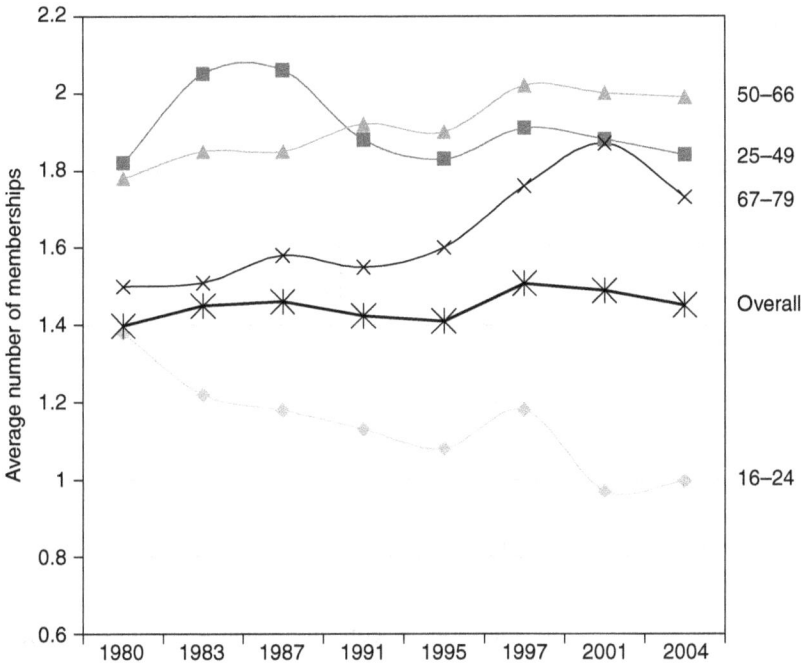

Figure 4.3 Average number of organizational memberships 1980–2004, by age group (sources: Active memberships: Survey on Level of Living (1997 and 2004); CNP (1997/2004); (Sivesind, 2005)).

Note: Includes only organization categories included at all observation points (union, professional or business association, sports group, area association, housing association, health association, choir/marching bands, political party, religion, local interest group, women's organization).

young people since 1980.[13] By contrast, membership rates have increased substantially in the oldest age bracket (age 67–79). Thus, an overall decline in memberships is postponed by increased activity among the elderly. But if this turns out to be a generational rather than a life-cycle phenomenon, the consequence will be a decline in participation rates in the near future.[14]

If we focus on *active* memberships (Figure 4.4), the overall decline and the greying of the sector become even clearer. Between 1997 and 2004, active membership fell for the first time in the post-war era. However, not all age groups are affected equally. Once again, the pensioners are holding their ground, while young people are turning their backs on organizational activity.

Structure

Figure 4.4 also reveals an important structural change: there is a proportional increase of volunteers. Intriguingly, youths and pensioners are more active. To a greater extent than active membership, volunteering seems to be compatible

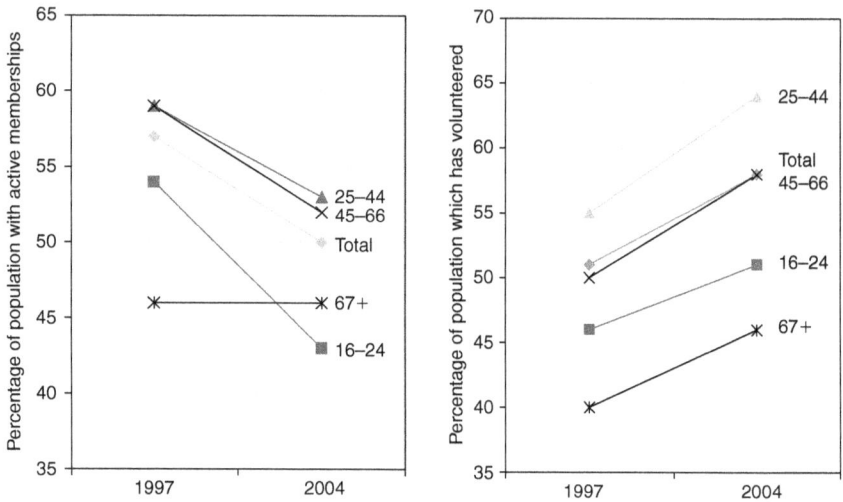

Figure 4.4 Active memberships and volunteering in organizations 1997–2004.

with reflexive identities, the rejection of collectives and shortened attention spans. The decline occurs, therefore, within the segment of organized civil society which is based on the classical membership-based secondary model with its more institutionalized ties between participant and organization, i.e. the most distinctive trait of the Norwegian organized civil society.

Volunteering outside the membership institution was until recently an alien idea to Norwegian civil society. Social democrats, in particular, viewed unpaid work with scepticism; it undermined the rights of paid workers and was associated with middle/upper-class Anglo-American ideas of charity, which was seen as incompatible with the universal welfare state.

In recent years, however, the ideological resistance has mellowed. Individual surveys reveal that younger volunteers place much less emphasis on being members than their older counterparts (Wollebæk and Selle 2003). Many organizations, therefore, actively recruit 'drop-in' volunteers and emphasize that no membership affiliation is needed. Furthermore, young people care less about which organization they participate in – if another organization offered the same activity, they would readily shift allegiance – and they see democratic structures as less of a necessity than older participants (op. cit.).

The decoupling of the member and volunteer roles implies an increased emphasis on the service-function of voluntary organizations and less focus on its democratic role, as well as weaker ties between participant and organization. In contrast to active members, volunteers have no ownership or formal right to vote in the institutions for which they offer their time, and they are more likely to drift between different causes and interests. This declining loyalty is documented by Ødegård (2007), who found that concerning young people, the average length of an organizational membership declined dramatically during the 1990s. Analogously, at the organizational level, the turnover of organizations almost tripled from the 1980s to the 1990s (Wollebæk and Selle 2002a).

Even more fundamental, the classical secondary model itself is starting to crumble. It is challenged by a two-part organizational society without institutional linkages between geographical levels. On the one hand, national organizations (especially newer ones) appear less interested in retaining vibrant local associations and in internal decision-making procedures, as there is a trade-off between efficiency and internal democracy. On the other hand, the proportion of 'freestanding' local associations is rapidly increasing. Half of the local Norwegian associations founded in the 1990s refrained from joining a national federation (Wollebæk and Selle 2002a). In all probability, we are dealing with a lasting generational, not a temporary life-cycle phenomenon. We know that freestanding associations very rarely join federations later on (Wollebæk and Selle 2002a). Furthermore, the total percentage of freestanding local groups increased from 20 to 30 between 1980 and 2000 (op. cit.).

Interestingly, the division between the local and national levels seems to occur simultaneously in several countries. Skocpol (2003) has documented the same development in the case of the United States. Similarly, Torpe and Ferrer-Fons (2007) show that in five of the six cities they have examined, the newest associations are mostly freestanding, and Wollebæk *et al.* (forthcoming) identify the same trend in Finland and Denmark. Thus, this is a real development with considerable consequences for the role voluntary organizations play in civil society. In the case of Norway, this development is particularly dramatic as the most typical trait of organized civil society is deteriorating.

Type

Above, we showed that broadly based ideological and public benefit organizations dominated the Norwegian organized civil society early on. These organizations are now losing ground in all the Nordic states (Jeppsson-Grassman and Svedberg 1999; Siisiäinen 2003; Wollebæk and Selle 2002a). In the context of our typology, there is a development from conflict to consensus and from collective to individual orientation. We are witnessing a transition from the type of civil society valued by public-sphere theorists and comparative associationalists to the type of civil society esteemed by the social capital direction and to some extent also by communitarians.

Figure 4.5 documents this development, based on the responses in the survey of local associations described above. In the absence of comparable questions that go back in time far enough, we use the founding year of the organizations that existed in 2000 as a proxy for historical development.[15] The placement of organizations within the typology is based on their responses to four ten-point scales (two items for each dimension) that are added up to an index.[16] Thus, Figure 4.5 shows the historical movement from conflict and public-benefit

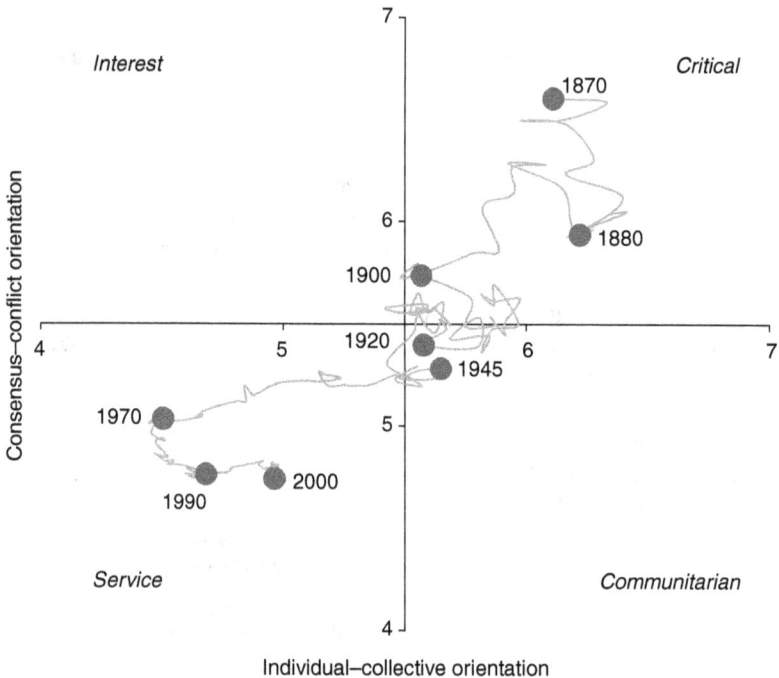

Consensus–conflict orientation (vertical axis)

Interest ... Critical

7

1870

6
1880
1900
1920 ... 6 ... 7
4 ... 5 ... 1945

1970
5
1990 ... 2000

Service ... Communitarian

4

Individual–collective orientation

Figure 4.5 The orientation of local voluntary associations by year of founding. Moving
15-year averages.

orientation towards consensus and member-benefit orientation, as moving averages for organizations formed in different years.

The long-term trend is a diagonal movement from the upper-right corner of
the figure towards the bottom-left. There is a shift downwards in the figure
(towards consensus-orientation) until 1945, as the innovation in organizational
society increasingly took place within social and humanitarian organizations.
From about 1965, organized leisure activities, both for adults and children, represent the main areas of growth. From 1980 to 2000, there is a minor shift
towards public-benefit orientation, which is related to proliferation of local
community and cultural heritage groups. On the consensus–conflict dimension,
the level of conflict-orientation remained at an all-time low after 1990.

Obviously, there are great variations within each period. The movement in the
figure understates some developments running counter to the main picture. We have
witnessed extensive proliferation within one conflict-oriented organization type
during the 1980s and 1990s, namely organizations for the sick and disabled. There
has also been some innovation within the critical category, as the environmental
movement and other NSMs experienced a short period of growth in the 1970s and
1980s. While politically important, these developments are far too small in terms of
number of members and organizational entities to offset the main picture.

One type of organization is worth particular mentioning. There has been a comprehensive growth in neighbourhood and area associations, in some cases founded on the initiative from municipal authorities.[17] We also see an increase in consultative councils (for children and youth, or the elderly) that have supplemented or replaced voluntary associations as channels of influence (NOU 2006: 13). These initiatives reflect changes in local government strategies inspired by imported New Public Management ideals, in which the individual is seen as a client rather than a citizen. These directly imported management ideas reinforce the emphasis on the individual over the collective and widen the structural divide between the local and national level – in short, again the most typical traits of organized civil society in Norway are challenged.

Discussion and conclusion

There are at least two different conceptualizations of the social democratic model, and our results challenge the aptness of both. First, the idea that a strong welfare state is anathema to civil-society institutions for various reasons (crowding out, loss of initiative or 'colonization'), is quite simply not in tune with the empirical reality and should be regarded as falsified.

Second, regime theories, such as the social origins approach, succeed better in capturing typical traits of current organized civil society. Nevertheless, we argue that these characteristics have less to do with social democracy than with the periods preceding and following the predominance of this ideology. First, the hegemonic hierarchical structure, the movement-based character of the sector, in which cultural, professional and political interests were intertwined, and the tradition for mass mobilization were established well before the breakthrough of social democracy. Furthermore, in the prime of social democracy, it was the 'wrong' organizations that expanded, namely welfare-oriented social and humanitarian groups, not the expressive organizations predicted by social-origins theory. Finally, the recent developments, which with regard to type constitute much of the growth in Salamon and Anheier's 'expressive' organizations, are more aligned with neo-liberal than with social democratic ideals. However, the relatively low degree of social inequality and high educational levels which social democratic governments have fostered, have without doubt contributed to maintaining extensive participation.

Changes in volume, structure and type indicate that the uniqueness of the Scandinavian countries is diminishing. Our findings have documented a transition from criticism and opposition to service of members' interests. This must lead to a reassessment of what to expect from voluntary organizations in civil society and democracy. From a social capital perspective, what we have observed is not necessarily negative. The horizontal linkages within local groups are still present and show only early signs of decline. Thus, the generation of trust, civic engagement and networks, the main resources for a viable democracy, should continue, or even be strengthened by the attenuation of conflict.

There are two objections to this interpretation. First, it is questionable whether this local, face-to-face activity actually generates the resources that the social capital perspective presupposes. Empirical tests of this hypothesis usually have turned out to be negative so far (Mayer 2003; Stolle 2001; Wollebæk and Selle 2002b, 2007). Rather, Wollebæk and Selle (2007) emphasize the role of organizations as *intermediary institutions*, and assert that visible, outward-reaching organizations, which demonstrate the rationality and utility of collect-ive action, are what matters to social capital formation.

Second, even if the face-to-face hypothesis was supported, it is questionable whether establishing trusting local communities would be sufficient. The vision

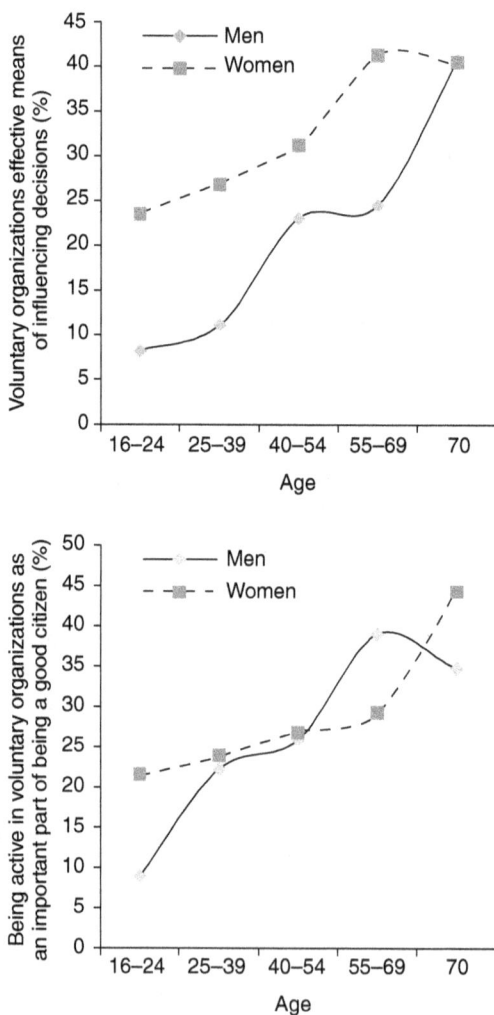

Figure 4.6 Public perceptions of the role of voluntary organizations in civil society, by age.

of civil society advocated by comparative associationalists, emphasizes the importance of organizational structure, a dimension which is absent not only in the thinking of social capitalists, but also in regime theories focusing solely on volume and type. Solving micro-problems at the local levels cannot constitute the type of civil society envisioned by the more conflict-oriented approaches to democratic theory. Given the fact that government is multi-level, organizations need to be vertical and hierarchical in order to function as real intermediary structures.

Figure 4.6 shows that the public perception of the democratic role of organizations seems to be changing along with the developments at the organizational level. Only a small minority of young people see organizations as effective means of influencing decisions, while this belief is quite entrenched among pensioners. This is indicative of the shift from conflict to consensus within organized civil society, as well as the decline of hierarchical structures. A similar pattern applies to the question concerning whether organizational engagement constitutes an important part of being a good citizen. This shows that older generations regard organized civil society as a collective endeavour, while younger cohorts see it as an arena for individual fulfilment.

Organized civil society in Norway increasingly functions as an arena for socializing and pursuit of personal interests – very positive things, of course – but it serves to a decreasing extent as intermediary structures between citizen and political system. Both, the starting and end point of this development has little to do, in our view, with social democracy. It reflects that a tradition which has held a dominant position for almost a century is challenged by global trends such as individualization, marketization and a changing conception of time. These developments are likely to reduce the uniqueness of the Scandinavian model, and more generally, the explanatory power of regime theories even further in the future.

Notes

1 The other categories are liberal, statist and corporatist.
2 However, see note 17.
3 *Formannskapslovene* (1837) established the municipalities as political entities. The abolition of the Conventicle Act in 1842 and the Dissent Law (1845) increased religious freedom.
4 In the 44 years that have passed since then, the party has been in government only 23 years.
5 For a broader analysis of this integration, see Tranvik and Selle (2005).
6 It is worth noting that non-socialist governments have shown more interest in the voluntary sector than social democratic ones, and voters and members of non-socialist parties, especially the parties at the political centre, are in general more interested in and are more often members of voluntary organizations (Grendstad *et al.* 2006; Wollebæk *et al.* 2000).
7 It goes without saying that this organizational structure is also crucial in order to explain the comparatively high amount of trust and social capital found in the studies that include Norway.
8 57 per cent of the associations surveyed by Torpe and Ferrer-Fons (2007) are affiliated with regional or national organizations, compared to 74 per cent in Norway.

9   This does, of course, not imply the lack of power distinction or even paternalistic structures within some organizations. However, important enough, formally they are all democratic in structure.

10 We do not imply, of course, that social democracy has had any problems with adapting to such structures or that the structures themselves in any way are alien to social democracy.

11 9.6 per cent of Norwegians, 4.8 per cent of Swedes and 4.2 per cent of Danes volunteered for a social and humanitarian organization. The average for all countries was 1.9 per cent.

12 The issues raised by NSMs soon became integrated into the programmes of the political parties and public bureaucracies, which made it difficult for the movements to remain radical and to mobilize widely (Grendstad *et al.* 2006).

13 The figures exclude five categories that have been changed or added between 1980 and 2004. This does not introduce an age bias. The average number of memberships in the removed categories was 0.25 among 16–24-year-olds in 2001, compared to 0.43 for the entire sample.

14 However, even if it should not primarily be a generational phenomenon, it will mean a comprehensive change in the dynamics of the voluntary sector.

15 We cannot know if organizations have changed over time, or if organizations that have disbanded have differed from survivors. However, the basic characteristics of organizations are imprinted in them at 'birth' and unlikely to change radically (Hannan and Freeman 1984). Furthermore, the developments we describe are in alignment with what can be learned from other sources (see Selle and Øymyr 1995; Wollebæk and Selle 2002a and 2004 for more detailed overviews of the historical developments).

16 Individual–collective orientation is measured by relative agreement/disagreement with the following statements:

   1 Most of the organization's activities are open to members only vs. most of the organization's activities are open to all.
   2 The organization works primarily for the benefit of its members vs. the organization works primarily for the benefit of the local community. Agreement with the latter alternatives is interpreted as collective orientation.

   Conflict-consensus orientation is operationalized by the two statements:

   1 It is not important for us to convince others of our values vs. it is very important to us to convince others of our values.
   2 We are not in opposition to dominant attitudes in society vs. we are in opposition to dominant attitudes in society. Agreement with the latter alternatives is interpreted as conflict orientation.

17 This explains some of the movements in Figure 4.5 since the late 1980s. However, most of these organizations are not typical communitarian organizations. They are mainly consensus-oriented, but many of them place themselves in the middle of the individual–collective axes and show a narrow interest in what is going on outside their own neighbourhood (see Wollebæk and Selle 2002: 176).

References

Baer, D. (2007) 'Voluntary association involvement in comparative perspective', in L. Trägårdh (ed.) *State and Civil Society in Northern Europe: The Swedish Model Reconsidered*, New York and Oxford: Berghahn Books, 67–125.

Bellah, R.N., Madsen, R. and Sullivan, W.M. (1985) *Habits of the Heart: Individualism and Commitment in American Life*, Berkeley: University of California Press.

Berger, P. and Neuhaus, J. (1996) *To Empower People: From State to Civil Society*, Washington, DC: American Enterprise Institute.

Cohen, J. (2007) 'Civil society and globalization: rethinking the categories', in L. Trägårdh (ed.) *State and Civil Society in Northern Europe. The Swedish Model Reconsidered*, New York and Oxford: Berghahn Books.

Cohen, J., and Arato, A. (1992) *Civil Society and Political Theory*, Cambridge: MIT Press.

Dahl, R.A. (1961) *Who Governs? Democracy and Power in an American City*, New Haven: Yale University Press.

Della Porta, D. and Diani, M. (2005) *Social Movements: An Introduction*, Malden: Blackwell Publishing.

Edwards, M. (2004) *Civil Society*, Cambridge: Polity.

Esping-Andersen, G. (1990) *Three Political Economies of the Welfare State*, Cambridge: Polity.

Etzioni, A. (1988) *The Moral Dimension: Toward a New Economics*, New York: Free Press.

—— (1995) *The Spirit of Community*, London: Fontana Books.

Fukuyama, F. (1995) *Trust: The Social Virtues and the Creation of Prosperity*, New York: Free Press.

Gaskin, K. and Davis Smith, J. (1995) *A New Civic Europe? A Study of the Extent and Role of Volunteering*, London: Volunteer Centre UK.

Grendstad, G., Selle, P., Strømsnes, K. and Bortne, Ø. (2006) *Unique Environmentalism. A Comparative Perspective*, New York: Springer.

Hannan, M.T. and Freeman, J. (1984) 'Structural inertia and organizational change', *American Sociological Review*, 49: 149–164.

Ibsen, B. (2006) 'Foreningslivet i Danmark', in T.P. Boje and B. Ibsen (eds), *Frivillighed og nonprofit i Danmark – omfang, organisation, økonomi og beskæftigelse*, København: Socialforskningsinstituttet.

Janoski, T. (1998) *Citizenship and Civil Society*, Cambridge: Cambridge University Press.

Jeppsson-Grassman, E. and Svedberg, L. (1999) 'Medborgarskapets gestaltningar: insatser i och utanför föreningslivet', in E. Amnå (ed.) *Civilsamhället SOU 1999: 84*, Stockholm: Fritzes.

Lundström, T. and Svedberg, L. (2003) 'The voluntary sector in a social democratic welfare state – the case of Sweden', *Journal of Social Policy*, 32 (2): 217–238.

Maloney, W.A. and Rossteutscher, S. (eds) (2007) *Social Capital and Associations in European Democracies*, New York: Routledge.

Mayer, N. (2003) 'Democracy in France: do associations matter?' in M. Hooghe and D. Stolle (eds) *Generating Social Capital. Civil Society and Institutions in Comparative Perspective*, New York: Palgrave Macmillan.

NOU (2006) *Fritid med mening. Statlig støttepolitikk for frivillige barne- og ungdomsorganisasjoner*, Oslo: Barne- og likestillingsdepartementet.

Putnam, R.D. (2000) *Bowling Alone: The Collapse and Revival of American Community*, New York: Simon and Schuster.

Rokkan, S. (1967) 'Geography, religion and social class: crosscutting cleavages in Norwegian politics', in S.M. Lipset and S. Rokkan (eds) *Party Systems and Voter Alignments*, New York: The Free Press.

Salamon, L.M. and Anheier, H.K. (1998) 'Social origins of civil society: explaining the non-profit sector cross-nationally', *Voluntas*, 9 (3): 213–247.

Salamon, L., Anheier, H.K., List, R., Toepler, S. and Sokolowski, W. (eds) (1999) *Global Civil Society: Dimensions of the Nonprofit Sector*, Baltimore: Johns Hopkins Comparative Nonprofit Sector Project.
Schofer, E. and Fourcade-Gourinchas, M. (2001) 'The structural contexts of civic engagement: voluntary association membership in comparative perspective', *American Sociological Review*, 66 (6): 806–828.
Selle, P. and Berven, N. (eds) (2001) *Svekket kvinnemakt? De frivillige organisasjonene og velferdsstaten*, Oslo: Gyldendal akademisk
Selle, P. and Kuhnle, S. (eds) (1992) *Government and Voluntary Organizations: a Relational Perspective*, Aldershot: Avebury.
Selle, P. and Øymyr, B. (1995) *Frivillig organisering og demokrati: det frivillige organisasjonssamfunnet endrar seg 1940–1990*, Oslo: Det Norske Samlaget.
Siisiäinen, M. (2003) 'Vuoden 1997 yhdistykset', in S. Hänninen, A. Kangas and M. Siisiäinen (eds) *Mitä yhdistykset välittävät: tutkimuskohteena kolmas sektori*, Jyväskylä: Atena, 11–37.
Sivesind, K.H. (2005) *Seniorers deltakelse i frivillig arbeid. Betydningen av alder og livssituasjon*, Oslo: Institute for Social Research.
Sivesind, K.H., Lorentzen, H., Selle, P. and Wollebæk, D. (2002) *The Voluntary Sector in Norway – Composition, Changes, and Causes*, Oslo Report/Institute for Social Research, 2.
Skocpol, T. (1999) 'Advocates without members: the recent transformation of American civil life', in T. Skocpol and M. Fiorina (eds) *Civic Engagement in American Democracy*, Washington, DC: Brookings Institution Press.
—— (2003) *Diminished Democracy*, Norman: University of Oklahoma Press.
Smith, D.H. (1993) 'Public benefit and member benefit nonprofit, voluntary groups', *Nonprofit and Voluntary Sector Quarterly*, 22 (1): 53–68.
—— (1997) 'The rest of the nonprofit sector: grassroots associations as the dark matter ignored in prevailing "flat earth" maps of the sector', *Nonprofit and Voluntary Sector Quarterly*, 26 (2): 114–131.
Stolle, D. (2001) 'Clubs and congregations: the benefits of joining an association', in K. Cook (ed.) *Trust in Society*, New York: Russel Sage Foundation.
Torpe, L., and Ferrer-Fons, M. (2007) 'The internal structure of associations', in L. Trägårdh (ed.) *State and Civil Society in Northern Europe: The Swedish Model Reconsidered*, New York and Oxford: Berghahn Books.
Tranvik, T. and Selle, P. (2005) 'State and citizens in Norway: organizational society and state–municipal relations', *West European Politics*, 28 (4): 852–871.
—— (2007) 'The rise and fall of popular mass movements: organizational change and globalization – the Norwegian case', *Acta Sociologica*, 50 (1): 57–70.
van Deth, J.W. and Montero, J.R. (eds) (2007) *Citizenship and Involvement in European Democracies: A Comparative Analysis*, New York: Routledge.
Weisbrod, B.A. (1977) *The Voluntary Nonprofit Sector*, Lexington: Lexington Books.
Wolfe, A. (1989) *Whose Keeper? Social Science and Moral Obligation*, Berkeley: University of California Press.
Wollebæk, D. and Selle, P. (2002a) *Det nye organisasjonssamfunnet: demokrati i omforming*, Bergen: Fagbokforl.
—— (2002b) 'Does participation in voluntary associations contribute to social capital? The impact of intensity, scope, and type', *Nonprofit and Voluntary Sector Quarterly*, 30 (1): 32–61.
—— (2003) 'Generations and organisational change', in P. Dekker and L. Halman (eds) *The Values of Volunteering: Cross-cultural Perspectives*, New York: Kluwer.

—— (2004) 'The role of women in the transformation of the organizational society in Norway', *Nonprofit and Voluntary Sector Quarterly*, 33: 120S-144S.

—— (2007) 'The origins of social capital. Socialisation and institutionalisation approaches compared', *Journal of Civil Society*, 3 (1): 1–14.

Wollebæk, D., Selle, P. and Lorentzen, H. (2000) *Frivillig innsats. Sosial integrasjon, demokrati og økonom*, Bergen: Fagbokforl.

Wollebæk, D., Siisiäinen, M. and Ibsen, B. (forthcoming) 'Local associations in Norway, Finland and Denmark', in R. Alapuro (ed.) *Nordic Civicness Revisited in the Age of Association, volume 1*: European Voluntary Association Network.

Ødegård, G. (2007) 'Troløs ungdom. Endringer i ungdoms deltagelse i frivillige organisasjoner fra 1992 til 2002', in Å. Strandbu and T. Øia (eds) *Ung i Norge. Skole, fritid og ungdomskultur*, Oslo: Cappelen.

5   Civil-society debates in India

Civil society against political society?

Bruno Jobert

Civil society has been a key issue in Indian public debate ever since the state of emergency period in the 1970s. The state of emergency was declared by Indira Gandhi in June 1975 in order to cope with internal disturbances, and it ended in March 1977 with the election victory of the opposition. During that 19-month authoritarian interlude, when Prime Minister Indira Gandhi ruled by decree and civil liberties were suspended, civil society provided a symbolic framework of opposition to the authoritarian practices of the government. In order to fully understand the significance of this upsurge of a civil discourse, we need to go back further in history, however, to the phase of tutelary modernization and even to the struggle for independence.

We share the hypothesis exposed in the writings of Partha Chatterjee (2001) that the Indian case can only be understood by making a distinction between *civil society* and *political society* and by analysing its inter-relationship. The *civil society* appeared in the small circle of the elite leading the national struggle: 'these elites were thoroughly wedded to the normative principles of modern associational public life and criticized the colonial state precisely for not living up to the standards of a liberal constitutional state' (Chatterjee 2001: 175). The *political society* corresponded to a mode of political mediation that had first developed in the anti-colonial struggle and then in Indian democracy when mobilization spread to broader circles of the population, well beyond the elite. The modes of action in political society were profoundly different from those of associational life. Demands stemmed not from citizens but from a population struggling to 'survive by side stepping the law' (Chatterjee 2001: 177). These demands were expressed in terms of collective rights attached to a 'community'. As Chatterjee put it, state agents dealt with these people 'not as bodies of citizens belonging to a lawfully constituted civil society but as a population deserving welfare' (Chatterjee 2001: 177). We would add here the following nuance to Chatterjee's analysis: all the examples he gives refer to clear violations of the law by those in need – squatters, encroachers of public properties, unauthorized users of public utilities. But we should be more precise in that the most important source of uncertainty toward the law lies in the elites' frequently used strategy of denial of citizens rights to subaltern groups.

'Subaltern Studies' (Guha 1983), the well-known school of historiography from below, have shown that these competing modes of political mediation were present within the Congress Party from the time of the anti-colonial struggle onwards. This chapter will analyse this uncomfortable coexistence which persisted through the various stages of India's political evolution, although the configurations varied. We will start with the emergence of a tutelary model after independence, when civil society organizations were clearly subordinated to the political institutions. The following sections will delineate the various answers given to the ongoing expansion of political participation and their impact on civil-society frames. The political consecration of civil society after emergency was followed by alternative patterns of political mediation, when Hindu nationalism and the castes appeared on the political scene. Finally, the economic reforms of the 1990s modified the stakes and fields of action for the civil society organizations, bringing the question of the civilization of the state to the fore.

The tutelary model

Under the impetus of Mohandas K. Gandhi, the national movement set out to link the struggle against colonial domination to a social reform of Indian society. At the time of independence, this combination of political action and social work was the main subject of a debate between Gandhi and the party leaders J. Nehru and V. Patel on the future of the Congress Party. Gandhi wanted the Congress to devote itself to social work and to decentralize its efforts to bring about social reform. He envisaged the building of institutions bottom-up from the village level to the national level. The independence leaders, on the other hand, preferred a top-down approach driven and directed by the state. Contrary to many other cases, the groups spawned by the colonial state – in particular Indian civil service senior officials – did not play a significant part in the struggle for emancipation. Nevertheless, they were instrumental in the process of nation-building after independence.

This change of attitude toward the state bureaucracy can be partly explained by the challenges the Congress leaders were confronted with in the wake of independence: the crisis of the partition of the country, communist insurrection, the partitioning of federated states, and so on. The emerging state-centrism was not just a response to political events, however, but was firmly rooted in the conceptions of the founding fathers of the nation. For instance, the constitution adopted in 1950 put great emphasis on fundamental rights and on guarantees by the judiciary for upholding them, and it also assigned the state to play a key part in social reform. Besides the fundamental rights that were guaranteed by law, the constitution cited a long list of 'directive principles of state policy' asserting the economic and social rights of the citizens. Job reservation for 'scheduled castes and tribes' in public educational institutions and in the civil service was enshrined in it and it instituted the protection of minority rights. By combining universalism with the granting of collective rights connected to ascriptive identities, the constitution outlined the rifts and contradictions inherent in Indian politics.

The weak role conceded to the institutions of India's decentralized democracy was reflected in a top-down modernization project. It was not until the 1990s and 2000s that decentralization was significantly boosted. Until then, the reign of the district magistrate, inherited from the colonial period, was not only extended but even affirmed in a model of planned development that was based on the existing administrative apparatus. The Nehruvian model of development was devised at central-government level by an elite administrative body, i.e. the Planning Commission chaired by the prime minister, and its implementation in the states was carried out via the regular channels.

The tutelary nature of this development model was further accentuated by the modernization ideology that it conveyed. In an early book, Rajni Khotari (1970: 133, 134) defined the community development programme, which was launched in 1952, in the following terms:

> this combination of simple administrative expansion and verbal rhetoric, exhibiting high-minded conviction at the top, unrelated to the realities on the scene, was the biggest weakness of the community development movement. The rhetoric itself was ambivalent. It spoke of the innate capacities of the rural masses but decried their apathy; it wanted the people to come forward but also believed that only government action could produce results.

Throughout this period, most of the associational movements remained under party leadership. The neo-Gandhian social institutions received support from the Congress Party, while the Hinduists relied on Rashtriya Swayamsevak Sangh (RSS) volunteers (Weiner 1962: 65). Trade unions were divided along party lines and civil society was under state control and supervision, restricted by the particularisms and cronyism of political society. The significance of universal suffrage was limited by 'vote banks', i.e. the clientelistic control of a certain section of the electorate. In practice, the execution of the state's modernization programme was largely influenced by the negotiations that eventually took place between the political factions dominating the states and districts, and the administration that was supposed to implement it.

The authoritarian populist period of the first Indira Gandhi government (1966–1977) restricted the space open to civil society even more. Indira Gandhi owed her victory over the Congress barons to a campaign designed to capture the masses' votes by bypassing existing networks of factionalism, in the name of the war against poverty. But the policies adopted retained the top-down modernization model. Authoritarian family-planning and urban renovation policies increased the population's mistrust of state agents. In a context of economic crisis, social movements consequently started to challenge the legitimacy of a state known to be corrupt.

The return of civil society?

Against a background of unrest over prices and speculation, the neo-Gandhian leader J.P. Narayan became the head of a movement advocating 'total revolution'. He wanted to apply the lessons learned from the twofold failure of the state-centred development model and of the Gandhian movements through which Vinobha Bhave, another major Gandhian leader, had tried to achieve social reform by appealing to the dominant classes' sense of morality. The aim here was to bring about radical change through the people's own mobilization and to limit the discretionary power of the state and its representatives. The demands of Narayan's movement in Bihar and Gujarat were oriented towards the dissolution of the state assembly. Narayan:

> believed democracy was in danger. He felt that the weakening of democracy had reached a point where the mechanism of self-correction had completely broken down. It was necessary to develop Jan Shakti, people power. The right to recall the elected representatives was demanded, repressive measures to curb the agitations were opposed. And the right to speak, assemble and hold demonstrations was asserted.
>
> (Ghanshyam Shah 2002: 349)

Threatened by these movements and by a court ruling that challenged her election as a Member of Parliament, Indira Gandhi proclaimed the state of emergency, which suspended the freedoms guaranteed by the constitution. The state of emergency period (1975 to 1977) played a fundamental role in the return of a civil-society discourse within the Indian political scene. The state could no longer be presented as the guarantor of civil rights; instead, it was perceived as a threat to be countered by collective action. Human-rights movements grew rapidly during that period, especially the People's Union for Civil Liberties (PUCL) and later the Peoples' Union for Democratic Rights (PUDR). However, civil society did not find a suitable mediator on the political scene.

The political opposition united in the Janata Party won the 1977 elections. However, the government soon disappointed those who had hoped to see the beginning of a new political era with civil society playing a leading role. Participatory policies were boosted, nevertheless. The new discourse on these policies was grounded on the assumption that the success of redistributive policies was contingent on a collective organization of users: 'Critical for the success of all redistributive law, policies and programmes is that the poor be organized and made conscious of the benefits intended to them' (GOI 1978: 15). Planners, therefore, conceived of placing the implementation of all programmes under the surveillance of beneficiary organizations, including the sensitive area of land reform. This strategy is founded on Indian socialist traditions, but was also influenced by critical international currents, such as Paolo Freire's consciousness raising, for instance.

The forms of participation that were effectively implemented under the

Janata (the People's Party) government were far removed from this perspective of radical transformation. Projects for collective organization of the poor were opposed by conservative currents within the ruling party itself. Only those participatory devices endured that were no threat to the powers-that-be (Jobert 1984, 1985). They were, nevertheless, the first in a long series of programmes to promote participation in public policy-making. We will see below how these programmes used non-governmental organizations (NGOs) in a far more systematic way, in order to try to counterbalance the pressures of influential citizens and bureaucrats.

On the political scene, the civil liberties and popular organization rhetoric barely concealed the cracks in a governing coalition bound together by little more than their opposition to Indira Gandhi.

> The Congress-I abuse of power under the emergency regime gave the Janata government a historic opportunity to 'restore democracy' and non-partisanship in the use of public authority and resources. It restored the first, but its standards with respect to the second were hard to distinguish from those of the Congress-I.
>
> (Rudolph and Hoeber Rudolph 1987: 160)

Although it had been brought to power by rejecting the abuses suffered under the state of emergency, the Janata government, nevertheless, failed to alter the rules of the political game marked by particularisms and factionalism. Hindu militants did not want to be hampered by the civil-rights movements that they had supported as long as they were in the opposition. They tried to obtain the self-dissolution of the PUCL and were unable to accept the criticisms of the state governments that they controlled. They also refused to sever the umbilical cord binding their party, the Jan Sang, to their volunteer movement, the RSS. The divisions between other components of the Janata – senior Congress members, peasant leaders and socialists – ended up tarnishing the image of a completely fractioned party, thus allowing for Indira Gandhi's return to power in 1980 under the minimalist slogan 'government that works'.

Hence, the crisis triggered by the erosion of the tutelary model did not lead to the institutionalization of an alternative model for civil-society involvement. However, it initiated a new period in which different civil frames confronted each other in the political arena. From then on, the question of the social underpinnings of democracy was at the centre of controversies and revealed new rifts.

The Hindu nationalists called for a reconstruction of the Indian nation around its cultural majority. By contrast, the subordinate castes exerted strong pressure towards a stricter application and extension of the positive discrimination model established for the untouchables and tribes. The new social movements mobilized the victims and outcasts of the market-oriented development model of the mid-1980s. Thus, the difficulties and shortcomings of the administration opened a vast field in which protest movements rubbed shoulders with voluntary associations around a common reference framework: the civilization of the state.

Civil society and dictatorship of the majority

The crisis of the tutelary state had favoured the upsurge of Hindu nationalism. This ideology was embodied in organizations inspired by a particular version of democracy and civil society, based on the cultural majority's demand for hegemony. Arun Shourie, one of the thinkers of Hindu nationalism, synthesized the theses of this current in a widely-read book (Shourie 1997). He contended that the state's action had been perverted by 'minoritism', i.e. the granting of exorbitant advantages and exemptions to minorities, especially the Muslim minority. Shourie claimed that it was necessary to reconstruct the Indian nation around its cultural majority which, in his mind, had been marginalized for too long, through centuries of foreign domination. He postulated that its unity should not be based on the action of partisan or administrative elite, but on a cultural tradition binding peoples from the Ganges to the Southern end of the Deccan. He saw the Brahmins as the bearers and guarantors of this tradition who had to reverse a secular current: 'for seven hundred years, talking of the essence of tradition was blasphemy, for one hundred years a stupidity, and for forty years revanchism, jingoism and, finally, communalism' (Shourie 1997: 22). Shourie concluded, therefore, that the minorities should have their privileges withdrawn and should only be tolerated in the country on the condition that they comply with the rules of the majority.

The Hindu nationalist movement's power originated from its electoral base and its grassroots organizations, especially the RSS. If civil society was defined only in terms of associational life and the creation of social capital, these organizations could have been considered as powerful components of Indian civil society. But such a definition would conceal the absolutely uncivil nature of Hindu militantism, consisting of an authoritarian internal organization and paramilitary formation that subjected its members to the ideals of the organization, violently confronting and intimidating anyone standing in their way (Basu *et al.* 1993). The reconversion of tribal peoples or untouchables who had turned to Christianity or Islam was achieved through intimidation and violence. The repressions also did not spare cultural communities, in which artists who were deemed to lack respect for tradition were harassed. Hindu nationalist troops played a decisive role in the dramatic events in Gujarat in 2002, when the violence between Hindus and Muslims turned into a full-blown massacre. In all these areas, the collusion between militant Hindus and the government, that was controlled by the Bharatiya Janata Party, attested to the significance of this 'majoritarianism'. The political community that the 'Hindutva' militants wanted to build was not a 'civil' community, but rather a nation cleansed of what were considered to be 'foreign elements' spoiling it. The means used to that end met no criterion of civility whatsoever, even if the rhetoric of majority democracy was omnipresent.

Democracy through castes?

The parties based in the lower castes used the rhetoric of majoritarianism for different purposes. The victory of parties that advertised their caste membership in the large states of Northern India raised the question of whether the revenge of the oppressed was inevitably to be identified with an advancement of civil society. The Congress' inability to make the alliance between the upper castes, the untouchables, the tribes and the Muslim minority actually work, opened the field for new caste-based parties. Caste politics were fuelled by the debate on 'reservations' that aggravated the country in the early 1990s. The main issue was the extension of job quotas in the public service and education system, reserved until then for the untouchables (or 'scheduled castes') and tribal natives (or 'scheduled tribes'), to 'Other Backward Classes' (OBC). The V.P. Singh government's decision in 1990 to increase the quota to the benefit of the OBC from 23 per cent to 50 per cent, lead to what Indian observers have called the 'Mandalization' of political life (after the Mandal Report which inspired it) – a reference to a fragmentation of political life along the lines of caste. Competition was rife between the lowest castes, however, certain excluded groups, such as Christian and Muslim untouchables, and even members of upper castes in economic difficulties, also demanded reservations for themselves. The scramble for public positions and benefits intensified, as the liberal policies of state withdrawal got under way. But the starting economic growth of the country also facilitated the exit of the upper castes towards more lucrative positions in the private sector, which explains why the coalition led by the Bharatiya Janata Party (BJP) did not step down on the issue of reservations.

The intense competition was further enhanced by the parties trying to instrumentalize it in their election campaigns. According to Zohia Hasan, the main challenge to state governments elected by the lower castes was to obtain proportional representation of all groups in government, in the administration and in educational institutions (Hasan 2000). The formation of an elite derived from these subordinate castes took precedence over substantial policies to improve the fate of the lower castes in general. Sudipta Kaviraj noted that 'an enormous amount of the energy of the new politics of the disadvantaged is spent in symbolic acts of retaliation which have tended to replace substantive measures directed against inequalities' (Kaviraj 2001: 113).

This explains why the 'Mandalization' of political society put movements that were rooted in civil society in an uncomfortable position. Their discretion in this debate probably reflected the ongoing disagreements regarding the criteria for positive discrimination. While the Marxist currents argued in favour of affirmative action on the basis of economic criteria, those close to Gandhian socialism supported the 1990 reform. The growth of caste-based democracy had certainly called into question classical discourses on the virtues of empowerment for excluded groups. As Sarah Joseph explains, 'there seems to be an implicit assumption that social movements and political initiatives which genuinely involve the deprived would necessarily be radical, progressive and democratic in character. This assumption may not always be justified' (Joseph 2002: 302).

This mobilization seems to have impeded the constitution of collective actors capable of changing the social situation. Based on a study of two Indian cities, Frederic Landy *et al.* conclude that

> considering governance in general, it appears quite illusory that more open-ness in society brings more equity and efficiency. The segmentation of local society along religious and caste lines as well as the less visible faults made by economic disparities prevent users from behaving collectively and equally. The unity of civil society is a myth even at this local level.
>
> (Landy 2007: 27)

The structuring of political society along caste lines clearly represented an obs-tacle to the constitution of a public sphere open to civil-society organizations.

The transformation of civil society by the grassroots

It is not only Hindu nationalists that have invoked the notion of tradition, certain thinkers of the new social movements that have developed since 1980 refer to it as well. In fact, since then, militants disillusioned by the parties have initiated new forms of political actions, based on the decentralized mobilization of the oppressed. Theorized by R. Khotari (1988) and D.L. Sheth (2004), the concepts of 'non-partisan political formation' or 'grassroots politics' entered the political discourse. Their main claim is that the new movements should always be rooted locally. The positivist knowledge of experts, bureaucrats, capitalists or elected representatives is, thus, opposed to the knowledge derived from the practical experience and values underlying in traditional cultures, along with the ethnic assertion of oppressed groups.

From the emancipatory struggles of the marginalized segments of the popu-lation a new conception of democracy can emerge. The aim is not to replace representative democracy and political parties, but to tip the balance of power in favour of the most disadvantaged sections of the population. In order to do so, it is, nevertheless, necessary to overcome the risks of sectarianism and localism in the grassroots movements. Therefore, different networks aiming at coordinating the popular movements were set up. In the view of Rajni Khotari, the character-istics of the Indian tradition seem conducive to the integration of very diverse elements because it is based on social pluralism, on a conception of unity built on the dispersion of shared identities and values, as well as on the absence of a clergy and orthodoxy, and, consequently, on tolerance (Khotari 1988: 35). We can, thus, see the difference between the Hindu nationalists' perception of Indian tradition, and the one promoted by the theoreticians of grassroots politics. Nevertheless, they share the same basic assumption on the intrinsic virtue of the traditional society that they defend.

The new movements put their hopes in these communities' capacities to live on their own resources, and by the rules and values of their own cultures. They invoked a civil society as distant as possible from the state and the market. This juxtaposition of civil society and the state has been strongly criticized by Neera Chandhoke (Chandhoke 2003). Above all, however, it was challenged by the actual experience of the new social movements. The opposition to new economic policies of deregulation and liberalization triggered general protests from organizations claiming to represent civil society. Their efforts dealing with the destabilizing effects of new economic policies caused them to switch from global protest to more focused actions aimed at obtaining precise measures to protect the victims of globalization. For instance, the large federation of Indian voluntary organizations, VANI, initiated a vast debate on the structural-adjustment programme decided by the government in 1992. The climax of this campaign was the presentation of an alternative budget for the Union for 1993.

Mobilization has mostly been organized around the territorial dimensions of these liberalization policies, the aim being to defend the interests of those groups of the population that are victims of evictions and upheavals in their environment, due to development programmes concerning dams, mining, industries in the Special Economic Zones (SEZ), forestry or commercial fish culture. The social movements in question claim that such programmes destroy the resources and lifestyles of the concerned people. They defend the victims in two stages, first, by directly challenging programmes, although this has rarely prevented their continuation; and, second, by drawing attention to the needs of the affected group. The latter constitutes the core of the struggle and includes, among other measures, compensation and rehabilitation.

Another emblematic example is the renowned movement against the Narmada Valley dams (NBA). The movement's opposition to these cathedrals of modernization was acknowledged even by the World Bank, and the leader of the movement, Medha Paktar, was chosen to be one of the representatives of civil society on the 'world dam commission'. Faced with the fact that despite their protest, the project still was carried out in the end, the NBA organized local and national support for compensation and relocation of the inhabitants evicted from flooded areas. Summarizing, we can see that constrained by events, these movements have shifted from global protest to the struggle for the incorporation of the interests of disadvantaged people.

The civilization of state institutions

Against this background, a new reference framework of civil action emerged: the utopia of a stateless civil society was replaced by a vision of civil society as a transformation agent of the state. This new framework of reference was conveyed not only by the heirs of Gandhian socialism, but also by the militants of other ideological movements. The particular idea of this project of civilizing state institutions was not to compensate for the shortcomings of the state, but rather to pressurize it into becoming more civil-oriented. This framework applied to two different areas, the involvement of civil society in participatory policies and civil-society organizations' contribution to key political debates.

Bureaucratic shortcomings and voluntary organizations

Civil-society organizations' involvement in public policy-making has been justi-fied by the fact that the states are unable to provide basic services to those parts of the population that need them most. Hence, the blueprint for the 11th Five-Year Plan for 2007–2012 points out a fact that has been constantly repeated: in the sectors of primary education and health the diagnosis is severe, many posi-tions are vacant while at the same time absenteeism is a major problem among teachers and doctors (GOI 2006: 59, 68). One may assume that the poor quality of these services is the result of cronyism which strongly limits the emergence of professionalism. Notwithstanding that the quality of the service of both sectors is rated as very weak by the Planning Commission, there is no indica-tion, however, of the Commission's intention to address these well-known short-comings by implementing internal reforms in these sectors.

Recognizing the incapacity of centralized regulation to obtain more efficiency among staff, planners are calling, moreover, for a mobilization of decentralized authorities and committees of beneficiaries to monitor their performance. In this particular regard, civil-society organizations have been granted an important role:

> The CSO works in the remotest of remote areas where even the Government has no reach … In addition to capacity-building, many CSO have a proven track record of creating awareness, mobilising social capital and implement-ing programmes at the grass roots level … Recognising this experience, the 11th Plan should aim at encouraging partnership between CSOs and PRI [decentralized authorities] which also extend to joint implementation.
>
> (GOI 2006: 94)

In this respect, the 11th Plan is a continuation of its predecessors which intro-duced participatory measures in many fields, such as primary and secondary education, water management, or health services. But the problem of these pro-grammes harnessing local elites – political and social leaders, bureaucrats – still remains unsolved.

Therefore, an alliance is advocated between local councillors and associ-ations in order to spur the bureaucrats into action. For it to be effective, the councillors would have to oppose the cronyism that is hindering the work of civil servants in the field. In this respect, Kerala's experience, in which strong decentralization was combined with intense training and leadership by a militant organization, has attracted a great deal of attention. The 'Power to People Cam-paign' has been saluted by theoreticians as a model of radical democracy (Fung and Wright 2003). The particularity of this campaign was the combination of massive decentralization with mobilization and training of those concerned by militant networks – a paradoxical situation in which a party devoted to democratic centralism used planning services to achieve the decentralized participation of certain parts of the population. The interpretation of this operation is rendered even more controversial by the electoral defeat of the government that carried the reform (Chatukulam and John 2002).

In order to avoid to be caught in these games of connivance, certain movements have voluntarily situated themselves outside the bureaucracies that they want to monitor. In this respect, innovative practices have proliferated, from citizen juries to citizens' 'report cards on public services', initiated by Paul Samuel (2006) in Bangalore. Another example is the 'movement for the right to information', led by Aruna Roy, which prompted government to substantially amend the conditions of access to public documents. This movement resulted eventually in legislation allowing citizens to call state agents to account more easily.

Under pressure from donors who were eager to short-circuit the Indian bureaucracy and with the support of participatory programmes launched by the government, the associational sector has grown considerably since the 1980s. Currently, it comprises close to one million organizations, providing the equivalent of 2.7 million full-time jobs in 2002 (Planning Commission, Government of India 2005). Over the years this sector has structured itself around coordinating bodies such as the Voluntary Action Network India (VANI), which have the dual role of organizing the sector and negotiating the conditions of their collaboration with the government. The name adopted by this network is no coincidence, it is intended to distinguish it from the spurned world of NGOs. Denunciation of NGOs has become common in Indian political discourse, where arguments against 'NGO-ization' are always more or less the same (see, for instance, Khotari 1988; Chandhoke 2003). Certain NGOs are said to be nothing more than the hidden instruments of politicians, the so-called GONGOs (governmental non-governmental organizations). Others are alleged to be the new vehicles of neo-liberal hegemony, they are said to undermine the sovereignty of the state by short-circuiting the direct relations established with their financiers, and to legitimate the state's withdrawal by promoting private services in order to replace public services. It is, thus, claimed that by this depoliticizing development, NGOs impede the necessary opposition to the neo-liberal model, and they are seen to form an opaque sector which secures its leaders a good standard of living. These widespread allegations explain why many civil-society organizations take great care to refer to themselves as 'movement' or 'voluntary association'.

Grassroots at the summits of the state

While the Indian state has been willing to grant considerable space to the voluntary sector in the implementation of its policies, it has been far less tolerant of that sector's intrusion in the political debate. For at least a decade, national political mobilization has proliferated around the main topics of social protest. It has taken the form of campaigns bringing together multiple organizations in loose networks, for instance the national campaigns for people's right to information, or the right to food and to education, or campaigns driven by the National Alliance of People's Movements, coordinated by Medha Paktar, the leader of the movement against the Narmada dams. At the international level, these movements have actively participated in attempts to build a global civil society, primarily through world social forums but also via the committees created by international institutions.

This politicization of social movements is often not tolerated by the Indian state. Governments brandish the terrorist threat in order to justify tight regulation of foreign donations and even banning them for political organizations. But from the point of view of voluntary organizations, leaving the task of defining what a political organization is to the government, can lead to serious abuses. In some cases, these movements' support is, nevertheless, sought by certain public actors who wish to assert their autonomy. The experience of a 'judiciarization' of collective action and of the National Advisory Council chaired by Sonia Gandhi, is a telling illustration.

Judicial activism and civil-society organizations

With the support of a particular faction of the judiciary, human-rights movements were able to achieve an official recognition of the uncivil excesses of the Indian state. These judges wished to erase the memory of the judiciary's leniency towards the government during the state of emergency. By opening the door to public interest litigation (PIL), they provided civil-society organizations with a powerful lever for influencing government action. PIL enabled associations acting in the public interest to use the courts without pursuing a particular case.

The starting point was the case of People's Union for Democratic Rights (PUDR) versus Union of India (A.I.R., 1982, S C 1473), in which it was recognized that a third party could directly petition the court, whether through a letter or other means, and seek its intervention in a matter where another party's fundamental rights were being violated. In this case, referring to the Constitutional prohibition on forced labour and traffic of human beings, the PUDR submitted that workers who had been contracted to build the large sports complex at the Asian Games Village in Delhi were exploited. The PUDR asked the court to acknowledge that such work, under exploitative and overtly humiliating conditions, or work that was not even compensated by prescribed minimum wages, was a violation of fundamental rights.

Likewise, a petitioning of the Supreme Court was at the origin of the Right to Food campaign. The campaign began with a writ petition submitted to the Supreme Court in April 2001 by the People's Union for Civil Liberties (PUCL), Rajasthan. Briefly, the petition demanded that the country's gigantic food stocks should be used without delay to protect people from hunger and starvation. This petition led to a prolonged public interest litigation (PUCL versus Union of

India and Others, Writ Petition [Civil] 196 of 2001). Supreme Court hearings were held at regular intervals, and significant 'interim orders' issued from time to time. The result was direct Supreme Court intervention in monitoring the various programmes set up by the Indian government to combat malnutrition.

Due to the court's action, problems were put on the government's agenda, that would have hardly emerged had they been raised using the regular means of representative democracy. But judicial responses have always been constrained by the strategic orientations of the executive, and the Supreme Court has challenged neither the large investment projects nor the reinforcement of the repressive arsenal created in the context of the government's war on terrorism.

The movements at the parties' bedside: the NAC

The same types of constraint seem to have weighed on the National Advisory Council (NAC) for the implementation of the Minimum Common Programme. This body was set up by the United Progressive Alliance (UPA) government around left-wing parties and Congress after their victory in the 2004 elections. It was composed of experts and personalities from civil society and had the mission of making proposals to ensure the implementation of the government's common programme. Militants had already been invited to forums in which government policy orientations were discussed. The Planning Commission and central-government ministries had extensive experience in this respect. But this was the first time that a body so close to decision-making and with such general competence was formed.

This convergence of civil activists and Congress was facilitated by the former Hindu nationalist government. Its wait-and-see attitude in the case of the Gujarat massacre was strongly condemned and caused some of the voluntary movements to move closer to the 'secular' political coalition formed by the Congress and the left. The political fate of the NAC was closely linked to that of its president, Sonia Gandhi. Having given up the idea of being prime minister, the president of the Congress could use this institution to claim the merit of having initiated important measures. Examples were the Right to Information Act and, especially, the National Rural Employment Guarantee Bill, passed unanimously by Parliament on 23 August 2005. In both cases, these bills were promoted within the NAC by senior social activists who had driven a national campaign on these topics. The laws that were promulgated did not entirely meet the demands advanced during these campaigns, and the final legislative result was severely criticized by some activists and these leaders.

However, this involvement of civil-society actors in circles close to government's decision-making bodies depended largely on the strategic position of the chairperson of the NAC. Sonia Gandhi's resignation from the NAC in March 2006 was rapidly followed by the withdrawal of active militants, such as Aruna Roy and Jean Drezes, from this institution – with the result that it suddenly seemed marginal.

Thus, although movements rooted in civil society have found new allies in the Indian state, their influence on the Indian political scene should not be over-emphasized. Whenever the core strategies of the state are concerned, that influence is slim. Economic liberalization has been pursued without any major changes. The construction of dams has continued despite protest and, like the other major projects, has generated a steady flow of evicted persons. According to these movements, guarantees of compensation and reinsertion remain insufficient. Likewise, the rule of law is undermined by the lasting dread of terrorism in the country. The armed conflicts overwhelming Kashmir and the North-east of India, and the pressure of the Maoist armed struggle in the Central East have triggered the introduction of highly repressive legislation. However, political society remains largely insensitive to the alarm bells set off by these measures among human-rights movements.

Conclusion

If we consider only the discourse on civil society, the evolution of the Indian debate echoes more general tendencies cited at the beginning of this book. But when the place of civil society in political society is examined, the terms of the Indian debate differ profoundly from this broad trend. The hypothesis that civil society becomes a point of reference whenever established politics enter into crisis, is illustrated by the return of civil society after the state of emergency in the late 1970s. The framing of alternative references for relations between the state and civil society has borrowed much from the international discourse on good governance and, particularly, on the crucial role of voluntary associations in the empowerment of beneficiaries, in the activation of bureaucracies and in the defence of the environment. This discourse, which is close to a version of the 'third way model' for the states of the South, has been fiercely criticized by those social movements – oriented or not towards a radical transformation of society – which have actively participated in alter-globalization forums. Nevertheless, a shift in strategies can be witnessed among these groups. Although they still condemn the liberal development model, they tend to be more focused on means of civilizing the state, attempting to limit harmful impacts of globalization on the most disadvantaged groups.

The saga of social movements in India has received much attention on the international scene. However, this should not cause us to forget the modest role of this civil associational world in the reality of daily life in India. Even in a modern city like New Delhi, John Harris found associations only play a very minor part in the solution of citizens' problems (Harris 2005). In the same vein, a book entitled *Democracy Without Associations* (Chibber 1999) generated much debate in India, but no one could question its testimony to the weakness of formally established organizations. It clearly indicates the fact that:

> for the lowest strata of Indian society, associational channels ... are not easily available: their repertoire, which has considerable range, stretches from acceptance of patronage of politicians to wary support of local toughs;

from political mendicancy to spontaneous violence. All elements of this repertoire lie outside the definition of associational 'civility'.

(Kaviraj 2001: 317)

Yet, the fragility of the third sector is just one difficult facet among others, of the challenge to incorporate civil society into Indian political society. Civil society embodies a people consisting of *citizens*, whereas Indian political society is structured around inherited and imagined communities. Hindu nationalists base the political collective on the Hindu majority's revenge over centuries of foreign domination (including the Mughal Empire). The Scheduled Castes and Other Backward Castes also want to use the law of numbers to repair the injustices from which they have suffered. Hence, the minorities are also mobilizing to claim their fair share of public benefits. The strive for these particular advantages sometimes even takes precedence over the quality of the service delivered by bureaucracies.

Certain currents of civil society have not been insensitive to the charms of particularism and have argued around a mobilization of traditional identities to oppose the steamroller of globalization. The universalism of the right to vote has thus led to a confrontation between particularist groups for the sharing of the spoils of the state. The battle for public resources is intensifying as liberal policies for controlling public expenditures prevail. The new market prosperity is, nevertheless, enabling the middle and upper-classes to turn elsewhere, to find more attractive services and jobs in the private sector. Over and above these different particularisms, unity is sought through an activation of Indian or Hindu nationalism.

The place that particularist actors have in political society puts civil society into an awkward position. The unity that civil society could promote would be founded on the creation of a common base of civil, political and social rights, cross-cutting boundaries of caste and tradition (Gupta 2003). In Indian political discourse, homage is ritually paid to the recognition of human rights in the constitution, in jurisprudence and even in the programmes of the different Plans, aimed at meeting essential needs. But this definition of a common base is obscured by the dynamic of collective rights.

The consolidation of this common base depends, in turn, on the existence of a network of different, open and secular institutions. According to André Béteille (Béteille 2003: 202), it is the autonomy of these institutions that guarantees the possible vitality of civil society. Several observers have celebrated the 'silent revolution' (Jaffrelot 2003) that Indian democracy is said to have experienced with the growing movement of the untouchables. To be sure, greater participation by the working or poor classes in the elections is a remarkable feature of Indian democracy, yet it remains to be seen whether this 'revolution' will bring civil society and political society closer together.

Bibliography

Basu, T., Datta, P., Sarkar, S. and Sen, S. (1993) *Khaki Shorts and Saffron Flags: A Critique of the Hindu Right*, Hyderabad: Orient Longman Limited, 126.

Baxi, U. (2000) 'The avatars of Indian judicial activism: explorations in the geography of (in)justice', in S.K. Verma and K. Kusum (eds) *Fifty Years of the Supreme Court of India*, Delhi: Oxford University Press.

Béteille, A. (2003) 'Civil society and its institutions', in C. Elliot (ed.) *Civil Society and Democracy, a Reader*, New Delhi: Oxford University Press, 191–210.

Chandhoke, N. (2003) *The Conceits of Civil Society*, New Delhi: Oxford University Press, 278.

Chathukulam, J. and John, M.S. (2002) 'Five years of participatory planning in Kerala: rhetoric and reality', *Economic and Political Weekly*, 37 (49): 4917–4926.

Chatterjee, P. (2001) 'Postcolonial civil and political society', in S. Kaviraj and S. Khilnani (eds) *Civil society: History and Possibilities*, Cambridge; Cambridge University Press, 165–178.

Chibber, P. (1999) *Democracy without Associations: Transformation of the Party System and Social Cleavages in India*, Ann Arbor: University of Michigan Press, 304.

Fung, A. and Wright O.E. (2003) 'Deepening democracy: innovations in empowered participatory governance', *Politics and Society*, 29 (2): 5–41.

Government of India (GOI) Planning Commission (1978) 'Draft – VI five year Plan revised', New Delhi.

—— (2006) 'Toward a faster and more inclusive growth. An approach to the 11th Five Year Plan 2007–2012', New Delhi, 109.

Guha, R. (ed.) (1983) *Subaltern Studies: Writings on South Asian Studies*, Oxford: Oxford University Press.

Gupta, D. (2003) 'Civil society or the state. What happened to citizenship?' in C. Elliot (ed.) *Civil Society and Democracy, a Reader*, New Delhi: Oxford University Press, 211–237.

Harris, J. (2005) 'Political participation, representation and the urban poor: findings from Delhi', *Economic and Political Weekly*, 40 (11): 1041–1054.

—— (2007) 'Antinomies of empowerment. Observations on civil society, politics and urban governance in India', Draft Paper for the Berkeley CSAS Conference on Local Governance and Empowerment May 2007, http://ias.berkeley.edu/southasia/democracy07/docs/jharris.pdf (accessed November 2007).

Hasan, Z. (2000) 'Representation and redistribution', in F.R. Frankel, Z. Hasan and R. Bhargava (eds) *Transforming India: Social and Political Dynamics of Democracy*, New Delhi: Oxford University Press, 146–175.

Jaffrelot, C. (2003) *India's Silent Revolution*, New York: Columbia University Press.

Jobert, B. (1984) 'The testing of the alternative: two major innovations in Indian social policy', *Social Science Information*, 23 (6): 921–954.

—— (1985) 'Populism and health policy: the case of Community Health Volunteers in India', *Social Science and Medicine*, 20 (1): 1–28.

Joseph, S. (2002) 'Society vs state? Civil society, political society and non party political process in India', *Economic and Political Weekly*, 26 (4): 299–305.

Kaviraj, S. (2001) 'In search of civil society', in S. Kaviraj and S. Khilnani (eds) *Civil society: History and Possibilities*, Cambridge: Cambridge University Press, 287–323.

Khotari, R. (1970) *Politics in India*, New Delhi: Little Brown Company and Orient Longman, 459.

—— (1988) *State Against Democracy: In Search of Human Governance*, Delhi: Ajanta Press, 308.

Landy, F. (2007) 'Vertical governance: brokerage, patronage and corruption. The case of the public distribution system of foodstuffs', unpublished contribution to the APUG seminar, Mumbai and Hyderabad: University of Nanterre, 29–30 May 2007, 27.

Planning Commission. Government of India (2005) 'PRIA voluntary sector in India. Scale, impact & potential', New Delhi, 9 September 2005, planningcommission.nic.in/data/ngo/csw/csw_4.pdf (accessed October 2007).

Rudolph, L. and Hoeber Rudolph, S. (1987) *In Pursuit of Lakshm: The Political Economy of the Indian State*, Chicago: University of Chicago Press, 529.

Samuel, P. (2006) 'Public spending, outcomes and accountability: citizen report card as a catalyst for public action', *Economic and Political Weekly*, 41 (4): 333–340.

Shah, G. (2002) 'Direct action in India: a study of Bihar and Gujarat', in G. Shah (ed.) *Social Movements and the State: Readings in Indian Government and Politics*, London: Sage, 335–360 and 475.

Sheth, D.L. (2004) 'Globalisation and new politics of micro-movements', *Economic and Political Weekly*, 39 (1): 45–58.

Weiner, M. (1962) *The Politics of Scarcity*, Chicago: University of Chicago Press, 271.

6 China

Creating civil-society structures top-down?

Thomas Heberer

Civil-society discourses in China

Since the 1990s an ongoing discourse on civil society and on the application of this concept has arisen among Chinese intellectuals. This debate is strongly interlinked with the discussion on the causes of the decay of the former Soviet Union, China's further political development, and the issue of establishing a new framework for state–society relations. Whereas in the early 1990s many academics wanted to 'learn' from this 'Western concept', meanwhile the focus has shifted to whether the concept is applicable to China's conditions and, if so, how to implement it. One group argues that political change requires a bottom-up process in which society gets stronger vis-à-vis the state; the other group holds that under China's authoritarian conditions the party-state itself will have to activate civil-society structures.[1]

Since the end of the 1990s, proponents of the civil-society concept have linked it to the protection of interests of specific social groups, an independent judicial system, the freedom to establish social organisations and associations and of press and opinion (He Baogang 1997; Zhang Ye 2003; Wang Ming 2003; Yu Keping 2003a, 2006a, 2006b, 2006c).[2] One strand of discussion argues that the emergence of a middle class is the precondition for a civil society; others suggest that public intellectuals are necessary for building such a society. Altogether, a strong majority believes that only the rise and increase of social associations and NGOs (civil-society organisations) would provide the premises for a civil society.

Although at first sight many arguments sound quite familiar, the perception of the civil-society concept differs significantly from Western notions. Even its conceptuality is distinct from Western concepts: the Chinese terms used for civil society are *shimin shehui*, referring to the urban sphere only, and *gongmin shehui*, which means 'society of public people' and focuses upon the responsibility of citizens in terms of public goods and good behaviour. It is, therefore, not concerned with the issue of political power. Accordingly, civil society is perceived as a non-confronting model that should not pose a challenge to the state.

Furthermore, without doubt, social and political conditions differ from 'Western' countries. In China we find a strong interweaving between state and society. The party-state, for instance, not only integrates the existing associations into bargaining processes, but also strictly controls them. It bans associations which apparently attempt to act autonomously from the government. However, as sociologist Ding Xueliang points out, society infiltrates the party-state via social associations and thus initiates processes of change. This Janus-faced nature of associations, which Ding called 'institutional amphibiousness', on the one hand illustrates that associations through countless threads are closely connected with party and state structures (even to the point of 'institutional parasitism', i.e. their interests and financial means frequently are bound to the party-state), while, on the other hand, party and state institutions can be infiltrated and changed by these associations ('institutional manipulation and conversion'). Party members and cadres are represented in all social institutions, which finally leads to mutual interconnectedness. Ding argues that Western concepts of civil society hardly grasp this dual character since, for the most part, they insist on civil-society's autonomy and thus underrate the effects of state–society interaction (Ding Xueliang 1994: 198–300).

Differences of political systems are not the only reason for diverging conceptions. China is still in a process of both state- and institution-building. Institutions governing the coexistence of people and providing certainty of expectations are only gradually evolving (for instance in terms of rationalisation, juridification and creating a legal system). There is a strong lack of civilisational competence, i.e. a deficiency of a complex set of rules, norms and values, of a law system, law security and civic liberties. Among people, groups and organisations there is a lack of respect for the law, a mistrust vis-à-vis authorities, deficiencies in terms of institutionalised rules and double standards with regards to speaking and conduct. In China's rapidly changing society new rules of social behaviour will have to be learned and internalised. A public sphere which controls the state bodies, a process of 'civilising' in the way of dealing with co-citizens, and a state which treats its citizens respectfully will still have to emerge. In states like China, in which institution-building is still in progress, the state exerts an overpowering control and subsequently monitors and restricts the activities of its citizens. We can, therefore, hardly expect the existence of an *autonomous* civil society.

It is open to debate whether, under authoritarian conditions, a gradual development of civil-society structures is feasible and prone to facilitate the transition to a democratic system. I side with those authors who claim that key patterns of a civil society can also evolve under different political systems (Schmitter 1997: 293–262; Alagappa 2004; Howell and Pearce 2001). Accordingly, I am specifically interested in the type of social actions that are emerging in China, which are at first not fully autonomous, but are not congruent with the party-state, either, and which finally may become nuclei of autonomous social fields, beyond state control.

Hence, I define civil society in the Chinese context as the emergence of a public sphere beyond the party-state. I will provide evidence that the Chinese state plays a particular role in activating structures of a latent civil society top-down. Furthermore, I argue that under conditions of civilisational incompetence and the prevalence of traditional structures like *danwei* (the traditional work or social unit), clan and kinship, the state has to operate as an engineer of those structures. I agree with Joel S. Migdal who has pointed out that in the case of weak societies facing strong states and underdeveloped civil society structures, a state may have to function as a 'political architect' (Migdal 1988).

This chapter is organised around three main hypotheses. First, basic structures of a civil society are gradually evolving; second, those structures are engineered top-down by the party-state. Third, an authoritarian (illiberal) type of civil society is emerging, which the party-state attempts to control. It is illiberal in the sense that it is activated and regulated by state interference and not yet by law. Thus, a public space within which people may pursue their interests exists only in a restricted way. A civil society requires structures and institutions and the core argument is that the Chinese party-state is facilitating these prerequisites in order to solve major social and political problems. This does not automatically lead to a civil society worth its name, but may enable democratic structures and thus the transition to a civil society in the future.

Enhancing civilisational competence

Since I take civil society as a political ideal which can only be realised in the long run, I will focus on the conditions and actor strategies that are likely to effect the development and functions of civil-society structures in the specific socio-political context of modern-day China. Following Bourdieu, I classify civil-society structures as 'fields', i.e. as an ensemble of social arenas which are both strongly inter-related, and at the same time preserve their independence in terms of each field sticking to its own principles and rules which affect all actors involved in the specific field (Bourdieu and Wacquant 2006: 124–146).

Likewise, the Polish sociologist Pjotr Sztompka (1993: 88–89) has delineated four different fields in which a society might engender 'civilisational competence'. With reference to the post-socialist societies in Eastern Europe he suggests particular preconditions for the emergence of a civil society under conditions of post-socialism. These are:

- an *enterprise culture* as a precondition for participation in a market society;
- a *civic culture* indispensable for an enhanced citizen participation and the evolvement of citizens with citizens' awareness;
- a *discourse culture* as a prerequisite for participating in a free intellectual discourse and;
- an *everyday culture*, i.e. a civilised individual behaviour.

If we apply Sztompka's fields of civilisational competence to China we find, first, that since the 1980s a private economy and private entrepreneurship and along with it an *enterprise culture* have evolved at a rapid pace. Second, proto-citizens are gradually emerging; we witness an increase in citizens' participation in the public sphere, be it individually or collectively, e.g. in villages and urban neighbourhood communities or in associations and NGOs, which amounts to a rise in *civic culture*. Third, an intellectual debate on social and political issues is arising and spreading via the Internet, giving impetus to a *discourse culture*. Last, but not least, a civilised way of behaviour is propagated and evolving, both concerning individuals (as, for instance, the development of empathy and self-restraint) and the state, supporting an *everyday culture* fitting for a civil society.

Below I am going to examine four major fields where conditions for the emergence of civil society structures in China might become more favourable:

1   the private sector;
2   citizenship, social associations and organisations;
3   intellectual discourses, including the use of the Internet;
4   the efforts of the state to push a new value system and new standards of moral behaviour.

Field 1: resurgence of a private economic sector and entrepreneurship (enterprise culture)

Until the 1990s state ownership was the predominant form of ownership. In the 1980s China returned to private cultivation in agriculture (though without privatising arable land). This was the starting point for the admittance of different forms of ownership not only in agriculture, but also in commerce, services and handicrafts. Quite rapidly, the impetus of the private sector turned this sector into the driving-force of economic development. Self-employment and setting up of private enterprises were increasingly encouraged and facilitated by the party-state. Commencing from rural areas, millions of people established small stores and workshops, individuals and groups began to set up enterprises of different sizes. Many of them rapidly developed into larger enterprises. Concurrently, many state-owned enterprises lost their competitiveness in the market and began to operate in the red. This was the reason why in the 1990s the state began to sell or lease the majority of the small and medium enterprises to private persons. Currently, more than 90 per cent of all enterprises are owned by private persons and more than 50 per cent of all workers and staff are employed by the private sector, with an increasing tendency (Heberer 2003: 17–28). This bottom-up privatisation has considerably widened existing income disparities and led to the rise of new social strata (entrepreneurs, the middle-classes). Step by step, the state tolerated and later even encouraged the establishment of interest and professional associations. By getting organised, entrepreneurs reinforced their bargaining capacity vis-à-vis the party-state. In 1997 the 15th National Congress of the Communist Party elevated the private sector to equal that of the state sector. The 16th Congress in 2002 announced that entrepreneurs constitute an important part of China's socialist market economy (*Renmin Ribao* 18 December 2002). Accordingly, since then they have been permitted to join the Communist Party. This further strengthens those who are engaged in the private sector. By engaging in political institutions (e.g. parliaments) and media campaigns, by enhancing social relationships to officials and even by way of corruption they were successful in broadening their social impact.

Field 2: emergence of citizens and civil organisation (civic culture)

The existence of citizens and citizenship is a principle prerequisite for a civil society. One of the crucial issues is whether a civic culture is gradually emerging in China. By civic culture I mean forms of voluntary participation, civic awareness, a sense of citizen duty and a public spirit of the people.

Drawing on Thomas H. Marshall (1976: 71–73) I discern four basic criteria for an emerging citizenship in China:

1   increasing opportunities for people to participate in social and political affairs;
2   the prospect of a rising living standard for the majority of the population;
3   voluntary involvement in public and societal issues including the formation of associations;
4   civic liberties.

Again, it is the party-state that expands and constrains the opportunities for participation and the emergence of a sense of citizenship. Whereas openings to participation and voluntary engagement have increased dramatically over the last years, so far civic liberties exist only in a limited way.

First, concerning participation, in recent years new opportunities have evolved, for instance by establishing legally-binding grassroots elections in villages and urban neighbourhoods and by fostering social participation in neighbourhood communities, social associations and welfare institutions. Meanwhile, village leadership has to be elected by the population in direct and secret ballots. On the levels of towns/townships and urban neighbourhoods we find experiments with direct elections of local officials. The success of rural elections gave rise to the transfer of rural experiences to urban areas. The Ministry of Civil Affairs, responsible for grassroots elections, argues that elections are to strengthen the degree of the population's participation and the legitimacy of the political system. In many respects this may not yet work in a satisfactory way (local authorities, for instance, intervene in the ballots, arbitrarily remove elected village heads; in urban neighbourhoods elections are primarily by indirect ballots, i.e. only representatives of the inhabitants have a voting right). My own research and surveys in China prove, however, that people increasingly conceive elections as their 'right' (Heberer 2006a: 19). Rational voters emerge, who have realised that a correlation exists between balloting and the responsibility of the elected toward their voters. Many interviewees argued that elected persons had a stronger sense of accountability, because they want to be re-elected and therefore have to show engagement for the demands or interests of the residents, who in turn increasingly put forward suggestions and voice their opinions. Moreover, even indirect voting (by delegates) requires the elected to take the interests of their constituents into account if they want to be re-elected.

On the whole, grassroots elections are a new phenomenon that will foster a learning process, the internalisation and training of voting and participation. On the one hand, this will enhance the citizens' demands for information and participation. On the other hand, candidates are increasingly pushed to present themselves in a more substantial way in order to generate trust. The introduction of direct elections would therefore be supportive in spawning legitimacy.

Second, we can ascertain a rising standard of living among the majority of the people, particularly in urban areas. As long as people are primarily concerned with their personal survival they are unable and unwilling to participate. In more developed areas, better-off people might increasingly engage in social and welfare issues. Nevertheless, the figures available support the assumption that the majority of better-off people are primarily involved in their jobs and lack the time to engage socially (Heberer and Schubert 2008).

In China's increasingly differentiated and sophisticated society it is acknowledged that the state is unable to undertake and operate all societal tasks. A new social-security system is still underdeveloped and market regulation does not produce yet the outcome sought after. Therefore, the party-state is very strongly encouraging engagement in social activities, such as taking care of weak social groups in villages and neighbourhood communities. 'Volunteers' are requested to look after old-aged, disabled persons and fringe groups. They should also take care of the environment and cultural life in their communities. Yet, interest in participation and the number of volunteers is meagre. According to the party newspaper *Renmin Ribao*, at the end of 2005 merely 3 per cent of all urban inhabitants had been involved in voluntary social activities (*Renmin Ribao* 6 December 2005 and 17 July 2006) whereas in Western societies the percentage hovers between 35 and 40 per cent of the entire population (Gensicke 2006: 9–16).

A Chinese report elucidated that around 80 per cent of the volunteers in urban neighbourhood communities were members of the Communist Party or the Communist Youth League or public servants (compare *Shequ* 2005: 15). In Peking in 2005 just 300,000 persons were registered as 'volunteers', about 2.3 per cent of the entire population. However, according to a document of the State Council of 2006 this share shall be increased to 8 per cent by 2008 (*Renmin Ribao* 17 July 2006). So far, 40 per cent of the volunteers are linked to the party, and 70 per cent were over 50 years old (Goujian Hexie 2006: 50). Thus, predominantly party members and welfare recipients (people who require support from the state and are obliged to attend social activities within their neighbourhood communities) could be mobilised to attend public activities and to take care of the socially weak.

The Chinese party-state is activating citizenship top-down in several ways: it opens windows for political participation by introducing direct and indirect elections at grassroots level. Furthermore, it takes responsibility for assuring a rising standard of living and gradually institutionalises property rights. At the same time, it is encouraging voluntary participation and accepting the formation of private associations. A rising standard of living and the enhancement of participation is expected to spawn the empowerment of people (not least via reinforcing internal efficacy) and participatory activities are likely to promote a gradual increase of a sense of citizen duty.

Finally, the party-state supports the surfacing of citizenship by a turn in ideology and the use of a different terminology: instead of talking about 'masses', the dominant term in the former political concept, it is now propagating the notion of 'citizens' which has the connotation of legal and participation rights. Recently, a journal published by the Ministry of Civil Affairs noted that China needs conscious citizens electing and monitoring their own administrations and who consciously participate in public affairs of their communities (Chen Weidong 2004: 11). Here, participation and a public spirit are conceived as a part of citizenship, a concept relatively close to Western notions.

In line with this reasoning is the spread of associations and interest organisations. According to the Ministry of Civil Affairs, which is responsible for the registration of associations, at the end of 2006, 355,000 'non-state organisations' from the county-level upward had been registered, i.e. associations, foundations, private non-profit enterprises and other organisations like NGOs or GONGOs (government-organised NGOs).[3] Those figures do not include associations at the township and village-level as they are not required to register. However, the term 'association' is rather imprecise as it encompasses organisations founded by the party-state as well as those set up by citizens. Furthermore, unlike in democratic systems, in China such organisations can not be set up autonomously. They have to be registered and the 'Regulations Concerning Registration and Administration of Social Organisations' of 1989 stipulates that registration is only possible with the help of a patron institution (e.g. offices, state or party institutions, public enterprises), which has to apply for the admission and takes over the formal patronage and a monitoring function. This, however, does not mean that associations primarily represent the interests of the party-state.

Although the majority of associations are concerned with sports, health, recreation, professional, cultural, scientific–technical, and similar activities, in recent years a broad range of social organisations and foundations have emerged that are active in more politically sensitive fields. For instance, an environmental movement and environmental NGOs are gradually evolving, albeit the latter are widely locally organised and oriented. They mainly originate in larger cities and areas affected by evident ecological crises. According to official Chinese data in 2005, more than 2,000 such NGOs existed, an amazing number since none of them existed prior to the 1990s (Worldwatch Institute 11 January 2006). They are involved in various areas, such as environment protection, endangered animal species, fringe groups, support of Aids sufferers, ethnic minorities, protection of cultural relics, consumer issues, or nature and landscape preservation. Furthermore, there are also NGOs involved in the extension and enhancement of grassroots elections, participation in urban neighbourhood communities, or the improvement of the labour conditions of rural migrant workers. Among the successful social movements in recent years were, for instance, movements against hydroelectric power plants in the Yunnan province, against the relocation of the Beijing zoo or the movement 'air-conditioning 26 degrees' (aiming at limiting energy waste by air conditioning), to mention just a few. Moreover, network organisations evolved which are composed of a larger number of individual organisations (e.g. the China NPO Network or the Chinese Association of NGO Cooperation CANGO) (Guobin Yang 2005: 46–66; also Lehrack 2004). Most notable is the environment domain, where an increasing number of student groups have come forward to perform a monitoring function. According to reports in 2006, such groups existed at 176 universities in 26 provinces (Stalley and Dongning Yang 2006: 335).

As long as such organisations do not pursue political or politically sensitive objectives, the party-state (i.e. the central state) takes a benevolent attitude, since they address issues at the local level, which the central state is unable to solve. Both government officials and the broader public attribute them the capacity to improve governance. In May 2006 *Renmin Ribao* explicitly emphasised that without the public participation of citizens there will be no improvement of environment protection (*Renmin Ribao* 18 May 2006). A survey of *China Development Brief* in 2002 in Beijing revealed that 80 per cent of the respondents assigned the task of supporting or complementing the work of the government to NGOs.[4] The majority of the respondents conceived social organisations not as independent, but rather as agencies to amend governance. Yet, frequently such organisations come into conflict with local authorities, particularly if they take up issues which infringe upon the interests of local authorities.

Beyond those official associations there are also 'underground NGOs' or informal networks. Some of these informal organisations are more traditional ones, for example clans, home-town associations, secret societies or beggar's guilds. Home-town associations are very active in China's larger cities. They comprise people from the same township, county or province and act as interest organisations. In part they control entire markets, live together in common living-quarters, and are obliged to mutual support of their peers. They function as self-protecting organisations of worker migrants and sometimes even as proto-trade-union organisations.

Thus far, peasant interest organisations do not yet exist. Accordingly, in rural areas informal 'opinion leaders' and 'peasant lawyers' are emerging, i.e. persons assigned by peasants of a single or several villages or even of a township, to convey problems to higher echelons or to draft and submit petitions (which is a legally confirmed right). Peasants even establish 'economic associations' and cooperatives, which in fact are to advocate the social rights of the rural population. As long as the party-state is reluctant to admit an official interest organisation of peasants, the grievances of the latter might continue to manifest themselves in informal organisations and collective action.

Religion is a contested field. The officially recognised religious communities are strictly controlled by the state. More traditional ones, like temple associations, sects and underground churches, that have spread in recent years, may function as social 'pockets of resistance' vis-à-vis the local state. But they are not tolerated by the party-state and, therefore, are unable to affect upon civil-society development.

Summing up, it is difficult to assess the importance of enhanced participation and associational life for a civic culture in China. Although wider patterns of participation and grassroots elections are evolving I do not argue that China is setting off for democratisation. Rather, it is the party-state which constitutes and sets the frame in the different fields for the structuring of a civil society. Nevertheless, people increasingly have the opportunity to participate and will learn to pursue their interests in an efficient and effective way. Unlike the Mao era, no individual is coerced anymore to attend political or social activities. The organisation of one's life is now a personal matter with little interference of the party-state. Thus, individual autonomy vis-à-vis the state and its agencies is increasing, which is considered to be a prerequisite for an autonomous social space.

With respect to autonomy, Chinese associations and NGOs clearly differ from their counterparts in Western societies. In China interconnectedness and interweaving between social associations and the party-state are helpful as they contribute to solve problems through informal channels and by informal bargaining. The Chinese 'bargaining society' in which interests of social groups are bargained in an indirect way in fact requires such interweaving in order to enforce interests more easily. Concurrently, such half-autonomous associations might function as precursors of genuine autonomous economic and political associations. At the moment, associations have a rather ambiguous character: on the one side they are subject to the supervision and control of the party-state, on the other side they may exhibit certain elements of independence as long as this does not challenge the party-state.

It is open to debate whether more independently operating social movements such as the environment movement will have a greater impact. Some argue that they are prone to come into conflict with the party-state and thus might become a proponent of political change. Others argue that due to rigid state control their political effect will be rather limited and that confrontational behaviour would just provoke tighter party-state surveillance (see, for instance Qiusha Ma 2007).

Field 3: intellectual discourse on social and political reforms (discursive culture)

In order to explore the potential for the development of a discursive culture in China I will assess three distinctive fields:

1 the social and political leverage of intellectual ideas and conceptions;
2 the party-state acceptance of diversity and pluralism of concepts and political opinions;
3 the degree of open-mindedness in policy discussions.

What is particular about the Chinese situation is the exchange and interdependence of these three fields. There exist constant flows between the party-state and various intellectual circles and fields. The party-state benefits from new reform ideas developed by leading intellectuals and think tanks. Furthermore, it has to take public opinion more into account. Yet, the tolerance of the political leadership is limited by one crucial imperative: every actor has to adhere to the principles of 'political correctness', i.e. to refrain from challenging the leading role of the party. In fact, the majority of the intellectuals agree that the improvement of the well-being of the people and social and political stability are crucial for China's further development and that the current political system is the guarantor of stability.

The growing autonomy of Chinese society in the reform process favours an increasing independence of intellectuals. Open debates on the future of China's political system have become possible and even pronounced critical statements are tolerated as long as the discourse participants still keep within an implicit 'contract' between the party leadership and intellectuals, which entails political correctness in the Chinese sense has to be maintained, i.e. the power of the Communist Party and the political system should not be openly challenged.

The public intellectual discourse on corruption provides a telling example of public debates. Participants argue that democracy, associated with public control, an independent public sphere and the rule of law are decisive for fighting corruption efficiently. Thus, in the academic debate, corruption is conceived as a political and at the same time a systemic phenomenon and – in contrast to the standpoint of the party leadership – not merely as an individual, moral issue. As far as the discourse on corruption reinforces the discourse on political change and democratisation, the inner Chinese-debate on corruption will finally support and facilitate the conversion into a rational power system based on law. Yet, apparently, the consequences of this debate reach far beyond this argument. Albeit it might not always be expressed in an open manner, it is quite obvious that not only the deficits of the legal system are revealed, but rather the political structures and the very foundation of the political system are at stake.

Such critics clearly trespass the above-mentioned official borderline, e.g. when the adviser of the central leadership Yu Keping argues that the political system constitutes the structural foundation for political corruption. Without control by citizens, overt political channels of information (transparency) and political contestation, corruption might not be contained (Yu Keping 2003b: 170). Thus, the discourse on corruption becomes an important feature of the discourse on political change and democratisation in China. It is an indication of an increasing political maturity of the Chinese society. It acknowledges a distinction between public and private spheres, and the demand for corresponding laws and transparent and rational administrative rules. Accordingly, the state is more and more conceived as a body which has to serve general and public interests (Heberer 2006b: 26–28).

The Internet is another field of interest that in recent years has spawned new forms of publicness. It has an effect on the emergence of the public space, the development of (virtual) social organisations and of widespread Internet protest activities. Furthermore, by encouraging public debates and the articulation of problems, it functions as a tool of social transparency (Guobin Yang 2006: 196–214; also Shanthi Kalathil 2003: 31–46).

At the end of 2006 the number of Internet users in China accounted for more than 137 million, although this figure does not say much about how it is used (*Renmin Ribao* 19 July 2007). The China Internet Network Information Center ascertained in 2003 that 46.2 per cent of the users are using the Internet for information and 32.2 per cent for entertainment (CNNIC 2003).[5] Certainly, Internet access provides an alternative source of information on domestic and international developments. Accordingly, some Western and Chinese scholars argue that the Internet might function as a tool for political change (Kluver 1999; also Chase and Mulvenon 2002). Some scholars even speak of an evolving *cyberdemocracy* (Saco 2002).

Recently, sociologist Yang Guobin has pointed to the particularities of the Internet in China: thanks to the Internet, politics is no longer perceived as an abstract factor of political power but – in connection with the entertaining surfing the net – represents a new form of a (voluntary) political everyday discourse and leisure-time activity (Guobin Yang 2003a: 7). Insofar it differs greatly from the political–ideological sessions of the Mao era in which people were coerced to participate.

Undoubtedly, in recent years the number of Internet portals with news, up-to-date information and of virtual communities has significantly increased. Particularly better educated and younger people in urban areas participate in public debates in the public space of the Internet, thus redefining the relationship between state and society. The anonymity of the Internet has spawned a new critical public. Proactive users, called *Wangmin*, cyber-citizens or netizens (deduced from the term *citizen*) pick up information on social injustice, on the hush up of local disasters, criminal activity or corruption, they spread the news and put it up for discussion.

A prominent example was the case of a worker who after a flagrant misjudgement was executed in Shaanxi province in 2002. This provoked a public debate on the death penalty and legal procedures in China. Not only jurists and the party newspaper *Renmin Ribao* but also thousands of citizens participated online in the debate. The discussions were rather heated and many participants expressed fury and outrage. Albeit the party leadership finally stopped the discussion, it requested the legal authorities to decrease the number of executions. Meanwhile, the Supreme Court was ordered to re-examine each death sentence. Certainly, the death penalty is not yet abolished. But this case reveals that people increasingly use the Internet to disseminate information and to vent their grievances. Moreover, the Internet contributes to forming public opinion and making trends more transparent.

Another noticeable case was that of Sun Zhigang, a rural college graduate, who was seized by the police in Guangzhou because he could not prove his identity by an identity card. He was detained and put into custody where he was finally beaten to death. Immediately after that a discussion on the general behaviour of the police, the freedom of the press and a reform of the legal system arose on the Internet. Jurists demanded a revision of the law provisions on the treatment of rural working migrants in Chinese cities and wrote to the national parliament (the National People's Congress) demanding to cancel or revise the existing regulations, to investigate this incident and to punish the policemen responsible.

Such Internet movements are a form of *collective action* that is new to China: a more or less spontaneous concurrence of individual or group actions, which represent common interests and have an impact upon policies. Political scientist Wu Qiang even speaks of 'e-social movements'. Meanwhile, he argues, organised patterns of interest expression had emerged, such as online petitioning (e.g. against 'software regulation' [2001/2002], against the censorship of Internet publications [2002], in support of the Tian'anmen-mothers [an initiative of mothers whose children were killed during the 1989 'Tian'anmen incident'], or the 'Living Buddha A An Zhaxi', who was detained due to alleged 'terrorist activities' etc.) (Cooper 2006: 123–126; also Qiang Wu 2004). Furthermore, since the mid-1990s autonomous virtual NGOs (*e-civic organisations*) organising online-congresses and online-parties were constituted on the Internet (Qiang Wu 2004). Even in terms of environment protection numerous websites and virtual NGOs have arisen, exposing environmental problems and disasters and thus inducing public debates.

Certainly, the party-state attempts to monitor Internet activities. It is blocking discussions it considers to be too sensitive or far too critical. As deterrence, from time to time people are arrested and sentenced to long imprisonments. Yet, those measures do not really impair upon the spirit of the Internet users or their debates.

However, recent research findings put into question that the Internet will develop into a tool of political change (Guobin Yang 2003b: 453–475; also Guobin Yang 2006: 196–214). The vast majority of the *Wangmin* does not oppose the political system. We therefore have to make a distinction between Internet contributions opposing the political system and those only critical of specific social developments. The exposure of scandals, corruption cases, social injustice and cases of environmental damage conduces to solving social problems and to canalise the discontent of citizens. Internet discussions do not necessarily pose a challenge to the political system. They may even contribute to its reinforcement. As Damm notes, Internet users are primarily younger people with a higher educational level and members of the new middle-classes who are not concerned with a change of the political system but rather want to make the system more efficient – in the sense of good governance (Damm 2003: 10).

Field 4: establishing a new value system (everyday culture)

The party-state is a leading force in the effort to promote a new value system and new patterns of behaviour. The rapid economic and social change has led to a considerable erosion of the traditional value system and moral standards. For this very reason the party-state has established a 'Programme for the Realisation of the Construction of a New Citizen Morale'. It was announced by the government in 2001 and from this point onwards, consistently propagated by the media (for example, *Renmin Ribao* 5 September 2003, 7 July 2004) In 2003, a particular day (20 September) was declared to be the yearly 'day to propagate the [new] citizen morale' (*Renmin Ribao* 19 September 2003). The party-state acts as a *moral state* which attempts to set and enforce new moral standards in a top-down approach.

To push up the government's objectives, *Renmin Ribao* regularly reports on citizens participating in the project of creating a new moral order. Villages and urban neighbourhood communities are advised to make their inhabitants adopt 'public conventions' in order to demonstrate that they are determined to adhere to appropriate moral standards relating to public behaviour within their community or towards co-residents (compare *Renmin Ribao* 9, 10, 11 September 2004).

In June 2004 deputy minister Chen Jichang of the Ministry of Civil Affairs has explicitly pointed out that the 'engineering of a new morale' particularly among the youth is a salient task of the new urban neighbourhood communities (*Renmin Ribao* 17 June 2004). The latter are conceived to be tools of the 'moral engineering' of society, raising the 'moral quality' of citizens and teaching them 'civilised behaviour', i.e. civic and political skills (Meng Gu and Bai Zhigang 2006: 3–10; Shi Chang and Zhuo Silian 2006: 127–136; also Tang Zhongxin 2006: 175–180). In establishing new values, a new public morale and public spirit the party-state assigns to urban neighbourhood communities the pivotal task of creating 'new citizens' top-down (Liu Jitong 2003: 105; Liu Lina 2004: 282–285; also *Renmin Ribao* 29 July 2004).[6]

Conclusion: is a civil society evolving in China?

While the role of society is certainly increasing, the party-state still plays a decisive and paramount role. At the start, in the 1980s and 1990s, the state took over the task of creating the institutional frames and preconditions for economic development and national modernisation. Local officials performed as local developing agents and established or took over enterprises and thus accomplished entrepreneurial functions. Correspondingly, the party-state created an incentive system so that economic activities started to spread. As a result, entrepreneurship was emerging and thus an enterprise culture. In the 1990s the party-state established grassroots elections in villages and urban neighbourhood communities, thus initiating a rudimentary civic culture. Meanwhile, the administrative bodies of villages and neighbourhood communities have to be elected regularly. The party-state has also established social associations and GONGOs as well as intellectual think tanks, thus engendering a discursive culture. Furthermore, since 2000 it has set up voluntary associations in urban communities and stipulated that students have to attend voluntary social work. Under the

condition that a sense of social responsibility is still lacking and that the majority of people are not yet interested in accomplishing voluntary work, it is the
state which mobilises people to participate in social activities. The underlying
idea is to develop a first contingent of proactive volunteers which might function
as a role model so as to stimulate other people to participate in social activities.

An article in *Renmin Ribao* indicates that the party-state is quite aware of
existing deficits in participation. The article argues that:

> the willingness and quality of participation of urban dwellers is not yet very
> high. Therefore, the government has to function as a driving force and initi-
> ate a top-down process in order to spur people on to participate. Moreover,
> it is the government's task to help people to enhance their capacity to
> participate.
>
> (Rong Sun 2005)

Thus the *party-state* is to incur the function of a teacher: it shall help the people
to learn the skills of participation and teach them to acquire the capacity and
internal efficacy to participate in social affairs. The objective of social mobilisation is quite obviously geared towards improving the social fabric of society.
The state assigns to the villages and urban neighbourhoods the task of fostering
and enhancing participation and voluntary social engagement in order to solve
urging social problems. This concept resembles the concept of communitarianism, as laid out for instance by US-sociologist Amitai Etzioni who calls for new
communities in order to create a new sense of responsibility and to invoke a
reinforcement of the moral foundations of society (Etzioni 1993, 1996). The
principle idea of communitarianism favours – under conditions of post-modern
service societies – a social order in which a sense of community is fully
developed and people identifying with their community. In contrast to Etzioni,
who is appealing to the mature citizen, the Chinese concept pursues a top-down
approach of creating (controlled) citizens. This is why I label the Chinese
pattern an *authoritarian communitarianism* and not a civil society (compare
Heberer 2005: 152–160).

As mentioned above, Migdal has pointed out that under the conditions of both
the weakly developed structures of a civil society and of a strong state facing a
weak society, a state may function as a political architect. Accordingly, the Chinese
state is not a 'developmental dictatorship' but rather a development agency. The
latter requires more than pure authoritarian mechanisms of enforcement, i.e. an
increasing involvement of social groups in processes of bargaining with the state,
participation in community affairs, and a corresponding institutional setting.

It is precisely the combination of mobilised participation and volunteers, the
top-down implementation of grassroots elections and the top-down establishment of neighbourhood communities, that is prone to generate the preconditions
of an illiberal, controlled and communitarian–authoritarian civil society. Yet,
already the 1997 *World Development Report* ('The state in a changing world')
has underscored that, on the one hand, the state has to initiate development

processes and, on the other hand, it has to delegate public tasks to citizens, NGOs or the private sector in the interest of greater efficiency and stronger citizen orientation (World Bank 1997). Accordingly, the Chinese state functions as an activating state, which takes care of social tasks: It is activating and motivating the people (citizens) to take responsibility and solve some of the social problems by themselves. Self-organisation and engaging participation of citizens generates more independence vis-à-vis the state – an essential factor of advancing civil-society structures.

Certainly, the opportunity to establish social associations or to participate in social affairs does not suffice for calling social relations in China a civil society in the sense of the Western conception. Thus far the party-state decides which associations and what kind of participation are 'good' or 'bad'. Under such conditions the emergence of a genuine public sphere between the state and the private sphere is under severe constraint. On the other side, ongoing developments in the various fields mentioned here may have a transformative impact, including the slow emergence of a public sphere and sustaining elementary structures of a civil society.

Notes

1 For an overview, see: www.lwwzx.com/Freepaper/Literaturetheory/2006–08–25/ Freepaper_20060825095421_29545.html (accessed 5 March 2007).
2 An overview on the discussion is provided via www.ccss.pku.edu.cn/ccss/Html/ xshd_xsjl/151128537.html (accessed March 2007).
3 www.chinanpo.gov.cn/web/listTitle.do?dictionid=2201 (downloaded 29 September 2007).
4 www.chinadevelopmentbrief.com/mode/157 (accessed 2 June 2006).
5 Further information is given by Liang Guo and Wei Bu (2002: 121–144).
6 There were similar efforts during the rule of Chiang Kai-Shek, see Robert Culp (2006: 529–554).

References

Alagappa, M. (ed.) (2004) *Civil Society and Political Change in Asia*, Stanford: Stanford University Press.

Bourdieu, P. and Wacquant, L. (2006) *Reflexive Anthropologie*, Frankfurt: Suhrkamp, 124–146.

Chase, M. and Mulvenon, J. (2002) *You've Got Dissent! Chinese Dissident Use of the Internet and Beijing's Counter-Strategies*, Santa Monica: Rand Corporation.

Chen Weidong (2004) 'Min ping guan: rang jumin chengwei gongmin' ['Citizen evaluate officials: let residents develop into citizen'], *Shequ [Community]*, 2–4: 11.

China Internet Network Information Center (CNNIC) (2003), *13th Statistical Survey on the Internet Development in China (2003)*. www.cnnic.net.cn (accessed 8 July 2006).

Cooper, C. (2006) '"This is our way in": the civil society of environmental NGOs in South-West China', *Government and Opposition*, 41 (1): 109–136.

Culp, R. (2006) 'Rethinking governmentality: training, cultivation, and cultural citizenship in nationalist China', *The Journal of Asian Studies*, 65 (3): 529–554.

Damm, J. (2003) 'Internet and the fragmented political community', *International Institute for Asian Studies (IIAS) Newsletter* 33 (March): 10.

Dickson, B. (2003) *Red Capitalists in China. The Party, Private Entrepreneurs, and Prospects for Political Change*, Cambridge: Cambridge University Press.

Ding Xueliang (1994) 'Institutional amphibiousness and the transition from communism: the case of China', *British Journal of Political Science*, 24: 298–300.

Etzioni, A. (1993) *The Spirit of Community: Rights, Responsibilities, and the Communitarian Thinking*, New York: Crown Publishers.

—— (1996) *The New Golden Rule. Community and Morality in a Democratic Society*, New York: Basic Books.

Gensicke, T. (2006) 'Bürgerschaftliches Engagement in Deutschland', *Aus Politik und Zeitgeschichte*, 12: 9–16.

Guobin Yang (2003a) 'Mingling politics with play. The virtual Chinese public sphere', *International Institute for Asian Studies (IIAS) Newsletter* 33 (March): 7.

—— (2003b) 'The Internet and civil society in China: a preliminary assessment', *Journal of Contemporary China*, 12 (36): 453–475.

—— (2005) 'Environmental NGOs and institutional dynamics in China', *The China Quarterly*, 181 (March): 46–66.

—— (2006) 'The Internet and emerging civil society in China', in Suisheng Zhao (ed.) *Debating Political Reform in China: The Rule of Law versus Democratization*, Armonk and London: M.E. Sharpe, 196–214.

Goujian Hexie (2006) *Beijing shi jianshe hexie shequ xin tan* [*To build up harmony. New discussion on the construction of new neighbourhood communities in Beijing*], Research Center for the important ideas of the Deng Xiaoping Theory; the Three Representatives of Beijing city and the 'Front' publishing house of the Party Committee of Beijing (ed.), Beijing: Xuexi Chubanshe, 50.

He Baogang (1997) *The Democratic Implications of Civil Society in China*, London: Macmillan.

Heberer, T. (2003) *Private Entrepreneurs in China and Vietnam. Social and Political Functioning of Strategic Groups*, Leiden: Brill, 17–28.

—— (2005) 'Soziale Sicherung und Sozialhilfe: Schritte zur 'Harmonisierung' der Gesellschaft im gegenwärtigen China', *China Heute*, 4–5: 152–160.

—— (2006a) 'Institutional change and legitimacy via urban elections? People's awareness of elections and participation in urban neighbourhoods (Shequ)', Duisburg: University Duisburg-Essen, Working Papers on East Asian Studies No. 68, 2006: 19.

—— (2006b) 'Discourses, intellectuals, collective behaviour and political change. Theoretical aspects of discourses', in C. Derichs and T. Heberer (eds) *The Power of Ideas. Intellectual Input and Political Change in East and Southeast Asia*, Copenhagen: NIAS Press, 26–28.

Heberer, T. and Schubert, G. (2008) *Von 'Massen' zu Bürgern? Partizipation, Regimelegitimität und soziale Stabilität in der Volksrepublik China*, vol. 1: *Der urbane Raum*, Wiesbaden: Verlag Sozialwissenschaften.

Howell, J. and Pearce, J. (2001) *Civil Society and Development: a Critical Exploration*, Boulder: Lynne Rienner Publishers.

Junhua Zhang and M. Woesler (eds) (2002) *China's Digital Dream. The Impact of the Internet on Chinese Society*, Bochum: Bochum University Press, 121–144.

Kluver, R. (ed.) (1999) *Civic Discourse, Civil Society and Chinese Communities*, Stanford: Ablex.

Lehrack, D. (2004) 'NGO im heutigen China – Aufgaben, Rolle und Selbstverständnis', Duisburger Arbeitspapiere Ostasienwissenschaften No. 57/2004.

Liang Guo and Wei Bu (2003) 'Internet use in China – a comparative analysis', in Junhua Zhang and Woesler, M. (eds), *China's Digital Dream. The Impact of the Internet on Chinese Society*, Bochum: Bochum University Press, 121–144.

Liu Jitong (2003) 'Guojia huayu yu shequ shijian: Zhongguo chengshi shequ jianshe mubiao jiedu' ['State utterances and shequ practice: explaining goals of community construction'], *Shehui Kexue Yanjiu*, 3: 105.

Liu Lina (2004) 'Shequ shi shehui gongde jianshe de zhongyao zaiti' ['Neighbourhood communities are important carriers of the creation of a social public morale'], *Xinan Minzu Xueyuan Xuebao*, 9: 282–285.

Marshall, T.H. (1976) *Class, Citizenship, and Social Development*, Westport: Greenwood Press, 71–73.

Meng Gu and Bai Zhigang (2006) *Shequ wenhua yu gongmin suzhi* (*Culture and Quality of Citizens*), Beijing: Zhongguo shehui chubanshe, 3–10.

Migdal, J. (1988) *Strong Societies and Weak States. State-Society Relations and State Capabilities in the Third World*, Princeton: Princeton University Press.

Qiang Wu (2004) 'From virtual community to real society: an online interrogation of eforum-based civic associations in China' (unpublished manuscript).

Qiusha Ma (2007) *Non-Governmental Organizations in Contemporary China. Paving the way to civil society?*, London and New York: Routledge.

Rong Sun (2005) 'Gaijin chengshi guanli, tuidong shequ fazhan' ['Reform urban administration, push forward the development of neighbourhood communities'], *Renmin Ribao*, 2 March 2005.

Saco, D. (2002) *Cybering Democracy: Public Space and the Internet*, Minneapolis: University of Minnesota Press.

Schmitter, P.C. (1997) 'Civil society East and West', in L. Diamond, M. Plattner, Y.-H. Chu and H.-M. Tien, *Consolidating Third Wave Democracies*, Baltimore and London: The Johns Hopkins University Press, 239–262.

Shanthi Kalathil (2003) 'The Internet and civil society in China and Southeast Asia', in Junhua Zhang and M. Woesler (eds) *China's Digital Dream. The Impact of the Internet on Chinese Society*, Bochum: Bochum University Press, 31–46.

Shequ (*Community*) (2005) *Shequ*, 11, 2: 15.

Shi Chang and Zhuo Silian (2006) *Shequ jiaoyu yu xuexixing shequ* [*Education of and learning neighbourhood communities*], Beijing: Zhongguo shehui chubanshe, 127–136.

Stalley, P. and Dongning Yang (2006) 'An emerging environmental movement in China', *The China Quarterly*, 186 (June): 335.

Sztompka, P. (1993) 'Civilisational incompetence: the trap of post-Communist societies', *Zeitschrift für Soziologie*, 2: 88–89.

Tang Zhongxin (2006) *Goujian hexie shequ* [*Engineering a Harmonious Neighbourhood Community*], Beijing: Zhongguo shehui chubanshe, 175–180.

Wang Ming (ed.) (2003) *Zhongguo fei zhengfu gonggong bumen* [*Non-governmental Public Sectors in China*], Beijing: Qinghua daxue chubanshe.

World Bank (ed.) (1997) *World Development Report 1997. The State in a Changing World*, Oxford: Oxford University Press.

Worldwatch Institute (2006) *State of the World 2006: China and India Hold World in Balance*. Online. Available HTTP: www.worldwatch.org/node/3893 (accessed 29 September 2007).

Yu Keping (2003a) *Zengliang minzhu yu shanzhi* [*Incremental Democracy and Good Governance*], Beijing: Shehui kexue wenxian chubanshe.

—— (2003b) *Quanli zhengzhi yu gongyi zhengzhi* [*Politics of Rights and Politics of Public Goods*], Beijing: Shehui kexue wenxian chubanshe, 170.

—— (2006a) *Minzhu yu tuoluo* [*Democracy and Top*], Beijing: Beijing daxue chubanshe.

—— (2006b) *Minzhu shi yige hao dongxi* [*Democracy is a Good Thing*], Beijing: Shehui kexue wenxian chubanshe.

Yu Keping (2006c) *Zhongguo gongmin shehui de zhidu huanjing* [*The Institutional Environment of China's Civil Society*], Beijing: Beijing daxue chubanshe.

Zhang Ye (2003) 'China's emerging civil society', CNAPS Working Paper, Center for Northeast Asian Policy Studies, August 2003. Online. Available HTTP: www.brook.edu/fp/cnaps/papers/ye2003.pdf (accessed September 2007).

Part II

Civil society and public policies

Dilemmas and ambiguities

7 Incantations and uses of civil society by the European Commission

Hélène Michel

Over the last decade, civil-society participation as a means to sustain and extend democratic governance has become an important political objective in many countries. Therefore, most political institutions have paid greater heed to civil society and have tried to enhance their relationships with civil-society groups, in particular with non-governmental organisations (NGOs). At the European level, a discourse on the involvement of civil society has emerged in the 1990s and several devices have been tried in order to encourage civil-society participation. The White Paper on European governance, published by the European Commission (EC) in July 2001, can be seen as a key moment formalising civil-society involvement in the policy-making process. It initiated the reinforcement of 'a culture of consultation and dialogue' (EC 2001: 428) in European governance. In 2002, the White Paper was supplemented by 'General Principles and Minimum Standards'. Furthermore, Article 47 of the Constitutional Treaty of 2004 specified, among other aspects, that 'the Union's institutions shall maintain an open, transparent and regular dialogue with representative associations and civil society' (European Union 2004: article 47–1).

A new generation of the European Union (EU) consultation regime was set up, characterised by the principle of 'participatory democracy' (Kohler-Koch *et al.* 2006). This policy was not entirely new. Many Directorates General (DG) had developed formal or informal consultations with economic and social organisations before, for example the DG Development with the European NGO Confederation for Relief and Development (CONCORD) (Sanchez-Salgado 2006), the DG Environment with the European Environment Bureau (BEE) and Friends of the Earth–Europe (Berny 2005). Also, the DG Employment and Social Affairs has been well known for both its fostering of social dialogue and its policy in favour of a structured dialogue with European NGOs. Taking this as good practice, the European Commission's general policy since the end of the 1990s implied that NGOs ought to be more involved in shaping and implementing policy processes. Civil-society participation had become synonymous with good governance. It was supposed to improve the democratic process of decision-making and to bring citizens closer to European institutions, thus tackling the so-called 'democratic deficit'.

Rather than recalling the history and narratives of the EU institutions, this chapter tries to give an account of the controversial nature of the various discourses on civil-society participation. We will explore why and how the European Commission's discourse became established. To this end, we opted for a sociological approach (Guiraudon 2002) based on interviews with different kinds of actors in order to trace how they deal with this new 'referentiel' (Jobert and Muller 1987) and we observed how this concept of promoting civil-society involvement was put into practice in order to disclose the factual appraisal of the policy by the relevant actors. This approach implies that we do not take the European institutions as a homogeneous entity, but as a 'field' (Kauppi 2006) where actors struggle to prevail with their own position. By analysing the interactions of players and taking into consideration their political and sociological backgrounds, it is possible to demonstrate what is at stake in this new policy towards civil society and how the promotion of civil society became a panacea to more democratic governance.

Against this background, this chapter analyses first the main conditions that have favoured the discourses on civil-society participation as a solution to the legitimacy problem of the European Union. In a second step, we will examine why the European Commission's discourse has prevailed over other stakeholders and how it has been turned into practice.

The call for civil-society participation at the European level

The literature on the rise of 'civil society' often describes a continuous and linear movement within some European institutions, particularly the European Commission and the European Economic and Social Committee (see, for example, Smisman 2003 and 2005). Dealing with social and economic issues, their members are said to be aware of the need to reinforce their relationships with civil-society organisations, who in turn are expected to be keen on fostering the acknowledgement of their role in European governance. Therefore, the success of 'civil society' is often accredited to the fact that civil-society's request for being involved in the policy-making process has met the strategic objective of legitimising non-elected institutions (Wallace and Young 1997; Armstrong 2002).

This perspective remains somewhat problematic because it suggests that institutions are a willing and homogeneous actor, disregarding the discrepancies among the entities on the conception of governance and their function in it. Furthermore, institutions are not as rational as it is assumed. Many decisions are taken without a clear design and many changes are put in practice step-by-step without an apparent rational strategy in view. Moreover, European institutions are competing with each other and certainly do not join in a single discourse on civil society. Quite on the contrary, what appears today as one homogeneous discourse of the European Union was rather dissonant at the end of the 1990s. This suggests that the publication of the White Paper in 2001 has been a crucial moment in formalising civil-society participation in the policy process because it provided a general framework guiding the relations between the EU and economic and social organisations, which served the initial interests of both civil servants and stakeholders.

Three main factors can be identified in order to explain why, at the end of the 1990s, civil-society participation became a major issue in European governance: First, there was the perception of a crisis after the fall of the Santer Commission, which deepened the so-called 'democratic gap' between European institutions and citizens. Second, some reformers within the European Commission, together with close supporters outside the institutions, pushed for 'civil society' as the solution to this problem. Third, despite the attempt to establish an institutional definition, the vagueness of the notion 'civil society' allowed for various conceptions and tied together grand ideas and pragmatic changes.

The context of crisis after the resignation of the Santer Commission

As argued by Bruno Jobert in the introduction of this volume, the shift towards civil society can be interpreted as an answer to a legitimacy crisis. For the European case this hypothesis seems to be highly relevant. Indeed, when the Santer Commission resigned in 1999, the European Commission was faced with a major crisis of legitimacy. Surveys from the Eurobarometer and electorate's participation rates indicated the increasing 'democratic deficit'. Scholars and commentators concluded that European citizens did not trust the European institutions any more, if they ever did. They emphasised the gap between European citizens and those in power and stressed the lack of political legitimacy of non-elected institutions. Likewise, national politicians' attitudes towards the EU were denounced as enhancing the distrust among citizens. The aftermath of the Nice Intergovernmental Conference in December 2000 and the Irish 'no' to the ratification of the Treaty were seen as further proof of the crisis and, therefore, the call for a reform of the European Union gained momentum.

When Romano Prodi came into power he had to face not only the next enlargement and the settlement of the New Europe, but also the flawed image of the institution he chaired. Thus, the reform of governance became one of his strategic priorities in his term of office and the publication of a White Paper his first launch at a new European political design.[1]

In the beginning, a small team of a dozen experts, headed by Jérôme Vignon, was asked to draft a proposal within the confines of the existing treaties. Jérôme Vignon had been a member of the French civil service and had participated in the formulation of the 1993 White Paper on 'Growth, Competitiveness and Employment'. He had also worked within the Forward Studies Unit, which he had established under the Delors Commission in 1989 and managed from 1995 to 1998. Within the newly established 'governance team' Vignon was joined by several members from the Forward Studies Unit, pursuing their previous work on European governance (Sloat 2004). Among the main issues they examined, civil-society participation was an important one because it referred to the social dialogue that had been set up several years earlier under the Delors presidency and it celebrated the role of intermediary bodies in the policy-making process. In the context of the legitimacy crisis of the European Union, such conceptions were supposed to promote the idea that civil-society participation could bring the European institutions closer to the citizens and their needs.

Reformers push for civil-society involvement

Although many politicians remained reluctant to the idea of participatory democracy, which they feared would become a substitute for representative democracy, and despite a strong opposition from the college of commissioners and from civil servants (e.g. from DG Competition or DG Internal Market and Services), Jérôme Vignon and his team finally succeeded in promoting the idea of civil-society involvement as a means for tackling the democratic deficit.

In this process, the main task of Vignon and his team was to gather potential supporters of governance reform and to reconcile the different views beyond the discrepancies and overall competition between institutions. A large range of actors, such as European administrators and representatives from economic and social groups, as well as members of think tanks and various experts contributed to this 'experiment'. On each issue working groups were established. The majority of participating officials were either members of the Secretary General, who were in charge of liaising with interest groups and civil society, or members of the DGs in charge of the issue of consultation and dialogue with social and economic organisations, namely DG for Employment and Social Affairs, DG for Regional Policy or DG for Development.

These officials were all strongly supportive of the initiative on the White Paper because it acknowledged their previous work as good practice and vitiated the recurrent accusations of promoting lobbying against public interest. Thinking about participation in civil society was an opportunity to turn the tables towards formalising their consultation practices in order to better meet citizens' needs and demands.

Civil-society representatives also largely agreed upon the acknowledgment of consultation as good practice. The group included members of large European networks of NGOs, like CPMR (Conference of Peripheral Maritime Regions of Europe), ECAS (European Citizens Action Service), the Forum of the Civil Society or the Social Platform of NGOs, who were all contented to be associated with this large working group on governance reform and eager to participate in order not to be left behind by the European Commission. Their general position was to promote the role of civil society in the policy process and to encourage dialogue with civil-society organisations. Therefore, they strongly supported the White Paper as an efficient device for achieving democratic governance and to legitimate decisions.

However, at this point no agreement could be reached on how 'civil-society participation' was to be implemented. Albeit each group and each official was able to describe specific experiments on particular issues in the DGs where cooperation had been successful, it appeared to be difficult to generalise and to elaborate a general frame that would fit with the various types of consultations. Therefore, the notion of 'civil society' and the form of 'participation' remained very vague.

The vagueness of the notion of 'civil society'

Many analyses on the rise of civil society at the European level, that link this development to the publication of the White Paper on European governance, emphasise that the vagueness of the notion of 'civil-society participation' has lead to controversies on the definition of the concept and on its role in the European policy process (Cohen and Arato 1992; Joerges *et al.* 2001; Keane 2006). According to some authors, this might even have hindered the establishment of a homogenous European civil dialogue. They stress the fact that the definition of 'civil dialogue' remained very ambiguous, as well, and they call for a clarification. Others hold that only associations of citizens or groups that promote general causes and public issues are to be considered members of 'civil society'. To them, civil dialogue only involves non-profit civil-society organisations, such as NGOs, while others maintain that all groups outside the European institutions are members of civil society and as a consequence, firms' representation bureaus, business associations, trade unions and NGOs should be considered as standing on the same level.

In this regard, the European Commission took up the all-embracing definition that had been suggested by the Economic and Social Committee.[2] This broad definition integrated trade unions, employers' federations, business associations, NGOs, CBOs (Community-Based Organisations) and religious communities. Economic actors, especially lobbyists and business representatives, appreciated this step (Michel 2005), but many stakeholders considered the inclusion of the social partners and market actors as a mistake. In particular NGO representatives and unionists claimed that civil-society participation should remain the prerogative of public associations.

We argue that, far from leading to confusion, this wide definition allowed for the setting of the idea. The vagueness of the notions of 'civil society', 'dialogue' and 'consultation' made room for consensus among both stakeholders and DG members. The terms covered various national conceptions, deeply rooted in the history of each member state. But beyond this heterogeneity, each actor was able to refer to a positive general conception of civil-society involvement as a democratic procedure. At the European level, 'dialogue' was a familiar term in the relations between civil society and European institutions because it referred to many devices and previous experiments, such as online consultations which had been used for writing the Charter of Fundamental Rights, for hearings in the European Parliament and in formal or informal meetings with officials and working groups. Furthermore, the involvement of civil society came across as a pragmatic shift in European governance, since it had long been implemented by some DGs. For the proponents, it was only a way to extend the existing practices and to officially acknowledge the role of civil-society organisations, whereas to the opponents, who were reluctant to the idea of including non-elected and lay people into the policy process, 'civil-society participation' only meant a form of 'policy shaping', but not the involvement of NGOs into the decision-making process. Although they all had in mind different definitions, on the surface all members seemed to share the same views on the benefit of civil-society partici- pation, agreeing on the idea of bringing citizens closer to the European institu- tions, and most of them also welcomed the pragmatic changes. However, officials and stakeholders still held very different opinions on the ways of imple- menting the civil dialogue.

The institutionalisation of civil dialogue

This second part exemplarily examines the practices of the officials of the DG for Employment, Social Affairs and Equal opportunities (DG EMPL) because for one, this DG has a long history of involving non-governmental organisa- tions, both in consultation processes and in implementing policies.[3] We will observe the officials' practice in order to understand how and to what extent they contributed to the institutionalisation of civil dialogue and the shaping of a pluralistic system of interest intermediation, as postulated by the White Paper and in the Constitutional Treaty proposal. The second reason for taking a closer look at DG EMPL is that this DG has been constantly in contact with social partners, such as UNICE (Union of Industrial and Employers' Confederations of Europe) and ETUC (European Trade Union Confederation).

Here, we are interested in how the new policy of civil-society involvement changed the relationship between the European Commission (EC) and the social partners, particularly in the social fields in which they were challenged by NGOs. The example of DG EMPL sheds light on the EC strategy of implement- ing participatory democracy in order to encourage a pluralistic system of interest intermediation in which trade unions and employers' associations no longer hold a privileged access to the European institutions.

DG EMPL's strategy in favour of civil dialogue

Among the DG EMPL's staff we interviewed, many supporters of participatory democracy stated some disappointment with civil society. They complained about many civil-society organisations lacking information and concern about the citizens' interests, and called for an increasing commitment and a more active involvement. One of the reasons behind this criticism is their reliance on participating NGOs to deliver expertise and information in order to discuss the DG's proposals and to develop a coherent European position on the main issues. Many European platforms, for example the Social Platform of NGOs, were set up with financial support from the EC for exactly this purpose.

For many DG officials 'civil-society participation' is equivalent to close col- laboration with civil-society groups. Choosing their dialogue partners for reasons of efficiency is an important part of the DG's strategy. Since this kind of relationship requires specific skills and a proficiency in the administrative jargon, in general, large networks and social partners are most likely to work with the European Commission. Unions seem to have an additional advantage over other groups because they are better structured, they have expertise on social issues and there has been a history of collaboration between the unions and the EC for many decades. However, at DG EMPL the situation appears to be different. Some of the officials consider unions as actors within the social dialogue and, therefore, maintain that they should not be part of the civil dialogue, even though unions are civil-society members by definition of the White Paper. According to these officials, the dialogue with civil society should include NGOs only. On the other hand, unions hold a large and useful expertise on social issues. Thus, another group of DG officers argued that they should be included in the consultations on social and civil issues in the same way as NGOs.

This conflict among the members of DG EMPL can be observed, for example, in policies dealing with elderly people. Since 1988, the European Trade Union Confederation (ETUC) had dealt with the issue of retired people and old age. In 1993, a new federation was founded by unionists in order to organise the representation of retired and older people. This new organisation, the European Federation of Retired and Elderly Persons (FERPA), was acknowledged as a social partner by the European institutions. At the end of the 1990s, DG EMPL decided to create a new European platform in order to gather all organisations in the sector. It was the aim of DG EMPL to set up a large intermediary body dedicated to the issues of the elderly, in parallel to the European Youth Forum or the European Women's Lobby. Along with physicians' associations, old-age pension funds, retired people associations and others, FERPA was asked to join this platform. Co-financed by the EC, yet another representative body, the NGO European Older People's Platform (AGE) was set up in 2001. It was supposed to provide expertise to the European Commission and to coordinate the work of the various organisations. However, FERPA representatives refused to cooperate, referring to the fact that a European organisation already existed. Moreover, they disagreed with the new concept of older people being represented by professionals and business organisations. FERPA, as a trade union, and AGE, as a European NGO, have been competing for the representation of retired and older people ever since the foundation of the platform.

In their effort to establish a dialogue, DG EMPL has been more inclined towards working with AGE than with FERPA. In our interviews the staff have been reluctant to indicate their first choice, but a marked preference for the NGO is obvious: AGE is invited to all meetings and public conferences on elderly people, it is automatically appointed to working groups relating to issues of the elderly and it is asked to provide analyses and to contribute to consultations. When AGE had not been appointed for the liaison group within the European Economic and Social Committee created in 2004, DG EMPL interfered in order to impose the NGO as the representative of the sector.

FERPA members regard AGE as a product of the DG, lacking any financial and political autonomy. In our interviews they maintained that AGE's representatives were often uncritical of the European Commission and merely defended DG's views in meetings,[4] in particular concerning their concept of civil-society involvement which conveyed a depreciative attitude towards trade unions. Taking a closer look at the backgrounds of platform representatives and civil servants, which appear to be quite parallel, the FERPA members' view might not be far-fetched: most representatives and officials are highly educated professionals with international experience and good management skills. They have followed similar career paths in the European institutions and, due to their administrative position in Brussels, they have built a large social network, exchanging opinions and sharing similar attitudes (Cavaillé 2005; Wagner 2005; Harabanski 2005). Both groups speak of 'civil society' as a solution – and sometimes as the only solution – to the problem of the democratic deficit of the EU. While they are in favour of promoting intermediary bodies and especially NGOs that arise from emerging social problems, they express little appreciation for trade unions, which they label as outmoded organisations that do not fit any longer into the economic and social reality of European societies.

In fact, for AGE representatives and DG EMPL members, social inclusion, the fight against poverty, equality between men and women or the problem of an ageing population are the main European issues. Their scepticism of the unions' capacity to resolve those problems is based on the unions' alleged approach to protect the insiders of the economic system instead of encouraging outsiders to enter the labour market. In the policy process, the social partners are said to insist on their conservative position on labour rights, unwilling to negotiate and, therefore, not to fulfil the objectives of their role within the social dialogue. In contrast, NGOs are seen by DG officials not only as being more innovative in developing new approaches to tackle social problems, but also as more effective and more experienced in presenting their ideas in an administrative language.

In our interviews, many members of DG EMPL stated that for these reasons they have chosen to cooperate with NGOs rather than with trade unions. This DG strategy of selecting their dialogue partner is not new, but with the implementation of the White Paper and its celebration of civil society, it has become easier for officials to justify this stance. The new paradigm of civil-society involvement has, thus, facilitated a way to bypass the unions and to strengthen NGOs. For obvious reasons the members of the unions are highly critical of the DG EMPL's strategy which, in their view, substitutes social dialogue by civil dialogue and favours relationships with organisations that lack formal representativeness.

Participation in civil dialogue and representativeness

With regards to the wider definition of 'civil society' and the implementation of a civil dialogue from which they were more or less excluded, FERPA representatives started to counteract the European Commission's attempts to promote a

pluralistic system of interests in which the special status of the unions is undermined. Each meeting with DG officials in working groups, committees or in
public hearings was an opportunity to underpin the union's claim of legitimacy:
they insisted on their status as a social partner and actor of the European integration according to Articles 138 and 139 of the European Treaty. What was clearly
at stake in these discourses was the general position of unions in the European
system of intermediation, their status as institutional actors with privileged
access to the European institutions and, last but not least, their monopoly on
workers' representation.[5]

Once again, the discourses within the elderly people policy domain are
emblematic. In the debate on who should take part in the consultations, FERPA
members raised the issue of representativeness and their decisive criterion was
membership. As ETUC was claiming to be 'the voice of 60 millions workers',
FERPA asserted to represent ten million affiliated retired people and emphasised
its grassroots associations all over Europe and beyond. In the attempt to
strengthen their position, FERPA tried to draw attention to AGE's presumable
lack of representativeness. They characterised the NGO as a group of representatives in Brussels with a 'computer network' in European capitals, but no constituency.

For DG EMPL, the representativeness of civil-society organisations has
never been a relevant issue. Following the principle of openness, the general
principles and minimum standards for consultation of interested parties do not
define any accreditation system (EC 2002). There is no official means of controlling or sanctioning access to the consultation process. In regard to civil
dialogue, moreover, DG officials speak of 'decision-shaping', not 'decision-
making', thus implying that, in contrast to social dialogue, it is not to be considered as a matter of accountability and representativeness. DG officials merely
talk about 'relevant' organisations, or as one of them put it: 'We don't need big
numbers, we need good ideas, and we don't care if they come from a little NGO
or from a big network'.

As their claim for representativeness in terms of membership numbers and
mode of interest representation appeared not to be a fruitful approach to regain
influence, FERPA focused on building up more professional expertise in order
to meet the DG's expectations. However, the leading idea of civil-society
involvement had permeated the discourses in a way that made the unions soon
change their strategy.[6] Rather than providing technical expertise, they adhered to
the policy of openness towards civil-society organisations by actively participating in social movements and by initiating other forms of collective actions, such
as demonstrations, petitions or public meetings. In 2004, FERPA launched a
petition and collected millions of signatures in support of their demand to be
included in the decision-making processes, this way remaining very visible and
making their point that they represented a significant number of people. More
recently, FERPA joined ETUC in a petition for higher-quality public service and
accessibility for everybody. They also sent open letters to European governments and organised European demonstrations in Brussels, Strasbourg and other

cities where European summits took place, in order to protest against various social policies. By means of emphasising their capacity of social mobilisation, the unions introduced a new dimension to their argument of representativeness, once again trying to marginalise groups with no constituency.

A similar debate on the definition of who is a legitimate representative of civil society and about the meaning of civil dialogue has taken place among NGOs. Their discourse on representativeness has been centred on questions of category, i.e. whether an NGO should aim to be identified with certain societal groups, such as elderly people or workers, or rather with specific issues, such as human rights or the struggle against poverty. AGE, for example, cannot claim high membership rates. Therefore, they regularly recall that the quantitative criterion of representativeness is not meaningful. Instead, they prefer to talk about 'qualitative representation'. In their view, a group is representative if it is able to provide valuable expertise, independent of its size.

Not all NGOs agree with this position because it does not provide a clear-cut definition in order to consolidate the NGO's legitimacy. Thus, some of them rather agree with the unions that representativeness should be defined on the basis of membership. When the European Civic Forum, for example, was set up in December 2005 in order to encourage higher civic involvement in the European policy process, its founders stated very clearly that they intended to make European officials aware of the existence of the large number of people who actually form 'civil society'. In the words of the president of the European Civil Forum: 'If we represent civil society, we have to show it'. Within the liaison group of the European Economic and Social Committee, Civil Forum members and unionists work together towards the same objective, i.e. to establish membership as the main criterion of representativeness.[7] Unlike European networks' representatives and large platforms who lack experience in managing social protests, Civil Forum members seem to be closer to grassroots associations and to fieldwork. They tend to come from backgrounds as activists rather than civil servants before becoming representatives at the European level and, therefore, are more likely to maintain their close links with the basis. From this perspective, the promotion of civil-society involvement contains a profound criticism of the established European pluralistic system in which all groups are supposed to have an equal voice, but through which in fact the European Commission selectively incorporates certain organisations into institutional processes, thereby neglecting the fieldwork at the basis of civil society.

Conclusion

The exemplary analysis of the respective discourses of the Commission, the unions and NGOs has demonstrated the conflicting nature of civil-society involvement, despite the overall consensus on the general idea. The broad definition of civil society in the White Paper reflects the European Commission's intention to integrate a range of very diverse organisations. However, when the consultation process was to be put in practice, in many fields the conflicts of interests soon became evident.

The Commission aimed at including the whole spectrum of interests and as many different point of views as possible and, therefore, supported the aggregation of the various groups in large platforms. Correspondingly, platform representatives became the preferred dialogue partners of the DG officials, which meant for the unions the loss of the privileged status the social dialogue had granted. Therefore, the unions raised the issue of legitimacy and defined representativeness according to the number of members and a close connection to the grassroots level, whose interests were at stake after all, so the argument went. This way, the conception of what constitutes civil society in Europe and who is entitled to participate is closely related to the definition of representativeness.

The European Commission prefers to structure the civil dialogue according to its requirements of expertise. By means of large platforms, a broad range of interests are included and the Commission is relieved from the task of interest aggregation. However, this 'state-aided' (by the EU institutions) concertation of pluralistic interests certainly cannot fulfil the function of a neo-corporatist system of interest aggregation, since hardly any of the participating organisations hold a mandate, thus lacking accountability towards their members or supporters.

Notes

1 Following Jacques Delors' footsteps, it quickly turned into a promotion of the European Commission and its president (Drake 2000).
2 See the presentation of the European Economic and Social Committee Liaison Group at http://eesc.europa.eu/sco/group/intro/index_en.asp.
3 Not all DGs are enthusiastic about institutionalising civil dialogue, as Rosa Sanchez Salgado (2006) shows in her dissertation.
4 According to the FERPA representatives, a telling example is AGE's contribution to the DG EMPL consultation on the 2005 Green Paper 'Confronting demographic change: a new solidarity between the generations' (EC 2005: 94). For the contributions to the consultation see: http://ec.europa.eu/employment_social/social_situation/green_paper_response_en.htm#13.
5 UNICE, the Union of Industrial and Employers' Confederations of Europe, has made similar claims in order to prevent the practice of wider consultations that have been launched by the DG. More recently, in July 2006, at the hearings on the *Green Paper on European Transparency Initiative*, unionists and representatives of employers' organisations jointly criticised the European Commission's strategy on the registration of interest groups. UNICE's representatives were highly concerned about the relationship of NGOs with the European Commission and the role of NGOs in the social field. The involvement of new actors in the European consultations threatened to disrupt the accustomed bargaining routines, therefore they stressed the importance of balancing the various positions in the consultation process. See European Economic and Social Committee, Events, European Transparency Initiative, 11 July 2006. http://eesc.europa.eu/sco/events/11_07_06_transparency/index_en.asp.
6 As Michel Offerlé (1998, 2004) noticed, collective action can resort to numbers (for examples, demonstrations), it can call on expertise (whether legal, economic or scientific) or it can rely on the resources of communication strategies.
7 Opinion of the European Economic and Social Committee on the representativeness of European civil-society organisations in civil dialogue, EESC 240/2006, SC/023, 14 February 2006.

References

Armstrong, K. (2002) 'Rediscovering civil society: the European Union and the White Paper on Governance', *European Law Journal*, 8 (1): 102–132.

Berny, N. (2005) 'Les groupes environnementaux français et l'Union européenne. Enjeux et dynamiques de l'activisme européens des groupes citoyens', unpublished thesis, IEP de Bordeaux/Université de Laval, Bordeaux.

Cavaillé, A. (2005) 'Salariées pour la cause. Carrières associatives au Secrétariat générale du Lobby européen des femmes', in H. Michel (ed.) *Lobbyistes et lobbying de l'Union européenne*, Strasbourg: Presses Universitaires de Strasbourg, 25–46.

Cohen, J. and Arato, A. (1992) *Civil Society and Political Theory*, Cambridge: MIT Press.

Drake, H. (2000) *Jacques Delors: Perspectives on a European Leader*, London: Routledge.

European Commission (EC) (2001) 'European Governance. A White Paper', Brussels: COM, 428, final 25 July 2001.

—— (2002) 'Toward a reinforced culture of consultation and dialogue – general principles and minimum standards for consultation of interested parties by the Commission', Brussels: COM, 704, final 11 December 2002.

—— (2005) 'Faced with demographic change, a new solidarity between the generations', Brussels: COM, 94.

European Union (2004) 'Treaty establishing a Constitution for Europe', *Official Journal of the European Union*, on 16 December 2004 (C series, 310), article 47–1.

Guiraudon, V. (2002) 'The constitution of a European immigration policy domain: a political sociology approach', *Journal of European Public Policy*, 10 (2): 263–282.

Harabanski, M. (2005) 'Lobbyistes agricoles et lobbyistes en agriculture. Recrutement et carrière des représentants d'intérêts au COPA', in H. Michel (ed.) *Lobbyistes et lobbying de l'Union européenne*, Strasbourg: Presses Universitaires de Strasbourg, 47–68.

Jobert, B. and Muller, P. (1987) *L'Etat en action. Politiques publiques et corporatismes*, Paris: Presses Universitaires de France.

Joerges, Ch., Mény, Y. and Weiler, J. (2001) 'Mountain of molehill? A critical appraisal of the Commission White Paper on Governance', Jean Monnet Working Paper 6/01, Symposium The Commission White Paper on governance, New York: New York University School of Law.

Kauppi, N. (2006) *Democracy, Social Resources and Political Power in the European Union*, Manchester: Manchester University Press.

Keane, J. (ed.) (2006) *Civil Society: Berlin Perspectives*, New York and Oxford: Berghahn Books.

Kohler-Koch, B., Humrich, C. and Finke, B. (2006) 'Enhancing multi-level democracy by organizing civil society input', paper presented at the 20th IPSA World Congress, Fukuoka, 9–13 July 2006.

Michel, H. (ed.) (2005) *Lobbyistes et lobbying de l'Union européenne, Trajectoires, formations et pratiques des représentants d'intérêt*, Strasbourg: Presses Universitaires de Strasbourg.

Offerlé, M. (1998) *Sociologie des groupes d'intérêt*, Paris: Montchrestien.

—— (2004) 'About some backwaters of the research on social movements. French contentious politics in perspectives', in A.-M. Castrèn (ed.) *Between Sociology and History: Essays on Microhistory, Collective Action and Nation-Building*, Helsinki: SKS/Finnish Literature Society.

Sanchez-Salgado, R. (2006) 'L'européanisation de la société civile', unpublished thesis, l'IEP de Paris, Paris.

Sloat, A. (2004) 'Governance in the making. The future of the EU's (thought) experiment', in A. Wonka and A. Warntjen (eds) *Governance in Europe. The role of Interest Groups*, Baden Baden: Nomos, 66–76.

Smisman, S. (2003) 'European civil society: shaped by discourses and institutional interests', *European Law Journal*, 9 (4): 482–504.

—— (2005) 'European civil society: institutional discourses and the complexity of a multi-level polity', in S. Rossteutscher (ed.) *Democracy and the Role of Associations: Political, Organizational and Social Contexts*, New York: Routledge, 64–86.

Wagner, A.-C. (2005) 'Les représentants de la CES entre militantisme et expertise des affaires européennes', in H. Michel (ed.) *Lobbyistes et lobbying de l'Union européenne*, Strasbourg: Presses Universitaires de Strasbourg, 69–88.

Wallace, H. and Young, A. (eds) (1997) *Participation and Policy-making in the European Union*, Oxford: Clarendon Press.

8 State, civil society and public policy in Chile today

Raúl Urzúa

My task here is to examine in a recapitulary way the evolution of the inter-relations between state, civil society and politics in contemporary Chile from the viewpoint of the four civil society frameworks suggested by Bruno Jobert in Chapter 1 of this book. Taking into account the heterogeneous character of the concept, a definition of 'civil society' is called for. One that fits well the subject of this paper is by the Centre for Civil Society of the London School of Economics (2004):

> Civil society refers to the arena of uncoerced collective action around shared interests, purposes and values. In theory, its institutional forms are distinct from those of the State, family and market, though in practice, the boundaries between State, civil society, family and market are often complex, blurred and negotiated – Civil society commonly embraces a diversity of spaces, actors and institutional forms, varying in their degree of formality, autonomy and power. Civil societies are often populated by organizations such as registered charities, development non-governmental organizations, community groups, women's organizations, faith-based organizations, professional associations, trade unions, self-help groups, social movements, business associations, coalitions and advocacy groups.

This rather broad definition allows for linking the changes through time of the relative importance of various civil-society organizations, with reference to political, economic, social and cultural changes. After a brief reference to civil society in Chile before and during the military dictatorship of Pinochet, and against the background of the structural and cultural factors affecting the inter-relations under the present democratic regime, I will analyse two current cases of anti-poverty policies from the perspective of the four contending frameworks under discussion here. In conclusion, I suggest the emergence of frameworks somewhat different from the ones used up to now.

Civil society in Chile before the military dictatorship

The first civil-society organizations in Chile date back to the end of the nine-teenth century, when the country was still under a strongly oligarchic social and political system. Economic, social and cultural inequalities gave impulse to mostly spontaneous social movements, headed by artisans or workers and aiming at organizing collective action in the pursuit of commonly shared socio-economic, political, cultural or religious goals. Soon, these spontaneous movements became social organizations, most of which evolved into trade unions, that some time later joined forces in the National Confederation of Workers. The emergence of political parties representing lower and middle-class interests also originated from civil-society organizations. The socialist party was the first one, after a few years the communist party and other centre-left parties followed.

Since 1938 and until the 1973–1989 military dictatorship, all but one of the elected governments were centre-left. It was under those governments, and with the support of the governing political parties, that the middle-classes started social movements in defence of their rights. Employees from both public and private sectors organized associations, and successfully exerted corporate pressure towards the government approval of social benefits. During the last two governments before the military coup, the government took the initiative of establishing civil-society organizations in urban areas, such as neighbours' associations, meeting centres for lower-class women, youth and cultural centres etc.

In the 1960s, political debates in Congress led to agrarian reforms and to the official recognition of the rights of peasants and agricultural workers. These radical reforms that had been initiated by the socialist-communist government of President Allende, were opposed by the landowners and rejected by right-wing and centrist political parties, which, in turn, led to the emergence of new social movements, as well as to clashes between trade unions and civil-society organizations linked to different political parties.

Apart from the political parties, organizations created by the entrepreneurial class to defend their interests have always been important actors. Until the socialist government of President Allende, these organizations used their broad access to the government, attempting to influence decisions or to provide technical assistance in the formulation of policies, programmes and projects (Menges 1968; Urzúa 1973).

Civil society under the military government

The military government headed by General Pinochet put an end to most of the existing civil-society organizations. However, blue-collar and white-collar workers, as well as members of banned political parties, university professors and students, organized illegal associations and non-governmental organizations (NGOs) still remained active. The Catholic and evangelical churches launched a large number of organizations supporting and protecting those being persecuted by the government. Other NGOs also played an important role in the creation of grassroots organizations, defending human rights, organizing the opposition to the military government and aiming at re-establishing democracy by providing refuges for political discussions and negotiations. Studies on the subject estimate that in the 17 years of military dictatorship around 500 NGOs were active in the defence of democracy and human rights and contributed to increase social solidarity and community activities (Angell 2007).

Civil society in Chile after the return to democracy

A plebiscite in 1988 revealed a majority of the population to be in favour of a return to democracy. In 1989, the first democratic presidential election after the military dictatorship was won by the Coalition for Democracy, which integrated centre and centre-left parties that had fought against the military dictatorship. At the same time, former partisans of Pinochet created the Alliance for Chile, a political organization uniting two centre-right political parties: the relatively moderate Renovación Nacional (National Renewal) and Unión Democrática Independiente (Independent Democratic Union), which propagated a return to the dictatorship.

The presidential candidates of the Coalition for Democracy won four consecutive elections. Although these governments maintained the open global market economy adopted by the Pinochet regime, their policies marked substantial differences to their predecessors, to wit: the consolidation of the democratic regime; the eradication of extreme poverty; the reinforcement of political, civil and social citizenship; more support for the native people and for the feminist movement; political and economic decentralization; the strengthening of social participation in matters of public interest, and the achievement of growth with equity.

To state the obvious, the achievement of these goals is an ongoing challenge. The open market economy and the globalization process, as well as cultural patterns and lifestyles have affected the relationship between the state, the economy, civil society and politics. An analysis of the civil society–state relationship after the return to representative democracy in Chile needs to take into account both structural socioeconomic factors, as well as more subjective factors related to those changes. Neither trade unions nor NGOs were reinforced after the return to democracy. On the contrary, in part as a consequence of structural changes in the labour market and in labour relations, trade unions played a much weaker role than before the military coup, and many grassroots organizations that had emerged during the dictatorship vanished or just barely survived, due to a lack of interest or to drastic cuts of financial support from NGOs.

Structural, cultural and political factors affecting civil society

Structural, cultural and political factors have contributed to make civil-society organizations more vulnerable. Among the structural factors, the following seem to be the most relevant: first, the economic model has modified the way economic activities are organized and has contributed to a fragmentation within and between the economic sectors, which in turn has affected the workforce. The consequence for civil society is that it has become more difficult than in the past for workers to organize themselves. Second, a high proportion of manual workers are part of the 'informal sector', i.e. they are not covered by legal norms protecting their rights and mostly refrain from joining any organization out of fear of losing their jobs. Third, although family income has increased in all strata, financial inequality is still high. The striking differences in income perpetuate because they lead to inequality of educational opportunities, which in turn negatively affects the solidarity within civil society. Last but not least, even though extreme poverty has drastically declined, the definitions of poverty vary and the causes for different kinds of poverty are more difficult to identify. This is another factor undermining the sense of common plight and solidarity.

Cultural factors have been no less important than structural factors in affecting the participation in civil-society organizations. The combined effects over more than 30 years of a development strategy based on national and international market competition and wide access of middle and lower-classes to conspicuous market consumption, plus the symbolic integration into a consumption society through the mass media, have given high value to economic success via individual effort, which in turn had derogatory effects on participation rates in collective movements.

From the political point of view, public and private spheres have become more clear-cut in this process, the political class is much more isolated from the citizenry, and the leaders of political parties have little contact with party members. Public-opinion surveys show a high percentage of respondents declaring a lack of interest in politics, along with the loss of prestige of political parties (Urzúa and Agüero 1998). For many observers, these are indicators of a distrust of representative democracy and of a disenchantment with politics, that may negatively affect its governance (Tomassini 1998).

However, a closer analysis reveals that this interpretation is too bleak. If compared to electoral turnout rates in Western European countries, the average electoral participation in Chile is higher than in all but six of those countries (IDEA 1997). As was to be expected, in 1989 the voter turnout of the first democratic presidential election (plus 38 members of the Senate and 120 members of the Chamber of Deputies) after the coup d'état, was very high: 92.3 per cent of registered voters, which equals 86.8 per cent of the voting-age population. This high electoral participation in the first election after the peaceful end of 17 years of dictatorship, has declined in the following elections. Noteworthy is the lack of interest shown by the younger generation to participate in political activities. Recent studies (República de Chile, Servicio Electoral 2006) found 70.2 per cent of those between 20 and 24 years of age are not registered, and that the number of registered voters between 18 and 24 years of age has declined drastically from the first presidential election after Pinochet to the most recent election in December 2005. The overall voter turnout has not been lower than before the dictatorship, however (Navia 2004).

Moreover, low participation in political elections does not mean that the younger generation shows less interest in democracy than other age groups. On the contrary, as has been found in studies on the subject, the young generation shares a positive view of democracy, both as a way of living and as a channel for societal changes (Manzi and Catalán 1998). What they declare to resent is the inability of the Chilean democratic governments to implement more drastic changes towards a more equal society.

In sum, in Chile people's interest to join or promote movements and/or different civil-society organizations, as well as the way of establishing inter-relations between civil society and politics, are directly or indirectly affected by the modes of politics and the structural and cultural changes the country has experienced. It is important to keep this background in mind when we apply the models of civil society–politics relationships suggested by Bruno Jobert in Chapter 1 – to the Chilean case. In order to make the link clearer, I shall first examine the formulation of two policies against poverty during the present coalition government.

State, civil society and anti-poverty policies

The democratic governments' social policies have sought two main objectives. The first applies to sector policies, and aims at ensuring a certain level of services and benefits (education, health, housing and social security) for the entire population. The second is 'the development of specific programmes directed to poor and vulnerable sectors to give them access to use the opportunities offered by the central ring of social policy, by the growing economy, and by the development process in general' (Raczynski 2003). Elected governments from 1990 onwards have managed to maintain both, the universal character of social policies and the targeted policies and programmes aimed at eliminating poverty and establishing equal opportunities for all. The two cases to be examined here belong to this second type of policy, one of them is on the eradication of extreme poverty and the other on a housing policy for the poor.

The case of Chile Solidario (Chilean Solidarity)

Regular surveys carried out under Chile's system of national surveys on Socio-Economic Characterization (CASEN)[1] show that during the 1990s there was a continuous decline of poverty rates, and particularly of extreme poverty and indigence.[2] The numbers of poor people dropped from 25.7 per cent of the population in 1990 to 17.5 per cent in 1996 and 14.9 per cent in 2000, while the numbers of indigents went down from 12.9 per cent in 1990 to 5.7 per cent in 1996. However, the 1998–2000 surveys show the numbers of indigents stabilized at around 5.7 per cent.

When the figures on poverty and indigence between 1990 and 2000 became known, policy-makers declared it a matter of urgency not only to correct mistakes but also to review the existing assumptions and conceptual frameworks. The government's first reaction in May 1999 was to request an investigation of the Planning Ministry (which carries out the CASEN surveys on the situation of Chilean families) by the Ministerial Committee on Social Affairs. The most disturbing element of the CASEN report of 1998 was that the households classified as extremely poor not only had lower independent incomes, but also received lower levels of state cash subsidies than non-indigent households. In other words, the subsidies were misdirected and, therefore, a reform of the public policies against extreme poverty became a matter of urgency.

In 2000, the social division of the Planning Ministry, under the new government of President Ricardo Lagos, accepted the responsibility of designing an integrated strategy favouring families in extreme poverty. They created a task-force involving experts from the various state organs. The aim was to design an inter-sector strategy for action that would meet three requirements: to offer services before the demand for them arises, to work in networks, and to concentrate on the family as the focal unit.

Contrary to the usual centralization of policy formulation in expert groups working for the central government, in this case inputs from NGOs and local governments were taken into account. This was a significant change in the process of strategy definition. Ultimately, it was the government and its technical staff taking the initiative to create a system of social protection for families in extreme poverty, in reaction to negative indicators (i.e. lack of progress in further reduction of poverty) rather than to public demand. The outcome, however, was the result of the interaction between very different actors who nevertheless shared a common background in having held senior technical executive posts in public agencies or being members of consulting firms, universities or NGOs. Many of them were experienced in researching or directing social policies, and drew on their learning experiences in other policy fields and their theoretical–ideological preferences, in order to help design Chilean Solidarity. As the overall goal of the strategy they defined the creation of opportunities and provision of resources to allow families in extreme poverty to recover or gain access to resolve issues in their personal, family, community and institutional environment.

The strategy was first applied in a pilot project known as the Bridge Programme, designed by the Solidarity and Social Investment Fund (FOSIS), a state organ to finance plans, programmes, projects and special activities for social development and the reduction of poverty. Initially, the Office of the Budget of the powerful Finance Ministry was critical towards the project and blocked the nationwide implementation of the programme, but it finally agreed to finance a one-year pilot programme in four of Chile's 13 regions, to be extended once the results had been evaluated.

Parallel to the Bridge Programme, the national Office of the Budget designed and implemented another system of social protection for the poorest citizens. It aimed at a better coordination of sectoral and local aids, applying homogeneous criteria in order targeting and selecting beneficiaries. At the request of the Office of the Budget, the Presidential Office organized a seminar, in which university and non-university research institutions participated, along with advisers linked to the government and the opposition, ministers and government agencies involved in the issue, as well as the president and his advisers, in order to discuss the proposed system. There was general consensus on the viability of a plan to eliminate extreme poverty, but substantial disagreement on the strategy to achieve it.

While the government agencies worked on the drafts, Asesorías para el Desarrollo (Advice for Development), an NGO that is well known for its work on social policies, held a workshop to debate social protection and poverty. It was attended by experts from the Planning Ministry, the Office of the Budget, academics and by other NGOs. The workshop played an important role in bringing the opposing views closer together. Thus, a team formed by members of the Planning Ministry, the Solidarity and Social Investment Fund, the Office of the Budget and presidential advisers were finally able to write up the Chile Solidario System. It was presented by the president in his State of the Nation address to Congress on 21 May 2002.

Today, five years after its implementation, the programme is mostly in the hands of NGOs and it has proved to be quite successful. The combination of immediate aid and skills development components has meant that Chilean Solidarity was able to create conditions that allow more and more participating families to overcome their situation of extreme poverty. By the end of 2006, almost 300,000 families (around one million individuals) had been included in the system, and extreme poverty had declined from 5.7 per cent in the year 2000 to 3.2 per cent by the end of 2006 (Ministerio de Planificacion 2007; Encuesta Casen 2007).

Chilean Solidarity and contending frameworks

Chilean Solidarity can be considered a case of transit from a state-centralized anti-poverty policy to a new, more decentralized policy in which civil society played an important role. The failure of the former anti-poverty policies forced the government not only to find new answers to extreme poverty, but also to design an integrated approach in which different ministries, the central government and local governments, NGOs and the poor families themselves were involved in the different steps towards the elimination of extreme poverty. The question that needs to be raised now is whether Chilean Solidarity and the process of formulating the policy corresponds to one or another of the contending frameworks identified by Bruno Jobert (Chapter 1, this volume).

The analysis of Chilean Solidarity reveals that neither the Neo-Conservative model, nor the Organized Civil Society model, nor the Tutelary Modernization model are close to the aims and results of Chilean Solidarity. The Neo-Conservative model fits Chile under the dictatorship of Pinochet, who tried to minimize the role of civil society and to monopolize the formulation and implementation of policies, to restore traditional family and religion, and to establish a techno-bureaucratic elite that was loyal to the military regime. Poverty was expected to be eradicated via economic growth derived from a withdrawal of the state, not by state social policies. Likewise, all elements of the Organized Civil Society Model are very far from Chilean Solidarity, as well. The Tutelary Modernization model fits partly the state–civil society relations in Chile before the military coup, in regard to the establishment of a welfare state.

Although Chilean Solidarity does not fit entirely with the Third Way model, either, it does coincide with it in many respects. First, there is a common interest in moving from political citizenship to social citizenship: the overall aim of the strategy adopted by the taskforce was to provide resources and to create opportunities for families in extreme poverty. Second, Chilean Solidarity has contributed to reinforce civil society in two ways: by inviting civil-society organizations to participate in the elimination of indigence, and by supporting members of indigent families to organize themselves in order to solve problems. Third, Chilean Solidarity has played a role in establishing a beneficial partnership between the state and members of civil society. Last but not least, Chilean Solidarity has contributed to redefine the role of NGOs, from the defence of the poor under the military regime to the education of social citizens.

The case of civil society and housing for the urban poor

The housing policy during the 1990s focused on the massive production of houses, which for some time helped reducing the housing problem in most large cities. However, deficient programme targeting, socio-spatial segregation, inability to solve the various problems of the very poor, and failure of the credit system for housing, contributed to intensify the negative reactions of the people concerned. As a result, in 2000 the Ministry of Housing formulated a new housing policy, aiming at four main objectives: the drastic reduction of the housing deficit, support for the extreme poor, the establishment of a socio-spatial equilibrium, and the improvement of the quality of the houses and the surrounding environment.

To that purpose, a Solidarity Housing Fund was established, that was targeted at families below the poverty line. Intending to reinforce social networks among those families, participation in the programme was tied to the condition that they are organized in a communal group assisted by 'organizing entities', such as municipalities, foundations, corporations or NGOs. The Minister of Housing and Urbanism expected the solidarity housing fund to become 'a programme based on the joint participation of the civil society, the State, local governments, and the private sector, thus creating an environment of innovation and imagination previously not existing in the housing environment' (Surawski and Cubillos 2005).

The analysis of the origins and implementation of the housing programme leads to more balanced conclusions, recognizing its innovative character, as well as the positive role of the private sector in financing and building the houses. The formulation and implementation of the programme required to take into account social and cultural factors, usually ignored by builders of houses for the poor. However, contrary to the inter-sector approach of Chilean Solidarity, the Solidarity Housing Programme was formulated only by experts from the Ministry of Housing and private constructing firms. Civil-society members, such as organizations of the public-housing system, associations of tenants, NGOs, foundations and other entities, were excluded from the formulation of the programme. Furthermore, at local levels, neither the Association of Municipalities nor the major municipalities involved or other regional authorities, participated in discussions on the subject. In spite of the formal recognition of the need for decentralization and an inter-sectors approach, the definition and formulation of the new housing policy and the Solidarity Housing Programme were centralized exclusively in the Ministry of Housing.

Without entering into too much detail, it is instructive for our purposes to take a closer look at the eligibility for the programme: in order to apply for the benefits of the programme, no less than ten families have to be legally established. On top of family savings, the government provides subsidies for housing and the equipment of the surrounding environment and of other common initiatives. The participation of different actors in the process of finding a house or deciding on the type of houses to be built and on the surrounding environment, can either be via formal channels or informal relations with potential actors. Once that stage has been reached, the applicants can further participate by establishing a housing committee or by taking part in projects fostering the integration with neighbours.

Overall, the programme has been successful (Surawski and Cubillos 2005). In the first place, the fact that in 2005 there were 82 per cent more housing projects than in 2000, and that the number of families taking part in the programme today is 192 per cent higher than at that date, indicates an immediate acceptance of it. Second, the programme has made evident the interest of the poor families not only in a decent house, but also in participating in community activities. The promotion and easy acceptance of cooperation between families, the establishment of, and the participation in, associations, plus their interest in keeping good relations with local authorities, are all signs of new ways of becoming active members of civil society.

The Solidarity Housing Fund and contending frameworks

The Solidarity Housing Fund policy is another example of state–civil society inter-relations that are contributing to new ways of modelling civil society. The driving force behind this policy was the Ministry of Housing and Urbanism, which had recognized the inadequacy of some existing programmes to solve the housing problems of the urban poor. Ricardo Lagos, Chile's president from 2000 to 2006, supported the initiative. His approach to social policies was based on four Third Way referentials: striving for a new state–market–civil society relationship, the establishment of a social citizenship, an increase of citizens' participation, and the equality of opportunities. The Solidarity Housing Fund incorporates these ideas to a large extent. Although the formulation of the programme was in the hands of the Ministry of Housing, it was implemented primarily by regional governments cooperating with municipalities, NGOs, private construction firms, members of housing committees, local authorities and, most

importantly, the persons concerned. Connecting the poor with social entrepreneurs (most of them NGOs) and economic entrepreneurs thus contributed to
the goal of activating and consolidating civil society.

The Solidarity Housing Fund, therefore, fits with many elements of the Third
Way model suggested by Bruno Jobert: a main objective of the programme is
the constitution of civil society beyond the established social partners. In fact,
this is even the precondition for getting access to the programme. It is also a
good example of the use of civil society in the delivery of services and in the
activation of society, where social entrepreneurs may find new forms of social
involvement. The final responsibility for the management of the programme is in
the hands of the Ministry of Housing and Urbanism, but since then the implementation of the programme has been decentralized to regional and municipal
entities, NGOs and members of the private sector. Furthermore, all participants
are expected to assume their responsibilities and to defend their rights.

State–civil society relations under revision

Innovative as they are for political and institutional reasons, up to now the cases
summarized above are more an exception than the rule. One of the political
reasons is that, since the 1940s up to the military coup, the inter-relations
between state, civil society and politics were, mutatis mutandi, closer to what
Bruno Jobert calls the Tutelary Modernization model.

Although today two radically different models defined by Jobert, the Neo-
Conservative and the Third Way model, have become alternatives, the Tutelary
model still allows for many members of public and private bureaucracies to
maintain important roles in politics and the policy decision-making process. An
indicator for this is the – at least initially – reluctant attitude of government
experts towards the social policies discussed above: professionals working for
the Bureau of the Budget at first disapproved of the Chilean Solidarity programme, and in the formulation of the Solidarity Housing Fund experts from
outside the Ministry of Housing were excluded. But also for blue-collar workers
the Tutelary Modernization model is still considered a stronger guarantee of
stable wages and of higher respect for their trade unions than other models.
Businessmen may count on the support of the state as the guarantor or partner in
a joint effort to develop Chilean industry and commerce. On the other hand, for
supporters of the Neo-Conservative Market model (represented by members of
the present opposition parties and their followers) the Third Way model merely
represents a disguised way of attempting a return to a socialist government.

In fact, from the political–institutional point of view, in spite of deep structural socio-political changes, Chile still has a political system in which the
government controls most of the political power. This is partly due to the fact
that high-level posts within the government coalitions, in particular in the Ministry of Finance and its Bureau of the Budget, have been filled with very competent techno-bureaucrats. Important for our discussion is that, despite the formal
acceptance of civil-society participation, those government institutions for the

most part resist it in the formulation and implementation of policies and pro-grammes. Conscious of that, in June 2004 President Lagos submitted a project proposal on associations' and citizens' participation in public management to the congress, which was met with very little interest. Only in early 2007, the Chamber of Deputies gave a general approval (the first step in the parliamentar-ian procedure of approving a law proposal submitted by the presidency).

This demonstrative lack of interest in citizens' participation in public man-agement shown by the members of the Low Chamber of Congress has been a drawback not only for the efforts of former President Lagos, but also for the long-standing association of political parties and civil-society organizations. However, despite this drawback, civil-society organizations today are continuing to contribute to existing programmes and to the formulation and implementation of new policies, as well remaining involved in social movements. On the con-trary, the attempts to avoid or retard more active civil-society participation in public management has fostered other kinds of civil-society involvement in poli-tics and policies. Most, if not all of them, have been established after Michele Bachelet took power as Chile's first female president in March 2006. She emphasized citizenship and social participation as two of the most important priorities of her government.

In May 2006, a series of student protests took place in some of the most pres-tigious secondary schools of the Chile's capital Santiago. The pupils requested a drastic reform of the Chilean school system. By 30 May 2006, around 800,000 pupils from all over the country were on strike. They were joined by university students, teachers, parents, public employees and leftist groups opposed to the governing coalition. Under pressure to avoid another strike, President Bachelet launched an advisory council for the quality of education. Among the 81 participants were youth leaders, school teachers, professors and presidents of universities, experts working for NGOs, religious leaders, mayors and members of congress. In December 2006, the council submitted its final report to the president. A smaller group working with the Ministry of Education has been since in charge of implementing the new system.

This movement, that had been started by pupils and was joined later on by members of many parts of civil society, differs from other more conventional movements in many respects. The youths who initiated the movement when the majority of them were non-partisans and not even eligible to vote, experienced that their movement as a way of reinforcing democracy. They regarded it as a fight for a more equalitarian and participatory democratic regime, and as a con-sequence, their representatives have requested the participation of new social actors in politics and policy formulation. They are strongly in favour of invest-ing in social capital and consider education and communication policies for all to be essential for a truly democratic regime.

The success of this civil-society effort in influencing government policies on better education for all stimulated other social groups to do the same. Their demands were centred on work and inequality. What had started as the usual bargaining between management and labour force, suddenly became a broad reaction not only of workers but also of other civil-society organizations against abysmal differences in income differentials. The Catholic Church came forward first with a formal public statement in favour of ethical wages and salaries. This was adopted very quickly by a large number of civil-society organizations all over the country, and the demands for more social equity led the president to convene an advisory council for social equity, responsible for elaborating proposals on better access to work, more wage equality, competitiveness and social equity. The council comprised 48 members chosen by the government, among them economists, businessmen, university professors, members of NGOs, members of congress and government experts. The council is expected to deliver its final report in March 2008.

As with the case of the advisory council for the quality of education, here political parties do not play an important role, either. Once more, priority is given to experts and members of civil-society organizations, as well as to social and civil dialogues. I would like to argue that the two cases under scrutiny here emphasize the need for a new type of democracy in Chile, in which civil society plays a more important role, where social and civil dialogues between politics and civil society are necessary and where active policies to consolidate civil-society organizations is needed. In other words, the government of President Bachelet, consciously or not, has opened the door to the fourth model defined by Bruno Jobert: the Organized Civil Society model. If this model becomes accepted, we have to acknowledge the coexistence of three models in Chile today: the Tutelary Modernization model, the Third Way model and the Organized Civil Society model.

Notes

1 The CASEN survey has been carried out periodically since 1985 by the Planning Ministry. Its sample framework is based on the most recent population and housing census, and represents the population in national private housing.
2 The poverty line is set by the minimum per capita income needed to buy a basic individual basket to cover food and non-food requirements. Indigence is found when per capita income does not cover a basket of food needs.

Bibliography

Angell, A. (2007) *Democracy After Pinochet: Politics, Parties and Elections in Chile*, London: Institute for the Study of the Americas.

Centre for Civil Society (2004) 'What is Civil Society?', London: London School of Economics (accessed on 30 October 2006).

Encuesta Casen 2006 (2007) Ministerio de Planificación y Cooperación.

IDEA (International Institute for Democracy and Electoral Assistance) (1997) *Voter Turnout 1945–1997. A Global Report on Political Participation*, Stockholm: Strömsborg, 18–19.

Manzi, J. and Catalán, C. (1998) 'Los Cambios en la Opinión Pública', in C. Toloza and E. Lahera (eds) *Chile en los Noventas*, Santiago de Chile: Dolmen, 524–533.

Menges, C. (1968) *The Role of Political Parties and Organized Interest Groups*, Ph.D. Dissertation, Columbia University.

Ministerio de Planificacion (2007) Encuestas Casen (caracterizacion national socioeconomica), www.mideplan.cl/casen/.

Ministerio de Vivienda y Urbanismo (2005) 'Bases generales 2001 del Programa Fondo Solidario de Vivienda', in A. Surawski and J. Cubillos, *Orígenes e Implementación del programa Fondo Solidario de Vivienda* [*Origins and Implementation of the Solidarity Housing Fund*], www.ciudadania.uchile.cl/informesprograma.html (accessed September 2007).

Navia, P. (2004) 'Participación Electoral en Chile: 1988–2001', *Revista de Ciencia Política*, 24 (1): 81–103.

Raczynski, D. (2003) 'Políticas Sociales y de superación de la pobreza de Chile', Centro de Política Social para América Latina. Online. Available HTTP: www.utexas.edu/cola/insts/llilas/content/claspo/PDF/overviews/chilsocpol90s.pdf (accessed September 2007).

República de Chile. Servicio Electoral (2006) 'Inscripciones por grupos etarios y sexo 1988–2006' ['Registered voters by sex and age'].

Saborido, Marisol, Fernández, Viviana, Villena, Mauricio (2006) Informe Final de Evaluación Programa Fondo Solidario de Vivienda, Ministerio de Vivienda.

Surawski, A. and Cubillos, J. (2005) 'Origen e Implementación del programa fondo solidario de vivienda' ['Origins and implementation of the Solidary Housing Fund'], www.ciudadania.uchile.cl/informesprograma.html (accessed September 2007).

Tomassini, L. (1998) 'Gobernabilidad y Políticas Públicas', in R. Urzúa and F. Agüero (eds) *Fracturas en la Gobernabilidad Democrática*, Santiago de Chile: Centro de Análisis de Políticas Públicas.

Urzúa, R. (1973) 'Notas Acerca de la Estructura de Poder en Chile', in R. Atria, A. Bardon, S. Molina, E. Ortega and R. Urzua (eds) *Hacia un Nuevo Diagnóstico de Chile*, Santiago de Chile: Editorial del Pacífico.

Urzúa, R. and Agüero, F. (eds) (1998) *Fracturas en la Gobernabilidad Democrática*, Santiago de Chile: Centro de Análisis de Políticas Públicas.

9   Activating civil society

Differentiated citizen involvement in France and the United Kingdom

Jacques de Maillard

In Western Europe, new urban policies have emerged that are characterised by contracting out, public deliberation, partnerships and participation of citizens. Participation, in particular, has become an almost consensual keyword in the context of the modernisation of political life and public administration (Papadopoulos and Warin 2007). From a broader perspective the question arises if these new urban policies are marked by a change of state–civil society relations. Do they imply a new techno-political device transforming the link between civil society and the state? This chapter presents an empirical analysis in order to explore these issues by taking the examples of citizen's involvement in policing and crime prevention in France and the United Kingdom.[1]

The fields of urban security and crime prevention provide a good illustration of the potential changes at work. In the last two decades an increasing number of actors have been engaged, local inhabitants, grassroots associations and voluntary organisations have become more and more involved in various types of joined-up government. Such changes challenge the traditional model of dealing with delinquency, close to what Bruno Jobert refers to as 'the tutelary modernisation model' (Jobert, Chapter 1, this volume). At the end of the 1970s, France and the UK could be depicted as 'penal welfare states', 'combining the liberal legalism of due process and proportionate punishment with a correctionalist commitment to rehabilitation, welfare and criminological expertise' (Garland 2001: 27). This penal welfare state was the result of a historical process dating back to the eighteenth century, which was characterised by the progressive state monopolisation of the responses to crime and by the increasing number of professionals acting in the field of policing, prosecution, judging and correction. These professionals developed and retained a specialised knowledge, in the name of which they established standards, created programmes or took individual decisions. Although civil society's mechanisms of social control still remained the backbone of the social regulation of these societies, the population progressively turned its requests to government institutions, rather than taking on the responsibility of crime control itself. As a consequence, this task shifted from civil society to state law enforcement and social-services agencies.

Both in France and the UK, the development of local security policies[2] was affected by various phenomena. The new policies were facilitated by new modes of governance with participatory features, such as the funding of grassroots initiatives or the implementation of consultation processes. In regard to one decisive aspect France and the UK seem quite different, however. While in France there has been no strong political discourse concerning the involvement of civil society in policing and crime prevention issues, the political debate in the UK has been marked by the omnipresence of a rhetoric on the involvement of communities, which just recently has been reactivated by New Labour. The ideological renewal orchestrated by Tony Blair and theorised by Anthony Giddens (Giddens and Blair 2002) explicitly supports the ideas of community participation and the reinforcement of social links. From this point of view, the policy field of public security provides an interesting test of the political and social effects of this new political rhetoric.

By examining the development of this rhetoric and the socio-political mobilisation it induces, we aim at analysing the political meaning of the discourses that may denote the return of civil society. Our hypothesis is twofold: first, we hold that the thrust towards civil-society involvement in the governance of security constitutes only a limited change compared to the previous model dominated by professionals and public institutions. If new settings, norms, instruments and actors are initiated and institutionalised in order to encourage the mobilisation of civil society, such a change will be constrained by professional, organisational and political dynamics. Second, drawing on the comparative dimension, we assume that the combination of a weak empowerment discourse in France and a dirigist tradition, in particular in the security sector, will produce a different kind of state–civil society relation than in the UK.

The first part of the chapter will focus on the political and administrative appeal to civil society in the two countries since the 1980s, which has meant a clear break from the traditional model. The second part analyses the involvement of civil-society representatives in policing and crime prevention policies and examines the contradictions entailed. Prior to this discussion, a semantic specification is called for: 'civil society' in our context is used as a general wording designating non-governmental and non-economic actors, i.e. associational groups, voluntary organisations, as well as ordinary people involved in urban policies. However, the categories used by actors do not always refer explicitly to civil society. In France, the prevalent term is 'the co-production of security', whereas in the UK, policy-makers speak of the 'community'.

Redefining state–civil society relations

Through new procedures, contracts and forums, criminal justice agencies have become involved in a multiplicity of programmes, in which they work together with other agencies and civil-society representatives. We will first sketch some explanations for these institutional and political uses of civil society. Then, we will examine more precisely the dominant rhetoric in each country, drawing attention to the contrasting political conceptions.

What accounts for the proliferation of the various innovations, aimed at involving civil-society representatives in new ways of governing? As Bruno Jobert proposes in this volume (Chapter 1), the appeal to civil society must be understood in a context of unresolved problems of legitimacy. Traditional policy instruments have become contested, the monopoly of professionals is criticised and political priorities are questioned.[3] Three elements, however, bear particular effects on the policy field in the countries studied here. The first one is a cultural aspect: in both France and the UK, the increase of cultural pluralisation has raised tensions, especially between the police and ethnic minorities. The second one is a political dimension: in the field of security, both countries have been marked by a decline of trust in political actors (Dogan 2005). In the UK, for example, some tabloid press campaigns have initiated strong mobilisations against alleged sex offenders (Edwards and Hughes 2002: 1–2). In France, in the fields of drug prevention or prostitution, for instance, inhabitants of particular neighbourhoods have been mobilised against the inaction of the state in regard to these local problems of drug markets and sex workers. The third one is an economic aspect: both countries have been affected by fiscal austerity since the 1980s, which led to significant cuts in spending on security and other policy fields. It is difficult to assess the impact of these three elements on the appeal to civil society in concrete terms, but they constitute the broader framework in which the increase of civil-society involvement has taken place.

Our central argument here is that the appeal to civil society has been framed differently by various policy actors in both countries. Therefore, we distinguish three underlying principles, each of them based on a specific conception of the role of the state and of the relation between state and civil-society actor:[4] the rationale of state overload, the rationale of the listening state and the rationale of the enabling state.

The rationale of state overload is based on the widespread belief among policy-makers that due to the financial burden and limited human resources, the state is no longer able to respond to high crime rates and, therefore, the appeal to civil society is seen as a redistribution of responsibilities between the state, the market and the community. In this regard, France and the UK experience similar problems with high crime rates and criminal justice systems that are widely considered by the public as too lenient and insufficiently concerned with public security (Garland 2001: 106–108; Roché 2003). As a consequence, governments encourage ways of tackling and preventing crime that go beyond the state apparatus. Some declarations of the respective ministries of interior are emblematic of this strategy to limit state responsibility: 'Every individual citizen and all those agencies whose policies and practices can influence the extent of crime should make their contribution. Preventing crime is a task for the whole community' (Home Office 1984).

> Security can not be the sole business of police and gendarmerie, the feeling of insecurity does not depend only on their action. It depends on various other factors: social cohesion, civic consciousness, etc. These factors are

affected by local authorities competences or initiatives coming from society itself.

(French Ministry of Interior 1997)

One may note that in the UK this move came earlier than in France. In the British case the limitation of the state responsibility may have been fostered by a general neo-liberal conception of civil society. For instance, John Patten, Minister of State at the Home Office in the 1980s declared: 'Scepticism about what can be achieved by the state acting alone has rightly become established in perceptions of economic policy; a similar realisation is needed in dealing with crime' (*The Guardian*, 9 April 1988). Despite the traditional conservative ideas on the role of the state in providing security, this call for a growing involvement of civil society has clearly a liberal connotation inasmuch as it stipulates a rolling back of the state (Savage 1990).

The second explanation, the rationale of the listening state, draws attention to the policy-makers' search for new modes of connecting state interventions and social demands. In a context of social crises and rising tensions between professionals and citizens, the traditional monopoly of professionals acting in the field was challenged, as they conveyed obvious difficulties to cope with some parts of the population and were no longer perceived as the only actors able to 'read' the expectations of the public. Thus, since the beginning of the 1980s, several influential public reports have called for more consultative strategies. In the UK, following the Brixton riots in 1981, Lord Scarman's often quoted report (1981) criticised the insufficient cooperation between the black community and the police in Brixton. As a consequence of this report, police community consultation groups (PCCGs) were set up in the 1980s in order to give a visible expression to the idea that police forces must not act independently from the rest of society and that 'policing cannot be left to the police' (Home Office 1993).

In France, until recently, the criticism has been less harsh over the years. However, the Bonnemaison report[5] of 1982, which had been elaborated in the aftermath of urban riots in the suburbs of Lyon, explicitly criticised the role of the police and social workers regarding the treatment of juvenile delinquency. The main innovation that derived from the report was that municipalities were given the opportunity to create local crime prevention councils (conseils communaux de prévention de la délinquance, CCPD), in which police forces, magistrates, municipality representatives, social workers and associative leaders worked together.

In the UK, with the diffusion of the Third Way ideology in the late 1990s, the criticism of the monopoly of professionals resumed and gave another strong impulse to the mobilisation of civil forces. The appeal to community may be seen as a way of redirecting the focus of highly professionalised and centralised police forces, in order 'to improve the quality of life and the behaviours of the members of the local community and increase civic sense' (Giddens and Blair 2002: 99). This idea also has been reflected more recently in the National Reassurance Policing Programme, a project aiming at increasing public confidence in the police. In France, again, the criticism has been less direct. However, the reform of the 'police de proximité', introduced by the socialist-led government in 1997, was directed towards a similar aim, i.e. to establish a closer contact between the police and the population (Roché 2005).[6]

From the state's point of view, forums and partnerships were seen as a way of improving communication and linking political institutions, professions and the population. Thus, encouraging the participation of citizens has been used as a way of containing social tensions.

In the third logic, the rationale of the enabling state, government is more dynamic, activating and supporting local communities. The manifesto of the Third Way clearly expresses its recognition of:

> the limits of the government in the social sphere, but also the need for government, within those limits, to forge new partnerships with the voluntary sector. Whether in education, health, social work, crime prevention or the care for children, 'enabling' government strengthens civil society rather than weakening it, and helps families and communities to improve their performance [...] New Labour's task is to strengthen the range and quality of such partnerships.
>
> (Blair 1998: 14)

According to Third Way rhetoric, the role of the 'enabling state' is more reflexive, accepting to regulate the actions of other actors without necessarily intervening directly.[7] It designs a changing pattern of governance in which state–society relations are regulated by contracts and 'the state is an enabling partner that joins and steers flexible networks' (Bevir and Rhodes 2003: 58). In this respect, Britain and France are very similar. In both countries civil-society actors have become important stakeholders, given their expertise on the issues treated.

The coexistence of the three rationales suggests that the appeal to civil society does not refer to a coherent ideology. It is rather the result of different, yet not explicitly contradictory, sets of beliefs.

Table 9.1 Three conceptions of state–civil society relations

	The overloaded state	*The listening state*	*The enabling state*
Objective	Rolling back the state	Linking governmental action and social demands	Activating civil society
State–society relations	Delegating state functions to private actors	Organising consultation in order to make institutions more responsive to society	Initiating public–private partnerships and creating networks
Procedures	Market, contracts	Forums, public meetings, consultation tools (pools etc.)	Contracts, co-financing

Political rhetoric: community versus proximity

As the call for citizens' involvement has been framed in political language, the concept of 'community' has become central to the discourse of New Labour, whereas it is quite absent from the French rhetoric. It is important to note that the use of 'community' in the British political rhetoric on security does not originate from New Labour, although under the New Labour government this policy discourse has gained importance. Yet, many conservative politicians have drawn on this concept before (Savage 1990). Strongly influenced by the 'communitarian moralism' of American communitarian thinkers, particularly A. Etzioni (Hughes 1996), New Labour has adopted this notion. Both in the Third Way manifesto and Etzioni's recommendations (1993), the need to restore communities and their moral voices is vigorously promoted.[8]

The absence of the notion of 'community' in the French public discourses is due to the French idea of 'community' as a potential threat to the legitimacy of political institutions.[9] The terms that are dominating the public rhetoric are 'proximité' and 'co-production'. Catchwords such as 'police de proximité', 'justice de proximité' and 'sécurité de proximité' are associated with recent administrative reforms, aiming at bringing political institutions closer to the public (Wyvekens 1996) and are used by local governments in order to legitimise their role in the local 'co-production' of security (Le Goff 2005).

The different uses of political rhetoric in France and the UK reveal the underlying political conceptions in each country. In France, public discourses are pervaded by republican symbols, emphasising the collective basis and the unity of French society. Therefore, any reference to 'communautés' is likely to be reduced to their ethnic dimension ('les communautés ethniques') or, just as any religious or cultural group, they are allocated to the private sphere. Concerning the UK, most British social scientists (see especially Crawford 2001; Hughes 1996; Lacey and Zedner 2000) see the political discourse on community as 'nostalgia disguised as modernisation' (Crawford 2001: 73–74). In their view, crime results from a breakdown of a community and of the rules attached to it. They follow that the reassertion of communities, within families, neighbourhoods and schools, helps to regulate deviant behaviour. This nostalgic re-imagining of communities, however, differs sharply from the general tone of the New Labour discourse concerning the 'inevitable modernisation'. One may also note that some New Labour theorists remain sceptical towards communitarianism (Giddens 2000: 62–65).

Given the extensive use of the terms 'community' or 'proximity' in the respective political discourses, it becomes apparent that rather than providing concepts guiding policy they are vague notions, 'feel good words' with unclear meanings. 'Community', for instance, may stand for a locality, or a specific neighbourhood, or it may denote non-geographical communities and identities of ethnic groups. 'Proximity' may be understood as spatial proximity (with public institutions localised in poorer neighbourhoods), or as temporal proximity (with a quicker penal answer), or as human proximity (by seeking to smooth the relations between these institutions and the public). In the same way 'co-production', a term often used in French administrative texts, is also a vague public category, which does not define if this includes ordinary citizens or only professionals and institutions to be involved. The uses of these terms reveal a high degree of ambiguity and uncertainty about the way the new relations between professionals, public institutions and civil-society representatives should be designed. Nonetheless, the vagueness of these notions is politically useful, because it leaves room for varying interpretations and flexible political practices.

Activating civil society: heterogeneity and contradictions

The use of civil society is a process fraught with tensions, ambivalences and contradictions. Here, we will focus on three complementary aspects: the various public forums, the partnerships between voluntary organisations and public institutions, and the experiments in which the state has given responsibility to civil-society segments in order to undertake tasks related to public security (see Table 9.2). Each of these strategies refers more particularly, but not exclusively, to one of the state–civil conceptions described above.[10]

Fragments of civil society in public forums: a limited impact

The creation of public forums is a frequently used and rather traditional way of incorporating citizens, association leaders and inhabitants, in brief what we consider here as representatives of civil society. The intent is to provide a platform for the people concerned to express their needs, debate issues and elaborate solutions. A closer look at the practice, however, shows that the involvement of civil-society representatives is restricted, guided and constrained by public authorities.

Table 9.2 Three institutional uses of civil society

	Delegation	Forums	Partnerships
Principle	Public competences delegated to non-state actors	Meetings organised by public authorities in which civil-society representatives are involved	Voluntary organisations, neighbourhood committees associated with public organisations, defining and implementing specific projects
Tools	Neighbourhood watches, special constables, informal social control exercised by the public	Group meetings, consumer-oriented studies, public meetings, citizens' panels	Formalised partnerships, co-financing contracts
State–society linkage	Overloaded state	Listening state	Enabling state

In the UK, many forms of consultation of the population have been established, such as police consultative committees (PPCs or PPCGs, police community consultation groups, see above), consultations of so-called 'hard to reach groups', or consultations in the framework of the Crime and Disorder Act.[11] It has been widely recognised that PPCGs are dominated by the police, whose expertise is largely unchallenged. The outcome of the consultation process is meagre because PPCG meetings are poorly attended and take the form of alibi exercises (Newburn and Jones 2002: 47–48). The community representatives often feel intimidated by the style and the 'professional' language of these meetings and get the sense that they are not heard because in the end decisions are taken elsewhere, as one community representative expressed his disappointment: 'We want miracles and they want an easy life' (quoted in Crawford 1997: 174). The purpose of these forums is to catalyse public expectations. According to a study of the Home Office, 29 per cent of the members of community and voluntary organisations criticised the 'tokenism' of some public institutions (Hester 2000: 2; see also HMIC 1999). Recently, Hughes (2007: 74) has stressed that 'most community safety partnerships [...] may be characterised as duopolies managed by the police and the local council'.

However, not all consultations prove ineffective or are perceived as failures by the participants. Another study revealed that almost 90 per cent of the partnerships reported involved 'hard-to-reach' groups and that almost half (45 per cent) of these consultations were assessed as 'successful' or even 'very successful' (Newburn and Jones 2002). In some cases, the partnerships have led to fundamental changes in the perception of the problems at stake, which in turn had an impact on the general strategy. This can be observed in particular with regard to young people 'because of the young people's input into the strategy we [the authorities] were able to stop considering young people as the problem. We were able to look at young people's views and consider them as the victims of crime, rather than the public perceptions of them [as offenders]' (quoted in Newburn and Jones 2002: 44). Similarly, recent developments in reassurance policing (which aims at a better accessibility and visibility of the police) have 'highlighted the importance of engaging with local residents, exploiting their knowledge about local crime and disorder problems, and providing them with a stake in their own community policing efforts' (Crawford and Lister 2004: 55).

On the other hand, this process of civil-society involvement can become problematic if it confronts the police with differing social demands: 'In developing links with marginalised and vulnerable communities, the police may face criticism from other groups that they are becoming driven by minority interests' (Jones and Newburn 2001: 48). Thus, an interesting point here is that the process of civil-society involvement contributes to making the conflicts between the various segments of civil society more apparent. The interests of young people are opposed to those of the elderly, religious and non-religious groups are confronted, territorial communities are challenging each other, etc. This way, the process of consultation has two sides, as it facilitates communication while at the same time revealing the internal contradictions of civil society, which is composed of various segments that have different views and stakes in public security (see also Stenson 2005).

Contrary to the British practice, there is no consultation undertaken solely by the police in France. Every meeting takes place in larger forums, in which local authorities, housing companies or other stakeholders are present. Research on the results of these forum meetings suggests different scenarios. The predominant outcome is that the needs that are expressed by the population are immediately rejected by the local authorities because the demands and suggestions are considered too individual, naive and unpractical (Donzelot *et al.* 2003; Donzelot and Wyvekens 2004; Roché 2002). The public is not in a position to successfully communicate the failures of public agencies, which in turn tend to use public meetings to teach citizens how to behave. In many meetings, a difficult situation arises because of contrasting expectations of the police, requiring specific information, and inhabitants who remain secretive. In a second, but less frequent, scenario participatory dynamics develop, in which, for instance, a process of consultation has been organised and a definition of a security policy has been formulated. As a result, however, the demands of the citizens remain at the margins of the institutional sphere because the experiments of local participation are cut off from the actual decision-making process.[12] A third situation is conceivable, which according to the research available is even much less frequent, however, where some initiatives induce a cooperative dynamic. One example is the case of Blanc Mesnil. The municipality of this town to the North of Paris has initiated various forms of civic involvement, such as public meetings, interviews, questionnaires, groups of liaison etc. In order to make these initiatives effective, it has enforced the massive presence of civil-society representatives in the committee that is in charge of checking the implementation of the local safety contract, despite the apparent reluctance of state representatives (Donzelot *et al.* 2003: 293; for other cases see DIV 2004: 32–37).

Thus, in the French case we are dealing with different institutional positions and approaches towards citizens' participation. In some towns, the mayor and the council appear in favour of a stronger participation regarding public security, whilst national government officials and professionals, i.e. prefects and police authorities, are less sensitive to security demands from below (Donzelot *et al.* 2003: 298). As a consequence, initiatives encouraging civil-society participation are rather led by municipalities than by the state government. This became significant when the national police was reformed between 1998 and 2002. The reform project aimed at the decentralisation of responsibilities within the national police and at improved contact with the population, but it did not imply any participatory mechanisms facilitating the exchange between the police and civil society.

In summary, we find in both countries that experiments with citizens' involvement often show disappointing results. Despite political claims about 'active citizenship' and the 'building of safer communities', the concrete processes of participation are characterised by uncertainty and instability. In some cases, especially in France, a lack of know-how concerning the ways of involving inhabitants in security issues is apparent. All in all, these findings underline that the cooperation between professionals and civil-society represen-tatives is often weak to non-existent and that the professionals tend to control the demands of inhabitants from the top-down. In France, there seems to be a slight contrast between local authorities that are more in favour of civic partici-pation and state professionals (i.e. policemen) who are less sensitive to the demands coming from below. In the UK, such a contrast is less evident, because the political system leaves less room for manoeuvre for local authorities, but also due to a more open attitude of the police towards citizens' participation. Moreover, in the UK the involvement of inhabitants, and more generally the issue of policing by consent, is a real concern for the Home Office, as well as for professionals. In contrast, the French system of dirigisme is mirrored in the pro-fessional ethos and institutional practices of French police officers. Thus, the French Ministry of Interior and police professionals do not consider themselves as being directly accountable to the population.

The involvement of voluntary organisations in partnerships: more flexible interventions?

As in other Western countries, in France and in the UK a vast array of voluntary organisations are involved in crime prevention partnerships. Most of the organi-sations are funded by public agencies in order to carry on various social preven-tion programs. However, in many cases these partnerships do not live up to the expectations.

In particular in the field of crime prevention, associations play an important role in the voluntary sector. In many French cities, they are an integral part of crime prevention strategies. In policy fields such as drug treatment and preven-tion, aid to prostitutes or aid to victims, many associations are endowed with public subsidies and act beside or in place of public institutions. In the UK, this development has been strongly supported by New Labour, in line with its con-ception of the 'enabling state'.[13] A good example is 'Crime Concern', a charity created in 1988 and partially funded by the Home Office, which supports a large variety of crime reduction programmes and aims at spreading good practices in the field of community crime prevention.

These examples of joint actions between civil-society representatives and public administrations provide more general insight into state and civil society relations in regard to security issues. First, they reveal a change in the way safety issues are treated. Like in other areas of public services, the distinction between 'purchaser' and 'provider' functions becomes more and more evident (see Osborne and Gaebler 1992; Deakin and Walsh 1996). Between grassroots initiatives and administrative control these partnerships as such remain ambiva-lent: on the one hand, they constitute a symbolic and financial recognition of civil society. On the other hand, they are supported by public administrations and, therefore, have to enter a specific framework that constrains their room for manoeuvre.

Second, these partnerships form an intermediate universe between civil society and political institutions. Members of civil-society organisations are improving their skills in order to negotiate with public organisations when looking for funding provided by various departments. The leaders of associations have to manage budgets and staff, in addition to being fluent in the administrative language,[14] which implies a managerialisation of voluntary civil society agencies. In France, managerial pressure is present rather in rhetoric than in actual practices, whereas in the UK, this managerialist approach is rather strong. According to Power's (1997) evaluation of the performance of service providers, the indicators of performance are key instruments for the distribution of public funding. Some authors (see Rhodes 2000 for the general picture, and Crawford 2001; Hughes 2007 for community safety) have stressed the contradictory dynamic at work: the central government tries to encourage local initiatives by letting local actors decide on local strategies, but at the same time it seeks to influence outputs and define guidelines. It aims at promoting trust within society and between citizens and public organisations, but the generalisation of auditing involves a closer surveillance. As it is summed up by Crawford (2001: 64), 'the reality of trying to separate purchaser/provider functions has been much more complex than managerialist gurus suggest, often fusing and blurring responsibilities and producing forms of government which are simultaneously 'at arm's length but hands on'.[15]

Third, at the local level a strong fragmentation of civil society along territorial, religious, ethnic and generational lines is taking place. This observation applies less to the UK, where two large national organisations, Concern and NACRO, have taken over the role of negotiating with national governments. Although their influence currently seems to be on the wane, it may also be seen as undermining civil society (Hirst 1997: 96–114).

Strategies of delegation

Parallel to the attempt of creating a dialogue between civil-society representatives and police forces, another strategy has been employed, which is close to what Garland has labelled a process of responsibilisation, i.e. 'a new kind of indirect action, in which state agencies activate actions by non-state organisations and actors' (Garland 2001: 124). In this process, the government hands over responsibility to private actors, while at the same time supporting them to develop the necessary competences. In regard to security, this strategy relies on the self-organisation of civil society by reactivating informal social mechanisms of control. In order to encourage various segments of civil society to take charge of their own security, the state promotes self-organised initiatives such as civil patrols, as well as technical tools. On this aspect, the two national cases differ deeply.

In the UK, the Home Office has recently developed different packs and toolkits for the communities to help them with safety issues. For example, an information pack for local groups on anti-social behaviour and a practical guide on crime reduction ('Be safe, be secure') was made available online. This way, the Home Office pursues a strategy initiated about 30 years ago when neighbourhood watches and special constables were installed. The concept of neighbourhood watches originated in the US in the late 1960s and was launched in the UK in 1982. It aims at helping people to protect themselves and their properties and to reduce the fear of crime by means of improved home security, greater vigilance, accurate reporting of suspicious incidents to the police and by fostering a community spirit. Five million households were covered by December 1993, and recent estimations suggest that one-quarter of the UK population are covered (Bennett *et al.* 2006).[16] Special constables are a force of volunteers who are trained by the local police force in order to support police officers. In 2005, there were more than 11,000 members. In addition, some experiments with civilian policing were launched, either supplementary patrols supported by the police or voluntary activities seeking to free the police of certain tasks. For instance, West Yorkshire police have recruited volunteers to undertake specific duties within police stations, such as providing information on the progress of cases to victims and witnesses, in order to enable police officers to spend more time on patrol (Crawford and Lister 2004: 33). The outcome of these experiments is questionable because most volunteers do not commit themselves on a long-term basis. Therefore, the British government has created new functions for residential patrol. Some local councils have set up neighbourhood warden schemes, where local people patrol their community, demonstrating presence on the street. These initiatives do not imply a 'delegation' to civil society in a strict sense, as the agents are employed by public authorities. They are emblematic, however, of the search for intermediaries between traditional police forces and the public.

Particularly striking is the voluntarism behind this process, the UK central government uses to reinforce local dynamics of self-protection. Civil-society participation is part of the state's strategy to pass responsibilities to civil actors. It is encouraged by the government as a way of reinforcing communities. Some authors have noted that these experiences, particularly neighbourhood watches, favour stronger ties within communities and anchor common values (Bennett *et al.* 2006). Others (Garland 1998; Lacey and Zedner 2000: 58; for a more general point on the Third Way, Jobert 2002) have stressed the contradiction at the heart of such a process: if the British government encourages the involvement of communities, it runs the risk that social and economic policies contribute rather to the disaggregation of these communities, by favouring individual responsibilities and inducing social exclusion.

In France, a much more reticent process is at work. The government might make some banks responsible for their own security or one can hear warning messages on the metro to be aware of pickpockets, but programmes like in the UK, or even a public discourse, hardly exist. Some exceptions to this observation are citizens' patrols sponsored by municipalities in periods of crises, for example during the riots in November 2005, or actions of self-protection that are organised by some religious communities, for instance the Jewish communities at times protect their buildings. Rarely, groups of inhabitants organise themselves more permanently (Body-Gendrot 2000; Borzeix *et al.* 2006). Borzeix *et al.* (2006) have stressed the role of a co-owners' committee in Grigny (a Southern suburb of Paris), that maintains some informal social control on teenagers committing incivilities. The committee members have the resources to act as intermediaries between the municipality or the police and the citizens and are thus able to translate some demands to these institutions.

Contrary to the UK, there is neither a national programme, however, to foster the self-organisation of civil society, nor do public authorities initiate mobilisations. One reason for this might be seen in French public opinion, which is strongly reluctant to passing actions related to security on to non-governmental actors.[17] In other words, solutions that rely on the self-organisation of society are not considered the best way to improve safety. The dominant idea among political and professional elites is that local authorities that encourage the self-organisation of citizens too strongly neglect their political duties. At the national level, it is regarded as the task of the Ministry of the Interior to reassure people, to hold a vigorous discourse and to listen to the demands of the population, rather than delegating public responsibilities to private actors.

Conclusion

The redistribution of powers from various political authorities to civil society has induced a form of network governance, interlocking private and public actors. The political and institutional appeal to civil society can be explained by the rationales of the state overload, the listening state and the enabling state, which each account for specific developments. In France and in the UK these rationales have been at work at different times. In the UK, after 15 years of neo-liberal policies, New Labour has put a significant political emphasis on the rebuilding of 'strong communities'. In France, policies toward civil society seem less politically controversial. Various governments have promoted new participatory devices without giving them a strong political impulse.

However, this move towards increased civic involvement might not be stable. Professionals, especially police officers, but also social workers or administrative officials, defend their past monopolies. They remain cautious about civil-society participation and they contribute to limit its amplitude, as is clearly evident in the public meetings of the police and civil-society representatives. The growing involvement also entails the creation of intermediaries between ordinary citizens and the state apparatus, as in the case of partnerships where professionalised leaders act between public organisations, by which they are financed, and the population, from whom they derive their legitimacy.

This presents a mitigated image of the so-called return of civil society. Moreover, the process contains contradictory elements, as public authorities may encourage the involvement of civil-society actors on the one hand, while limiting their role and impact on the other. Governments define the rules according to which civil-society representatives are encouraged to organise themselves. They propagate the leading idea of active and cohesive communities, while at the same time implementing social policies that rely on individual responsibility. Thus, the process of civil-society involvement has proven controversial and fragmented at times. Several segments of civil society advocate differing conceptions of public security and the building of partnerships is characterised by a dispersal of funding.

The specific national patterns that can be found in France and in the UK reveal that the respective initiatives are far more ambitious in the UK, both with regard to contacts between police officers and civil society and the attempted self-organisation of civil society. These processes reflect a delegation of power to civil actors to a degree that is unknown in France. The British system seems less professionally locked. However, various indicators and tools that have been developed for reasons of efficiency, have led to a managerialist orientation and have contributed to limit the freedom of civil-society initiatives. These two aspects, the opening of political institutions and the management of state–civil society relations, make the contrast related to the distribution of power within the state quite apparent: in the UK, both processes are led by the central state, whereas in France, in the fields in which the central state has retained central resources (especially concerning police forces), it no longer enacts a universalistic policy that local authorities have to implement. It is noteworthy that both developments go against the political traditions of each country.

What accounts for the differences? As mentioned above, the differing political cultures can offer an explanation. According to some polls, French people, including politicians, professionals and other opinion-makers, tend to be reluctant to cooperate with the police and to believe in the importance of state action in this field, thus showing only little support for a strong civil-society involvement. However, 30 years ago, France and the UK were rather similar, i.e. characterised by professionalism and statism. Why has the change been stronger in the UK than in France? It seems that in the UK, despite the official statements given by Conservatives and New Labour, the cumulation of policies conducted by successive governments and reinforced by the centralisation process over the last 30 years has had a large effect. The introduction of managerial reforms, the concern with policing by consent, and the process of responsibilisation of civil society have been relatively stable objectives over time. French governments have remained less entrepreneurial on this specific aspect. From this point of view, the ideas and normative discourses that have guided political actors and professionals for the last 30 years have played a decisive role.[18]

Notes

1 Special thanks are due to Gordon Hughes, Bruno Jobert and Beate Kohler-Koch for their comments on an earlier version of this chapter.
2 For a synthesis of other policy fields see Balme *et al.* (1999); Pierre (2000); Stoker (2004).
3 These processes are not specific to the public security sector, similar processes of delegitimation of traditional authorities are at work in the field of technology policies (Callon *et al.* 2001) and urban management (Bacqué *et al.* 2005).

4 The three different rationales explaining the return of civil society follow the framework proposed by Bevir and Rhodes (2003) on the various ways of explaining the changing frames of governance (i.e. 'the changing boundary between state and civil society' (2003: 42)), although we do not retain their primary focus on the political (socialist, liberal, conservative and Whig) traditions.

5 The chair of the Bonnemaison report (1982) was a socialist mayor of a town in the suburbs of Paris.

6 This challenge of professionals is linked to a declining trust in the police in both countries. Between 1996 and 2000, the percentage of respondents who are content with the work of the police declined from 56 per cent to 47 per cent in France and from 72 per cent to 66 per cent in the UK (Van Kesteren *et al.* 2001).

7 As will be shown later, however, the Third Way is also led by a centralising impulse.

8 The Third Way manifesto (Giddens and Blair 2002: 98–100), is clearly influenced by other American social scientists, as well. For example, the well-known book by Kelling and Coles, *Fixing Broken Windows* (1996), is quoted in order to assert the need to 'regenerate communities' and to reinforce partnerships between police and citizens.

9 When the former Ministry of Interior J.-P. Chevènement was told by a high civil servant about the successes of community policing in the US and Canada, he was appalled because to him 'police communautaire' sounded like a vital 'threat to the Republic' (Roché 2005: 46–47).

10 These three strategies are distinguished for analytical purposes only because in reality they overlap. Policing by the public, for instance, involves public meetings to organise the roles of the police and the public and is financed by public funding.

11 According to the Crime and Disorder Act (1998), the consultation of the following voluntary and community groups is compulsory: neighbourhood watch, victim support, groups established in the interests of women, young people, the elderly, the disabled, ethnic minorities, gay and lesbian people, religious purposes, residents, shopkeepers, co-operatives, partnerships and other relevant local agencies.

12 See monographs on Perpignan and Montreuil in Bailleau and Gorgeon (2000).

13 It should be noted that previous conservative governments did encourage the involvement of voluntary organisations in partnerships, too, and also created quasi non-governmental organisations (Quangos) in the field of community safety.

14 See Body-Gendrot (2000), about the professionalisation of community organisations.

15 Lacey and Zedner (2000: 164) have stressed the strategies of audit-avoidance by local actors, in which they try to 'make space' for the less auditable practices (such as social crime prevention).

16 The former conservative Home Secretary M. Howard did even publicly encourage the involvement of teenagers in neighbourhood schemes. Speaking at a neighbourhood watch scheme conference, he declared: 'I know that many young people are already actively involved. But the scope for more is enormous. One of the great challenges over the next few years will be to broaden the appeal to young people' ('Howard tells youth to fight crime', *The Independent*, 12 November 1995). However, his initiative was rejected by most professionals and experts in the field.

17 In a poll (Credoc-IHESI, quoted in Body-Gendrot 2000: 94), only a small part of the population thought that improving public safety depended on societal responsibility: in January 1998, 17.6 per cent thought it should rely on 'learning to be less exposed to risks', 3.8 per cent on 'self defence', 3 per cent on a 'call for private services'.

18 See, from this perspective, the explanation proposed by Bleich (2002) on the contrasting race policies in France and the UK, which underlines the differing policy ideas guiding governments in both countries.

Bibliography

Bacqué, M.-H., Rey, H. and Sintomer, Y. (eds) (2005) *Gestion de proximité et démocratie participative*, Paris: La Découverte.

Bailleau, F. and Gorgeon, C. (eds) (2000) *Prévention et sécurité: vers un nouvel ordre social?*, Paris: Editions de la DIV.

Balme R., Faure, A. and Mabileau, A. (eds) (1999) *Les nouvelles politiques locales*, Paris: Presses de Sciences Po.

Bennett, T., Holloway, K. and Farrington, D. (2006) 'Does neighborhood watch reduce crime? A systematic review and meta-analysis', *Journal of Experimental Criminology*, 2 (4): 437–458.

Bevir, M. and Rhodes, R. (2003) 'Searching for civil society: changing patterns of governance in Britain', *Public Administration*, 81 (1): 41–62.

Blair, T. (1998) *The Third Way. New Politics for the New Century*, London: The Fabian Society.

Bleich, E. (2002) 'Integrating ideas into policy-making analysis: frames and race policies in Britain and France', *Comparative Political Studies*, 35 (9): 1054–1076.

Body-Gendrot, S. (2000) *The Social Control of Cities*, London: Blackwell.

Bonnemaison, G. (ed.) (1982) *Face à la délinquance: Prévention, répression, solidarité*, Paris: La Documentation française.

Borzeix, A., Collard, D. and Raulet-Croset, N. (2006) 'Participation, insécurité, civilité: quand les habitants s'en mêlent', *Les Cahiers de la sécurité intérieure*, 61: 55–83.

Callon, M., Lascoumes, P. and Barthe, Y. (2001) *Agir dans un monde incertain. Essai sur la démocratie technique*, Paris: Seuil.

Crawford, A. (1997) *The Local Governance of Crime*, Oxford: Oxford University Press and Clarendon Press.

—— (2001) 'Joined-up but fragmented: contradiction, ambiguity and ambivalence at the heart of labour's "Third Way"', in R. Matthews and J. Pitts (eds) *Crime Prevention, Disorder and Community Safety: a New Agenda?*, London: Routledge, 54–80.

Crawford, A. and Lister, S. (2004) *The Extend Policing Family*, York: Joseph Rowntree Foundation.

Deakin, N. and Walsh, K. (1996) 'The enabling state: the role of markets and contracts', *Public Administration*, 74: 33–48.

DIV (Délégation interministérielle à la ville) (2004) *Politique de la ville et prevention de la délinquance*, Paris: Editions de la DIV.

Dogan, M. (ed.) (2005) *Political Mistrust and the Discrediting of Politicians*, Boston: Brill Academic Publishers.

Donzelot, J. and Wyvekens, A. (2004) *La magistrature social*, Paris: La Documentation française.

Donzelot, J., Mével, C. and Wyvekens, A. (2003) *Faire société. La politique de la ville aux Etats-Unis et en France*, Paris: Seuil.

Edwards, A. and Hughes, G. (2002) 'Introduction: the community governance of crime control', in G. Hughes and E. Edwards (eds) *Crime Control and the Community*, Cullompton: Willan Publishing, 1–19.

Etzioni, A. (1993) *The Spirit of Community: The Rights, Responsibilities and the Communitarian Agenda*, New York: Crown.

French Ministry of Interior (1997) 'Circulaire relative à la mise en oeuvre des contrats locaux de sécurité 7/1997', www.cls.interieur.gouv.fr/.

Garland, D. (1998) 'Les contradictions de la "société punitive": le cas britanniques', *Actes de la recherche en sciences sociales*, 124: 49–67.

—— (2001) *The Culture of Control: Crime and Social Order in Contemporary Society*, Chicago: University of Chicago Press.

Giddens, A. (2000) *The Third Way and its Critics*, Cambridge: Polity Press.

Giddens, A. and Blair, T. (2002) *La troisième voie. Le renouveau de la social-démocratie*, Paris: Seuil.

Hester, R. (2000) *Crime and Disorder Partnerships: Voluntary and Community Sector Involvement*, Home Office, Briefing note 10/00.

Hirst, P. (1997) *From Statism to Pluralism*, London: Routledge.

HMIC (Her Majesty's Inspectorate of Constabulary), (1999) 'Police integrity: securing and maintaining public confidence', London: Home Office.

Home Office (1984) 'Crime prevention. Home office circular 8/1984', London: Home Office.

—— (1993) 'Police reform: a police service for the twenty-first century', Cm2281, London: HMSO.

—— (1998) 'Crime and disorder Act', Home Office, 7/1998, www.opsi.gov.uk/acts/acts1998/ukpga_19980037_en_1.

Hughes, G. (1996) 'Communitarianism and law and order', *Critical Social Policy*, 49: 17–41.

—— (2007) *The Politics of Crime and Community*, London: Palgrave.

Jobert, B. (2002) 'Giddens et l'Etat-providence: une troisième voie très britannique', *Revue française de sociologie*, 43 (2): 407–422.

Jones, T. and Newburn, T. (2001) 'Widening access: improving police relations with hard to reach groups', Home Office, Police Research Series Paper 138.

Kelling, G.L. and Coles, C.M. (1996) *Fixing Broken Windows*, New York: Simon and Schuster.

Lacey, N. and Zedner, L. (2000) 'Community and governance: a cultural comparison', in S. Karstedt and K.D. Bussmann, *Social Dynamics of Crime Control*, Oxford: Hart Publisher, 157–169.

Le Goff, T. (2005) 'Les maires et la sécurité quotidienne: rhétoriques et pratiques de proximité', in C. Le Bart and R. Lefebvre (eds) *La proximité en politique*, Rennes: Presses Universitaires de Rennes, 197–214.

Newburn, T. and Jones, T. (2002) 'Consultation by crime and disorder partnerships', Home Office, Police Research Series Paper 148.

Osborne, D. and Gaebler, T. (1992) *Reinventing Government: How the Entrepreneurial Spirit is Transforming the Public Sector*, Reading: Addison-Wesley.

Papadopoulos, Y. and Warin, P. (eds) (2007), 'Innovative, participatory and deliberative procedures in policy making: democratic and effective?', *European Journal of Political Research*, 46 (4): 445–605.

Pierre, J. (ed.) (2000) *Debating Governance*, Oxford: Oxford University Press.

Power, M. (1997) *The Audit Society*, Oxford: Oxford University Press.

Rhodes, R. (ed.) (2000) *Transforming British Government*, London: Macmillan.

Roché, S. (2002) *Tolérance zero?*, Paris: Odile Jacob.

—— (2003) 'La répression en panne?', in S. Roché (ed.) *En quête de sécurité*, Paris: Armand Colin, 213–225.

—— (2005) *Police de proximité*, Paris: Seuil.

Savage, S.P. (1990) 'A war on crime? Law and order policies in the 1980s', in S.P. Savage and L. Robins (eds) *Public policy under Thatcher*, London: Palgrave, 89–102.

Scarman, L. (1981) 'The Brixton disorders 10–12 April 1981: report of an inquiry by the Rt. Hon. the Lord Scarman, OBE', London: HMSO.

Stenson, K. (2005) 'Sovereignty, biopolitics and the local government of crime', *Theoretical Criminology*, 9 (3): 265–287.

Stoker, G. (2004) *Transforming Local Governance*, London: Palgrave.

Van Kesteren, J., Mayhew, P. and Nieuwbeerta, P. (2001) 'Criminal victimization in seventeen industrialised countries', The Hague: Ministry of Justice, WODC. Onderzoek en beleid, 187.

Wyvekens, A. (1996) 'Justice de proximité et proximité de la Justice. Les maisons de justice et du droit', *Droit et société*, 33: 363–388.

10 Civil society and participatory governance in South Africa

The quest for socioeconomic equity in the post-apartheid era

Konstantinos Papadakis

Since the end of apartheid, South Africa has institutionalised the voice of civil society in the public sphere, particularly by including participatory governance processes in a range of different fields. In that respect, the first free elections in 1994 were 'payback' time for civil society due to the role it performed in providing grassroots legitimation to the anti-apartheid struggle. However, the ambitious plans for people-driven redistribution were to be dropped due to the turn of the new state to a market-driven agenda. Thus, after having been formally included in numerous participatory fora, civil society has increasingly felt that within these fora it performs a role of legitimacy-provider for the dominant market-driven agenda and has come to face a survival crisis. As a reaction, a number of social movements, which mostly act outside participatory governance structures, have emerged since 2000. The paradoxical effect is that these movements appear to be able to influence more effectively the functioning and outcomes of participatory fora.

The models proposed in this book might not fully explain the experience of South Africa. A fifth model of civil society which might be termed the 'radical civil society' model may be necessary for a better understanding of the notion and evolution of civil society in the specific political and historical context of this country. This model perceives *exclusion* from the formal policy-making sphere as a key element in the action of what has turned out to be the most combative segment of civil society, i.e. the post-apartheid social movements. Social movements provide an essential input to the participatory governance structures despite their operation outside these structures, thus leading to the revitalisation and reinforcement of civil society's critical voice, which in turn is a necessary precondition for the functioning of democracy in the context of South African post-apartheid politics, monopolised by a single party.

Since the mid-1990s South Africa has become a laboratory of innovation in the administration of public goods to the point that no country, in either the developed or developing world has gone further in the institutionalisation of participatory policy-making processes. The post-apartheid era witnessed the establishment of participatory structures within which civil society is called to contribute to the formulation and adoption of policies in a range of different fields, including two of the most serious challenges for the country, development and the fight against HIV/AIDS.[1]

We show that the civil-society organisations that have been included in the participatory structures of the post-apartheid era have not been able to maintain the vibrancy of their earlier initiatives, which consisted mainly of informal information-provision and awareness-raising, echoing the needs of the grass-roots and proposing solutions to build up the post-apartheid reconstruction agenda. This could be explained in part by the absence of appropriate financial support from the state and other donors but above all *by the very participation* of civil-society groups in policy processes which rely on consensus-building and function within a dominant policy framework characterised by a market-driven agenda.

The first part of the chapter provides a brief history of civil society in South Africa under the apartheid regime. It focuses on two of the most thriving civil society voices during the apartheid era, i.e. unions and 'civics', and highlights the difficulty of drawing a clear division between 'political' and 'civil' society action during this period. It then depicts the main characteristics of civil society during the transition to the democracy period (1990–1994) up to the first free elections in 1994, and analyses the notion of 'participatory democracy' as it appears in the official policy discourse of the new state, e.g. the Reconstruction and Development Programme (RDP). The second part highlights the shift of the new government in terms of (macro)economic strategy, towards a more market-driven agenda and the impact of this shift on the role of civil society in the reconstruction effort. In the third part, a brief description on the emergence of a new and more radical wing of civil society, i.e. the new social movements, is followed by the presentation of two case studies of institutionalised participatory structures: the National Economic Development and Labour Council (NEDLAC) and the South African National Aids Council (SANAC). This description highlights among other things the differences in terms of strategy and effectiveness between what we call 'embedded civil society' on the one hand, and the new social movements (or 'radical civil society') on the other. We conclude by putting forward the need for a new model of civil society, which we call the 'radical civil-society model', and which might be more appropriate in order to accommodate the experience of South Africa's civil society.

A brief history of civil society in South Africa

Political and civil society in the apartheid period

Civil society in South Africa has a long history, a detailed presentation of which goes beyond the scope of the present contribution. It might suffice to recall that the existence of a vibrant civil society in South Africa has been intimately related to the struggle against the apartheid regime and colonisation as well as the struggle for economic equity and political equality.[2] During this struggle, 'political' and 'civil' society shared common agendas and held mutually rein-forcing discourses. Indeed, the institutionalised exclusion of the black majority had created a situation where all kinds of grievances on behalf of this segregated majority were de facto perceived by ruling political elites as revolutionary demands. An important consequence of this background was that the civil-society sector was highly politicised, to the point that a clear line between 'political' and 'civil' society could not be drawn (Marais 1998: 200; Landsberg 2000; CAF 2000: 39).

During the apartheid era, political and civil-society organisations that managed to survive persecution (inside or outside the country), sought to develop a coordinated mobilisation. A spontaneous but coherent cooperation was thus developed among students, youth, women, workers and political organisations, aimed at influencing and utilising international public opinion with a view to putting pressure on the state to accept system change. Unions and civics took the moral and organisational leadership during this period and functioned as the main legitimating agents of the political struggle for democracy.

Unions

The fight for equity and justice in the workplace was the most pressing demand of the struggle in South Africa since key elements of the apartheid regime were based on a combination of colonial and racist principles which structured relations of production so as to make cheap labour available to a white-dominated economy (Campbell 1997; Standing *et al.* 1996: 12–16). The development of independent unions in South Africa and the mass mobilisation of workers were based on a twofold strategy of intense shop-floor organisation and grassroots action.[3] This two-track strategy of cooperating within and outside of participatory fora distinguished trade unions from other civil-society groups and social movements.

Civics

Along with the mobilisation of workers and organisations of students, women and youths, which were issue-specific and territorially more encompassing, another category of civil society, i.e. the 'civics', incorporated all kinds of interests at the community level, especially the townships. Thus, the civics were informally constituted associations of township residents dealing with all kinds of community issues. Civics fought day-to-day struggles for basic necessities such as housing, electricity, water, sewage and reasonable rents, to be made available to the grassroots. In addition to their protest-oriented activity, the civics functioned as the training ground of today's civil society and participatory democracy, since they constituted the platform through which professional bodies such as traders' associations, cultural clubs, schools, hospitals, clinics or old-age homes expressed their views on public projects that affected them (Botha 1992: 58).[4]

It should be noted that civics did not have (and perhaps did not need) a clearly defined organisational structure. They represented a diffuse and powerful social movement, which largely explains why it managed to avoid co-optation by the apartheid state. In the last years of the apartheid the mobilising power of civics was central not only for meeting the political and social needs of the excluded black majority, but also for creating a destabilising environment for the apartheid regime, and in turn strengthening the certitude (including of the apartheid regime) that democratic transition was inevitable (Botha 1992; Cawthra *et al.* 2001; Landsberg 2000; Seekings 1992; Lanegran 1995).

Transition to democracy (1990–1994)

The anti-apartheid struggle was officially terminated with the first free elections held in 1994, but a transitional period had already been initiated with the lift of the ban against the African National Congress (ANC) in 1990.[5] During this period the idea that active participation of civil society in the building of the new democracy was key to achieving a legitimate transition, gained additional ground with the largely spontaneous emergence of nationwide consultation processes around burning issues such as housing, healthcare, labour, women and youth. In these processes, set up by the ANC and other political organisations, civil-society organisations were asked to provide information about peoples' needs and make policy proposals in order to shape the forthcoming constitution and the policy priorities of the new state. Despite the close links of the various civil-society groups with the ANC, civil society managed to articulate its independent socioeconomic agenda and sought to promote it quite successfully.

These developments were followed by a twofold fundamental change in the composition and nature of the voluntary sector in South Africa, aimed at rationalising the contacts between the new state and civil society: first, the transformation of the so-called 'struggle' and 'welfare' organisations, which prevailed during apartheid, into 'developmental' organisations. Rather than providing a platform for fighting the apartheid discourses, or providing day-to-day assistance to the neglected majority, the new civil society was now asked to engage with the public sector at the local, provincial and national levels, so as to meet the huge reconstruction and development needs. The second change was the formation of national associations representing major civil-society segments – in particular civics, women and the youth – in order to ensure 'the continuity of an autonomous and institutionalized voice of grassroots movements' (CAF 2000; CASE and SANGOCO 2001).

Among the most important national umbrella bodies created during this period were those representing the community-driven demands of civics, i.e. the South African National Civics Organization (SANCO); women's interests, i.e. the Women's National Coalition (WNC); and youth interests, i.e. the (short-lived) National Youth Development Forum (NYDF).[6] These movements were to play a major role in the politics of transition to democracy. However, within the current context of the de facto monopolistic position of the ruling party in post-apartheid politics, they have come to represent the most dysfunctional part of civil society, which instead of providing legitimacy to the initially needs-driven socioeconomic agenda of the state, now functions as a legitimacy provider to the state's new market-driven approach (see below, pp. 160–163).

SANCO

SANCO was established in 1992, officially to secure an independent voice of civics in the transition politics. It played a key role during that period, both passively and actively. *Passively*, as it declined the option of direct negotiations offered by the apartheid regime in an effort to avoid splintering the unity of the mass popular movement (under the leadership of the ANC).[7] More *actively*, as in late 1993, it joined the electoral alliance comprising the ANC, the South African Communist Party (SACP) and the Congress of South African Trade Unions (COSATU). Most importantly, SANCO also participated in the drafting of the post-apartheid main political manifesto, i.e. the Reconstruction and Development Programme (RDP), which set the first political and socioeconomic programme for the new South African state (however, the RDP was abandoned in 1996 in favour of a more marked-driven approach – see below, pp. 158–160).

The presence of SANCO was crucial at the local level too, as it participated in various policy activities aimed at preparing the ground for new local government structures (such as the Local Government Negotiating Forum and the Local Government Transition Act) (CASE 2001; Seekings 1997: 10; Heller and Ntlokonkulu 2001: 15). Most importantly, SANCO's representatives became part of various participatory policy-making fora dealing with all sorts of issues, in particular the Housing Forum. These fora eventually led to a more institutionalised participatory processes such as the National Economic Development and Labour Council (NEDLAC), to which SANCO was also officially invited to become a participant (see below, pp. 161–163).

WNC

Similar responsibilities were given to the WNC, the national organisation formed during the transition period in order to ensure that gender equality was guaranteed in the new political system and reconstruction politics.[8] Among the successes of the WNC in the transition years was an agreement reached with the negotiating parties to include women in the negotiating process that led to the transition. More importantly, the WNC managed to push forward the idea of insertion of clauses guaranteeing gender equality and other socioeconomic rights for women (e.g. reproductive rights) in the future constitution.[9] Such ideas initially met with strong opposition from traditional leaders who argued that they conflicted with custom and tradition, laws and practices. But the WNC managed to resist pressures successfully and enjoyed during the first years of its existence a high profile as a non-partisan national women's organisation capable of 'breaking free of the divisive shackles of apartheid' (e.g. Gersharter 2001; Hassim 2000).

In sum, in the transition years platform organisations such as SANCO and the

WNC, incarnated the next most influential organised national social movements in South Africa, after that of the labour movement led by COSATU. Available literature and the numerous interviews conducted in South Africa between 2002 and 2005 testified that by the eve of the first free election in 1994, civil society's power of mobilisation associated with the activities of the union, civic, and women movements, delivered the needed legitimacy to the agenda of the ANC and contributed to building the degree of coherence between 'civil' and 'political' society which was crucial not only to the *peaceful* transition to democracy, but to transition *tout court*. It also paved the way to ensuring that the new constitution and reconstruction efforts would not ignore the needs of their constituencies, i.e. the socioeconomic needs of the people who suffered the most under the apartheid, as well as to warranting that the new political system would institutionalise their representation in policy-making.

The promise of participatory democracy and its impact on civil society (1996–2000)

Moves towards the institutionalisation of civil society's presence in the post-apartheid political life were not an historical accident or the outcome of an isolated political decision. Because of civil society's contribution to the anti-apartheid struggle, but also because large segments of the new state apparatus emerged from it, the first steps of the new democratic government were naturally directed towards demonstrating its willingness to actively involve civil society in the development and reconstruction process.[10]

The commitment to participatory democracy was embodied in numerous legislations and issue-specific policies.[11] Last but not least, the 'reconstruction programme' of the ANC that was articulated in the Reconstruction and Development Programme (RDP) and which functioned in the first year of the post-apartheid era as the overarching policy programme of the ANC, also highlighted the commitment of the new state to participatory democracy. It was itself negotiated and drafted by a wide spectrum of actors drawing on the ANC, COSATU and SANCO (ANC 1994).

In the early years of the post-apartheid period the RDP constituted the main political manifesto of the new democracy and the backbone of the post-apartheid socioeconomic policy in South Africa (CAF 2000). It was above all an attempt to advance the interests of the 'previously disadvantaged' by establishing a transition process towards economic, social and cultural equity. Meeting basic needs, redressing the rampant inequalities in terms of wealth, education, essential services and access to land, rebuilding and de-racialising the economy, developing human resources, as well as radically democratising the state and society have been its main objectives.

In order to overturn poverty and inequality, the RDP generally emphasised the role of the public sector and civil society at the expense of more market-driven approaches.[12] It advocated a state-interventionist approach coupled with an active participation of civil-society organisations in the design and delivery of RDP goals. The policy-making and planning process of the RDP was to include a variety of local, provincial and national 'development forums', in which all stakeholders, including the social partners, NGOs and grassroots organisations, would be represented.[13]

Overall, the first free elections of 1994 were not only historical for the ANC and other anti-apartheid movements but also 'payback' time for civil society, in particular the national umbrella organisations representing specific constituencies such as SANCO and the WNC. Not surprisingly therefore, the first years of democracy raised many hopes in civil society as it was invited to play an important role in the policy design and implementation of the new socioeconomic agenda. It also raised many hopes among 'radical democrats and reformed socialists around the world' who saw in South Africa the incarnation of models of 'associational democracy' (Baccaro and Papadakis 2004), reminiscent of Bruno Jobert's 'organised civil society' model in this volume (Chapter 1), albeit in a more radical form.[14]

Surprisingly, shortly after the transition to democracy and while being offered this unprecedented opportunity to formally participate in the numerous participatory fora, many civil-society organisations started facing a 'survival crisis'. This crisis was peculiar in the sense that it appeared in a context of overall healthy finances for the 'non-profit' sector as a whole, as abundant development aid came from both foreign and local, public and corporate sources (e.g. Swilling and Russell 2001; CASE and SANGOCO 2001). What was perceived to be a crisis for the sector could be explained to a certain extent by the following factors:

1   the redirection of the donors' priorities away from social-oriented civil-society groups[15] towards more marketable issues such as democracy promotion and awareness-raising around HIV/AIDS prevention;
2   the managerial drain or migration of former activists of the civil-society sector to either the market or the state sectors;
3   the lack of appropriate technical skills for participating in development endeavours since civil society had so far performed the largely political function of demand-channelling (Hearn 1999; Adler and Webster 1995; Marais 1998; Cawthra *et al.* 2001; Landsberg 2000; Pieterse 1997).

However, the main explanation underpinning this development is a fundamental change in terms of economic and social policy within the context of the dominant position of the new political elites in the post-apartheid state apparatus. These political elites opted after the initial years of the RDP for a market-driven approach, viewing civil society as less efficient than market actors in the reconstruction effort. Progressively, the ambitious plans for people-driven redistribution and structural transformation of the state and the socio-economy advocated by the RDP were to be dropped under the pressure of constraints associated to the dominant market-driven agenda (e.g. Marais 1998; Mattes and Thiel 199). Officially however, neither the government acknowledged this fact, remaining caught in its 'participatory' and 'empower the people' discourse, nor did civil society directly challenge the new policy, promoted by a monopolistic party/government apparatus which leaves little space for alternative discourses. As will be seen below, with the exception of trade unions, only one particular branch of civil society, i.e. social movements, challenged this policy shift by remaining largely outside the participatory apparatus, thus managing to maintain their vibrancy and the effectiveness of their action in defending the interests of the grassroots.

Shifting context and roles for civil society under the dominance of the market-driven agenda

From RDP to GEAR

The formal rhetoric of the new state officially focused on the political and financial empowerment of civil-society organisations so that they would be able to provide an effective input to the reconstruction effort. In spite of this, a new macroeconomic policy strategy which was abruptly adopted by the South African government in 1996 seems to question not only the technical relevance of civil-society groups, but also their legitimacy in designing and implementing the reconstruction policy.

In particular, the adoption of the Growth Employment and Redistribution (GEAR) programme, which established the new macroeconomic policy framework for the country and was negotiated *outside* the competent participatory structure (NEDLAC), implicitly made the case that 'unless the fundamentals are put in place', namely until structural adjustment policies were successfully put in place, the needs-driven policy of the state reflected in the RDP of the Alliance, where civil society had been called to play a key role, was going to be frozen.[16] It would be reactivated, once the market-driven setting had generated sufficient means for implementing the RDP objectives.[17]

The ultimate objective of GEAR was the creation of 100,000 jobs on average per year in five years, and 6 per cent growth rate. This was to be achieved through a stringent macroeconomic strategy which consisted of constraining government expenditure, lowering the fiscal deficit and inflation, increasing the pace of deregulation and privatisation, giving priority to attracting foreign investment, and establishing a minimal state intervention (the so-called 'fundamentals'). In essence, GEAR's 'orthodox' underlying assumption of 'first growth and then redistribution', proved to be a mere structural adjustment programme reversing the 'growth *through* redistribution' model suggested by the RDP.[18]

GEAR, which was drafted under the auspices of the Ministry of Finance in 1996, was described as a 'home-grown' structural adjustment programme. It was adopted immediately after its release as the official macroeconomic policy framework. More importantly, GEAR was adopted outside the available participatory process, i.e. the NEDLAC. It is widely believed that the document was indirectly shaped by the International Financial Institutions (IFIs),[19] the business intelligentsia and by technocrats.[20]

Ever since, GEAR has been viewed by many students of South African politics as one of the most controversial policy documents. Not only did it attract widespread criticism for the way it was adopted, namely without any consultation with civil society, but also, and perhaps most importantly, it did not demonstrate its effectiveness in terms of growth, employment generation and poverty alleviation. By the year 2000, GEAR had not reached its growth and employment targets.[21] By December 2005, GEAR had reached only its macro-economic targets as a stabilisation programme. Despite improved economic performance (e.g. 3.3 per cent real growth rate, strong exchange rate, controlled budget deficit and low inflation) widespread unemployment and poverty persisted (SARB).[22]

Concomitantly, the civil-society actors, academics and representatives of state development agencies we interviewed, had the assessment that GEAR had implicitly redefined the role of non-union civil-society actors: NGOs and grass-roots organisations were now entrusted with caring for the most deprived and most vulnerable groups until the growth and jobs targets were reached.

The field of employment creation provides a good illustration of the implied effects of GEAR. The state's function became primarily one of training-provision aimed at meeting labour market demands, rather than focusing on micro-sector activities and public works to create short-term employment opportunities.[23] In this context, civil-society organisations appear to have been assigned to the care for the 'primary unemployable', which is a category composed of roughly two million long-term unemployed persons. Addressing the needs of these people was not understood anymore as a 'job creation challenge, but largely a poverty alleviation one'.[24]

Admittedly, the shift from RDP to GEAR also influenced the working culture within public development agencies, now faced more or less explicitly with more market-driven (and less demand-driven) expectations. A good illustration of 'the encroachment of market principles into arenas that not so long ago were held to be governed by principles of justice and social citizenship' (Heller and Ntlokonkulu 2001: 40) was the case of government policies on 'cost recovery' in the provision of services and the increasing reliance on the private sector for housing delivery. In turn, this has been accompanied by political and administrative centralisation, the dissolution of local participatory spaces, and increasing reliance on a technocratic vision of development.

Perhaps with few exceptions (e.g. the National Development Agency), it was observed that development agencies (like Khula, Ntsika or the Usumbomwu Youth Fund) appeared to have internalised this shift. The staff of these agencies tended to perceive groups with private sector characteristics and strategies as far more appropriate for channelling their development funds in an 'effective and sustainable' way. On the contrary, they tended to perceive civil society (not-for-profit) groups as less effective and their intervention as 'rarely sustainable', despite the official discourse which described the active involvement of civil-society organisations in the implementation of their programmes as key 'due to the detailed knowledge of the field' and their 'proximity to the grass-roots'.[25]

Finally, GEAR's policies such as privatisation, deregulation and lowering of public spending were very costly in terms of social peace. In fact, unions were ferociously opposed to GEAR (COSATU 1999: Declaration on GEAR). COSATU's response to GEAR was a steadily escalating protest campaign, culminating in a one-day 'anti-privatisation strike' in late 2002.

While before 1996 civil-society organisations (both, those embedded in participatory structures, and those outside of them) were called to serve the reconstruction effort by implementing the RDP, they were now confronted with the challenges of the new state's macroeconomic choices which were viewed as costly in terms of social justice and socioeconomic equity.[26]

The impact of the new policy orientations on civil society: the emergence of the new social movements

The sequence of the collapse of the apartheid regime, the institutionalisation of civil society and the reorientation of the dominant macroeconomic framework had a twofold impact on civil society: first, the umbrella civil-society organisations which had been integrated in formal policy processes tended to internalise the official choices and new market-driven economic/technical approach of the post-apartheid state apparatus by remaining silent to the dominance of a new state discourse (in spite of the fact that this discourse directly affected the interests of their constituents). Civil society provided the state with legitimacy. The phenomenon of 'co-option' or 'capture' of most civil-society groups' interests, including those of SANCO and WNC, by the very same participatory processes that had given these organisations the opportunity to play an active role in the post-apartheid policy (e.g. NEDLAC, SANAC etc.), is critical. The absence of real opposition by the dominant civil-society organisations to the state-led economic policies pushed a number of civil-society organisations which were active *outside* the institutionalised policy fora to resume protest and mobilisation against those policies. In this context, one of the most interesting developments in the South African civil-society landscape has been the progressive emergence of 'new social movements' as the most vocal part of civil society and, de facto, the sole voice of opposition to the politically dominant governing party and its policies.

The term 'new social movements' in South Africa commonly refers to grassroots movements formed after 1994 (and in particular since 2000). They represent constituencies and interests operating outside the framework of the anti-apartheid liberation movement and the formal participatory processes. Most of these new social movements were founded in an effort to challenge policy choices often associated with the GEAR agenda (e.g. privatisation and 'cost-recovery') and/or the slowness of the post-apartheid government in responding to social crises (e.g. AIDS), which de facto exacerbated the vulnerability of the poorest segments of the population. While less structured and organised compared to the rest of the civil-society sector (e.g. unions, NGOs, community-based organisations), the new social movements enjoy massive support from poor South Africans living in townships such as Soweto in the Gauteng province and its informal settlements.

Among the most vocal new social movements in South Africa are the Anti-Privatization Forum (APF) and its affiliates like the Soweto Electricity Crisis Committee (SECC) and the Treatment Action Campaign (TAC).[27] These social movements were usually considered by traditional policy actors (i.e. the members of the former anti-apartheid struggle and current allies in the Tripartite Alliance, namely ANC, SACP and SANCO) as 'ultra-left' and were – at least rhetorically – ostracised from the sphere of institutional politics because of their 'extremist', 'revolutionary' and 'anti-system' views (e.g. Buhlungu 2005: 1). This ostracism was linked to the fact that their preferred means of action – mass street demonstrations, marches to parliament, civil disobedience campaigns – are reminiscent of the mass liberation movement during the apartheid era, and at odds with the participatory democracy tactics based on irenic consensus-building. Implicitly, the new social movements accused the new democratic intelligentsia of actually adopting an economic policy which resembled that of the dark years of the apartheid. In this context, on the one hand the new social movements regard the ruling party and its allies (including the union leadership and SANCO) as 'sold-out' elites who act in an effort of 'self-preservation'; on the other hand, the Tripartite Alliance leadership and supporters dismiss them as 'peace-time revolutionaries' and unorganised falling stars.[28]

The emergence of these new social movements in early 2000 marks a durable re-orientation of the civil-society sector in the post-apartheid era from development- to struggle-oriented activities, reversing the trend observed in the period 1994–2000.

Embedded civil society vs. social movements: the cases of NEDLAC and SANAC

In the post-apartheid years, participatory structures of policy-making such as the National Economic and Labour Council (NEDLAC) in the area of socioeconomic development and the South African National Aids Council (SANAC) in the area of HIV/AIDS initially constituted the best examples of participatory democracy in action. Progressively, however, these very same structures also stood as the best examples of ineffectiveness of civil-society groups in promoting the interests of their constituencies within institutionalised bodies of socioeconomic policy setting.

National Economic Development and Labour Council (NEDLAC)

Our field research in the period 2002–2005 demonstrated that more than 100 agreements had been successfully reached through the NEDLAC process on key socioeconomic legislation and policies.[29] However, the part of this institution which seemed to work best was the traditional social dialogue, which took place in all its tripartite chambers (i.e. labour market; trade and industry; public finance and monetary policy). The development chamber where the non-union 'community constituency' component of NEDLAC was allowed to participate (representing civics, women, cooperatives, disabled and youth) did not seem to work as well. It actually reportedly performed a purely symbolic role and was described as toothless and sidelined.

The key constituencies of the development chamber, SANCO representing civics and WNC representing women, made absolutely no difference in the policy-making process. Worse, it was observed on several occasions that despite the fact that these organisations were considered to be the natural allies of the union movement, the labour constituency was much more vocal and combative compared to the community constituency. During the Labour Relations Act amendments negotiations, for instance (aimed at rendering the South African labour market more 'flexible'),[30] the community constituency urged for more moderation and negotiations, before any action took place.[31] At the same time, trade unions adopted a strategy of direct confrontation and immediate mobilisation. Even more illustrative seems to be the case of GEAR which touched upon non-labour issues of crucial importance for the civics' constituents. With the exception of COSATU, the rest of civil-society organisations represented in NEDLAC had little to say about the adoption of market-driven policies by the ANC in the context of GEAR, which clearly ran against the interests of their constituencies.

There seem to be various reasons for this lack of activism and effectiveness:

1   the deep financial problems affecting all civil-society organisations in the development chamber;[32]
2   the constant challenge on behalf of the social partners, questioning whether or not the community constituency could claim to speak on behalf of particular groups (civics, women etc.);[33]
3   the fact that civil-society organisations were confined to the development chamber (referred to as 'a dumping ground for any issue'),[34] meaning that civil society was institutionally prevented from influencing discussions on trade, finance and labour issues, which are important for development;
4   more importantly, civil-society groups participating in NEDLAC lacked independence from the ANC.[35]

The lack of a critical voice and opposition capacity within SANCO and the WNC is in stark contrast not only to the history of these organisations, but also to the at the time prevailing attitude of their members who increasingly joined the new social movements. Local branches of SANCO and social movements such as the Anti-Privatisation Forum (APF), the Landless People Movement (LPM), or the Soweto Electricity Crisis Committee (SECC), not only supported COSATU's anti-privatisation strike; they have been continuously launching mobilisation campaigns in townships and undertaking protest action against water and electricity privatisation and other aspects of GEAR.[36]

It is interesting to note that the most prominent example of successful action by SANCO from 1994 to 2005 to the benefit of its main constituency, the poor township and informal settlement residents, has been a series of agreements reached between this organisation and ESCOM, the national electricity company. Students of civil society and social movements in South Africa indicate that SANCO's action and success in this field was *not* the result of SANCO's own strategy, let alone its political struggle. Rather, SANCO was called in at the last moment in order to sign this deal with ESCOM, apparently in an effort to obtain the official credit for the waiving of the residents' debts by the company. Mainly responsible for this spectacular 'success story' was the huge mobilisation action of township residents and their social movement which had previously created the momentum for this pro-poor agreement, i.e. the Soweto Electricity Crisis Committee (SECC).[37] In sum, without the key mobilisation, massive rent boycott and pressure coming from the social movement (SECC), ESCOM and the government probably would have never accepted to write-off such large amounts of electricity debts to the benefit of the poor township residents, the actual constituency of SANCO. This was confirmed inversely on at least one occasion (Zuern 2004: 20).

It should be noted that the above-mentioned campaigns against the flexibilisation of the labour market (1996 and 1999) and the privatisation of public assets (2000–2001) also seemed to have paid off for the trade union movement, as in both instances COSATU managed to either slow down the pace of implementation of these structural reforms, or mitigate their most pro-market components. In some cases, labour regulation became even more progressive.[38] Most importantly however, the success of the union movement during these campaigns was the consequence not only of the strong stance adopted by COSATU during negotiations in NEDLAC per se, i.e. in the framework of this participatory structure, but also because COSATU maintained the alternative of 'taking to the streets' and negotiated against a background of 'a persistently high level of strike activity' (Webster 1996: 4; Standing *et al.* 1996: 175).

In general, COSATU's strategy of combining protest-oriented activity outside institutionalised participatory fora with participation within these fora was a conscious and necessary choice in order to counterbalance the negotiating power of business and government representatives within a market-driven policy environment which decisively affected the balance of interests. COSATU believes that NEDLAC's arrangements and negotiations on their own, without outside pressure, are not sufficient to advance the unions' cause.

South African National AIDS Council (SANAC)

As in the case of NEDLAC's development chamber, the participatory forum aimed at addressing the HIV/AIDS issue, i.e. SANAC, and in particular the civil-society sector representing the National Association of People Living with Aids, has been frequently criticised for being too conciliatory with the state's policy on HIV/AIDS. The state policy has frequently been criticised for putting too much emphasis on education, prevention and other forms of pre-emptive intervention such as nutrition and counselling at the expense of a more proactive policy of treatment. Indeed, until recently, the government policy did not include any large-scale treatment campaign that is believed to decelerate the progress of AIDS by improving the immunisation system of the HIV-positive patient, and to prevent mother-to-child transmission of the virus (MTC). The government has often justified its position by reference to medical, economic and, at times, cultural considerations.

SANAC's silence and immobility on these crucial issues was impressive. Progressively, SANAC became the main (institutional) target of critiques coming from all parts of state and non-state representatives (many wished to remain anonymous) for not being able for instance to adopt a policy aimed to mitigate mother-to-child transmission (MTC) and its dramatic consequences.

Despite the presence of numerous civil-society groups representing various constituencies, the most ardent critic of SANAC has been the social movement Treatment Action Campaign (TAC), generally seen as the most influential and effective civil-society group in the HIV/AIDS field. In TAC's opinion, SANAC can do little to respond to the AIDS pandemic. According to TAC, civil-society representatives in SANAC 'have not been able to actively influence the agenda of this body and have remained *prisoners to the agenda of the government*'.[39]

In response to this immobility, TAC initiated litigation against the government. In August 2001, TAC launched a famous courtcase demanding of the government to provide the drug Neverapine to pregnant women so as to limit mother-to-child transmission. In July 2002, the Constitutional Court upheld the decision of the High Court and confirmed that failure to provide treatment violated the constitutional rights of women and babies.[40] However, the Department of Health delayed the rolling out of the distribution plan due to insufficient infrastructural capacities. TAC responded by launching a civil disobedience campaign, 'Dying for AIDS', and pressing manslaughter charges against the government in connection with AIDS deaths. Finally, in November 2003, the government issued an 'Operational Plan for Comprehensive HIV and AIDS Care, Management and Treatment for South Africa' (Department of Health 2003). In this plan, the government committed itself to roll out antiretroviral (ARV) treatment on a large scale. SANAC was to be responsible for the implementation.

Since the release of the Operational Plan, thousands of people (mainly in the Gauteng and Western Cape Provinces) have benefited from access to treatment. Yet, against a target of 50,000 people by March 2004, by October 2004 less than 15,000 people were being treated in public hospitals and clinics.[41] SANAC, like most institutionalised processes aimed to address HIV/AIDS-related issues, was still accused of immobility. In this context, TAC resumed its mobilisation and litigation activity aimed at the effective implementation of the Operational Plan. At the same time, TAC continued putting pressure on drug companies to lower the prices of antiretroviral drugs, and established a long record of success in this area.[42]

TAC's position and strategies has been in stark contrast to that of the various civil-society 'sectors' participating in SANAC, in particular the National Association of People Living with AIDS (NAPWA), which claims to represent between 200,000 and 300,000 members. While not rejecting the need for distribution of ARVs, NAPWA seems to have embraced the state's hesitant approach to treatment and appears to have adopted the more conciliatory view of the government and certainly a less confrontational approach. NAPWA argues that South Africa 'still lack(s) basic infrastructure which is conducive to effective administration of antiretrovirals' (NAPWA 2001). It focuses 'on the provision of care and support for people living with AIDS', on the 'facilitation of co-ordination' and the establishment of 'support groups for counselling', and finally on the 'enhancement of HIV/AIDS awareness through seminars and workshops throughout South Africa', but not on massive treatment.[43] NAPWA has accused TAC of promoting a hidden 'anti-governmental' (anti-ANC) and 'racist' (anti-black people) agenda and has officially distanced itself from TAC.[44]

In sum, NAPWA appeared to have embraced the official strategy in this area, that HIV and AIDS can be combated more effectively through prevention[45], although this argument has been turned down, *inter alia*, by the July 2002 Constitutional Court decision.[46]

It would seem that this conciliatory stance had applied to most other civil-society participants in the SANAC process. This was the case reportedly not because the participants were convinced by the arguments put forward by the state, but because of a number of structural problems associated with the SANAC process that prevented them from expressing their views forcefully including:

1   The lack of *political and financial independence* of the SANAC: despite the availability of some funds aimed at rendering SANAC more independent, the body's secretariat remained located in the Department of Health and funds were released only with difficulty.
2   The dominance of the government in the process of *agenda-setting* of SANAC sessions which accounted for the widespread conception that the agenda did not adequately reflect the specific and widespread demands of SANAC's participants, in particular in relation to the issue of swift and effective implementation of the treatment action plan provided for in the (Treatment) Operational Plan.
3   The *lack of clear terms of reference* and the obligation of many participants to subscribe to what some have described as 'implicit terms of reference', namely, 'talk in one voice' and 'don't criticise the government',[47] which obliged the participants to remain silent even when they disagreed with the agenda and priorities of the government and to refrain from openly criticising the government's opinion with respect to these issues.

Because of these drawbacks, SANAC could not function effectively, neither as a genuine advisory body nor as a monitoring mechanism of the country's

HIV/AIDS projects. In contrast, TAC's capacity to shape the agenda of the state from outside SANAC has been incontestable. TAC's influence was explained by the sole fact that it successfully confronted the government both in courts and in the street on human-rights grounds (for some replicating gay and lesbian groups' tactics in the United States) (see, for example, Mbali 2005). The decision of the Constitutional Court stated that the government had an obligation to design and implement effective policy in the area of MTC. Under such pressure, the government went beyond this obligation and decided to provide a *generalised* treatment plan. According to our field interviews, this was the result of the 'social movement' atmosphere created around the issue of treatment, of which TAC was and still is the linchpin. Street mobilisation, civil disobedience campaigns, marches to parliament, pickets and demonstrations appear to have constituted a necessary element for pushing the state to more commitment.

As the legal adviser of TAC in the *Mother-to-Child Transmission* courtcase argued, had it been an isolated successful litigation on behalf of a few NGO activists and not a grassroots social movement using protest, mobilisation and other agonistic methods, the legal precedents would have little resonance in government circles, let alone a chance to be generalised to all people living with AIDS (Bundlender 2002).[48]

Civil society outside the institutionalised realm of policy-making

The South African case tends to show that socioeconomic rights may be effectively implemented only as long as they are supported by social mobilisation, that is to say, when an active social movement plays the role of watchdog over the deliberation taking place inside institutionalised structures where embedded civil society is allowed to participate. In the absence of this safeguard, participatory bodies would tend to co-opt rather than empower civil-society participants.

Conclusion: towards a new civil-society model?

Experience in South Africa has shown that as a result of the need to respond to the market-driven strategy adopted by the ruling party – which is politically dominant due to its anti-apartheid struggle, thus leaving little space for new critical discourses – civil society came to be divided into two broad segments. *One part* of civil society, which is 'embedded' in participatory structures, has largely accepted de facto to serve as legitimacy provider to the state agenda. Even though maintaining a formal role for civil society in the policy-making process is presented as a core ingredient of the new political system, not least because the ruling forces are caught in their own 'participatory' and 'empower the people' rhetoric, embedded civil society has little impact. To a certain extent this is due to the fact that it is excluded from discussions over the macroeconomic and financial agenda-setting, lacks resources and has been depleted of its most experienced elements after having functioned as the training ground for the new political intelligentsia. Most importantly, however, it lacks an independent agenda now that the initial reconstruction and redistribution agenda, of which it was a key implementer, has been reversed by the government. Its incapacity to tackle this challenge vis-à-vis the dominant political party has led it to lose its critical voice and thereby its power.[49]

With the gradual abandoning of the initial promise of redistribution by the dominant party, *another part* of civil society, i.e. the 'new social movements', which could be described as 'radical civil society' has been moving away from the dominant political party's tutelary authority in the hope of influencing the state policies through protest and mobilisation. This part of civil society is represented by vocal new social movements putting pressure on the state to abandon or mitigate the dominant market-driven agenda, thus promoting the interests of their constituencies which are the poor and marginalised segments of society. The radical views of new social movements can successfully appeal to the collective memory of the liberated people in order to advance claims seen as legitimate by the grassroots, especially when they relate to reaffirming and pushing forward the promise for people's empowerment. In the absence of any real political force of opposition, the social movements represent the most effective voice in favour of grassroots interests. Thus, in the South African case, social movements operating outside the formal framework of participatory governance structures have played a central role in effectively influencing the agenda, the functioning and the outcomes of policies dealt with in the participatory structures of the state. It is interesting to note that the influence of radical civil society might be due to the very fact that it operates outside participatory structures while 'embedded civil society' which *did* participate in formal structures has not proven to be effective.

Therefore, ad hoc contest and resistance outside formalised models of civil-society participation can work as a safeguard against the risk of co-optation of civil-society groups within institutionalised frameworks by dominant discourses and pre-established agendas. By the same token, social movements (radical civil society) appear to play a key role for rehabilitating the embedded segment of civil society, so as to reassert its key role within formal structures. While inclusion of civil society is propagated by the South African government as an indicator of good governance in a healthy 'procedural' democracy, contestation by social movements (radical civil society) appears to be a key safeguard of 'substantive' democracy. It could therefore be suggested that social movements have perhaps given rise to a 'radical civil-society' model, which could be added to Bruno Jobert's four models presented in Chapter 1 of this book.

Notes

1 This chapter draws on empirical research, which was conducted in the International Institute for Labour Studies/International Labour Organisation (IILS/ILO) between 2002 and 2005, and aimed at collecting the perceptions and self-perceptions of policy actors and academics regarding the role of civil society in two participatory policy structures, the National Economic Development and Labour Council (NEDLAC) and the South African National Aids Council (SANAC). This chapter reflects the views of the author only and not necessarily those of the IILS or the ILO.

2 The Prohibition of Mixed Marriages Act, the Population Registration Act, the Immorality Act, the Reservation of Separate Amenities Act, the Group Areas Act, the Bantu Authorities Act constituted key pieces of apartheid legislation (Dewar 1985).

3 The Congress of South African Trade Unions (COSATU), founded in 1985, and the National Council of Trade Unions (NACTU), founded in 1986, became the linchpin of major strikes, longstanding *stayaways*, public protests, and civil disobedience campaigns (CAF 2000; Baskin 1991; Fine and Van Wyk 1996; Bezuidenhout 2000: 6; SAIRR 2000).

4 The first civic associations were formed in the early 1980s mainly as a response against rent increases and discredited white-imposed township councillors (see CAF 2000: 40; Campbell 1997). The larger civic associations included the Soweto Civic Association (1979) and the Black Civic Organisation (1979), followed by the Housing Action Committees in Durban (1980) and Cape Town (1981). See also, Nthambeleni (2003).

5 Many people in South Africa argue that, in fact, 1994 and the first years of democracy signalled a transition to democracy from a civil and political rights point of view. On the contrary, a transition to democracy from an economic, social and cultural point of view, the main indicator of which would be socioeconomic equity, is still an ongoing process and far from being concluded.

6 Due to capacity problems, its vague mandate, and absence of clear programmes the forum became redundant and collapsed in 1995.

7 SANCO rejected the specific offers made by the apartheid party to improve the well-being of the townships' residents, because its leadership acknowledged and internalised the ANC's fears that the National Party could co-opt the civic movement. This would have drifted away SANCO from ANC and its demands for system change (e.g. Lanegran 1995).

8 In an ambitious nationwide WNC public-hearings process which involved hundreds of focus groups, some three million women expressed their aspirations and grievances on their position in South Africa's society. On the basis of these hearings a 12-Article Women's Charter was drafted. This document was officially handed to the new President on 9 August 1994 with a view to determining the final Constitution of South Africa (adopted in 1996).

9 See: Beck, R. 'Women's rights in a new South Africa?', *Sister: Columbia University's Feminist Magazine*, www.columbia.edu/cu/sister/SouthAfrica.html (accessed 11 June 2007).

10 Interviews: Naidoo, J. [Former Executive Director of NEDLAC]. Interview by author. Tape recording, Johannesburg, Gauteng (South Africa)], 11 March 2003; Dexter, P. [Executive Director, National Economic Development and Labour Council (NEDLAC)]. Interview by author. Tape recording, Johannesburg, 26 February 2002; Mbongo, K. [Secretary General, South African Youth Council (SAYC); Convenor of the Development Chamber, NEDLAC]. Interview by author and L. Baccaro. Tape recording, Johannesburg, Gauteng (South Africa), 5 March 2002. Thoko Mkhwanazi-Xaluva [Director, Office of the Rights of the Child, The Presidency], Interview by author. Tape recording, Pretoria, 15 April 2002.

11 Including the constitution, the new Labour Relations Act (LRA), the Sector Education and Training Authorities (SETAS) of the National Employment Skills Act (in the field of employment creation), in local programmes regarding housing and water service development and other public works (e.g. Ntsime 2001), community policing (e.g. Rakgoandi 1995), and pieces of legislation regulating the various aspects of state–civil society relations per se such as the Non-profit Organizations Act No. 71 (1997), or the National Development Agency Act No. 108 (1998), see Swilling and Russell 2001.

12 Chapter Four of the RDP appears to be a more free market-driven analysis and is today often advocated by the government to promote a 'growth and redistribution'

agenda (Interview 17 March 2005): Dor, G. [General Secretary, Jubilee SA, coordinator, Alternative Information and Development Centre]. Interview by author and L. Baccaro. Tape recording, 17 March 2006).

13 For instance, under the heading 'Civil Society', one could read, '5.13.8. Forums such as the National Economic Forum constitute important opportunities for organs of civil society to participate in and influence policy-making' (ANC 1994: 132).

14 Another radical promise of the pre-1994 era was that of legislative reform to permit the representation of trade unions and other civil-society organisations on the Board of Directors of the Reserve Bank (Habib and Padayachee 2000: 251).

15 i.e. NGOs and CBO helping people to meet basic needs, provide essential services, access land, provide education.

16 e.g. Masilela, E., Dr. Todani, K., and Dr. Loewald, C. [Chief Director; Director; Director: Macroeconomic Analysis; Office of the Macro-economic Policy: Ministry of Finance]. Interview by author. Tape recording, Pretoria, Gauteng (South Africa), 11 March 2002.

17 The RDP came to be seen by GEAR proponents as a 'wish list' and electoral manifesto resulting from a problematic perception of the ANC regarding the resources necessary for its implementation.

18 More on the differences among these economic models between, see Swilling 1992.

19 It appears that at least some components of this policy may have been negotiated with the IMF or the World Bank as early as 1992–1994 as part of a 'largely unconditional loan' received by the South African government to address a drought crisis during these transition years (Keys, D. [Minister of Trade and Industry and responsible for economic coordination (1992–1994) and Minister of Finance of the first post-apartheid government]. Interview by author. Tape recording, Sandton, Gauteng (South Africa), 5 April 2002; see also Bond 2000).

20 Interviews: Naidoo, J., op. cit. Van Heerden, N. [Executive Director, South Africa Foundation (SAF)]. Interview by author and L. Baccaro. Tape recording, Johannesburg, Gauteng (South Africa), 7 March 2002; see also Bond 1997.

21 GDP growth should have been double of what had been achieved on average. Employment growth had been negative while it should have been 3 per cent per annum according to plan. The inflation and public deficit figures were lower than planned at the end of the period (2000). GEAR appeared to have fallen short of its targets, which was mainly due to the fact that interest rates were much higher than expected. In turn, this was linked to the need to protect the currency from speculative capital movements and capital flight. This overly restrictive fiscal and monetary policy depressed growth (Interview: Masilela *et al.*, op. cit.; see also Nattrass and Seekings 2001; Friedman 2002).

22 This observation draws on SARB (South African Reserve Bank), available at: www.reservebank.co.za. The phenomenon of 'jobless growth' is often seen as evidence of low employment absorption rates, rather than as the consequence of the economic policy choices as such (concerning this see, Torres *et al.* 2001). Having said that, in general, high rates of unemployment and poverty despite sound economic indicators (growth, inflation etc.), might also indicate that employment is not at the centre of the macroeconomic priorities (e.g. Bhaduri 2005).

23 Interviews: Masilela *et al.*, op. cit.; Naidoo, R., Horten, C., and Jarvis, D. [Director; Programme Coordinator Labour Standards; and Senior Researcher; National Economic and Labour Development Institute (NALEDI)]. Interview by author. Tape recording, Johannesburg, Gauteng (South Africa), 7 March 2002; Roberts, P. [Executive Director, Micro Enterprise Network of NGOs (MENNGOS)]. Telephone Interview by author. Manuscript notes, Pretoria/Cape Town (South Africa), 4 April 2002.

24 Interview: Bhorat, H. [Senior Researcher, University of Cape Town, Development Policy Research Unit (DPRU)]. Interview by author. Tape recording, Cape Town (Western Cape, South Africa), 22 March 2002.

25 Interviews: Mbatha, B. [Marketing Executive, Khula Enterprise Finance Ltd. (Department of Trade and Industry)]. Interview by author. Tape recording, Johannesburg, Gauteng (South Africa), 17 April 2002. Tabrizi, A. and Prof. Mlkandawire, R.M. [Chief Operating Officer; Senior Director Programmes and Research; Umsobomvu Youth Fund: Department of Labour]. Interview by author. Tape recording, Johannesburg (South Africa), 19 April 2002; Silo, P. [Divisional Manager: Co-ordination Division, Ntsika Enterprise Promotion Agency (NEPA)]. Interview by author. Tape recording, Johannesburg, Gauteng (South Africa), 27 March 2002.
26 Interviews: Ditlhake, A. [Executive Director, South African NGO Coalition (SANGOCO)]. Interview by author. Tape recording, Johannesburg, 9 April 2002; Tsele, M. [General Secretary, South Africa Council of Churches (SACC)]. Interview by author. Tape recording, Johannesburg (South Africa), 12 April 2002.
27 Interviews: Bond, P. [Professor of development economics at the University of Witwatersrand; participated in the drafting of the Reconstruction and Development Programme (RDP)]. Interview by author and L. Baccaro. Manuscript notes, Johannesburg, 3 March 2005; Habib, A. [Executive Director, Democracy and Governance, Human Sciences Research Council]. Interview by author, Tswane (Gauteng), 18 March 2005; Ngwane, T. [Secretary General, Soweto Electricity Crisis Committee (SECC)], Interview by author and L. Baccaro. Johannesburg (Gauteng), 15 March 2005; Mbele, T. [Secretary General, Anti-Privatisation Forum (APF)]. Interview by author and L. Baccaro. Tape recording, Johannesburg (Gauteng), 8 March 2005; Mnisi, M. [Chairperson, Landless People Movement (LPM)]. Interview by author. Tape recording, Johannesburg (Gauteng), 16 March 2005. The history of these movements is recent and has been analysed by Buhlungu 2005; Egan and Wafer 2004; Friedman and Mottiar 2004; Greenberg 2004; Oldfield and Stokke 2004.
28 Interview: Coleman, N. [Head of COSATU Parliamentary Office]. Interview by author. Manuscript notes, Cape Town, 25 March 2005.
29 e.g. the Labour Relations Act (LRA), the Basic Conditions of Employment Act (BCEA), or the World Trade Organisation (WTO) negotiations and trade policy positions of South Africa (interview: Dexter, op. cit.). NEDLAC also examined key legislative and policy proposals in the area of employment generation and poverty alleviation, among others, a Labour Job Creation Trust, Expanded Public Works Programmes, and the Draft Bill and Co-operative Development Strategy (NEDLAC 2004: 3; interview: Mkhize, op. cit.).
30 The proposed set of amendments aimed to allow for greater 'flexibility' in working hours, overtime and overtime pay (for more on the flexibility discourse, see Standing *et al.* 1996: 5).
31 Interview: Mbongo, op. cit.
32 Some civil-society participants could not even pay their taxi fares for attending the meetings taking place in NEDLAC, or their telephone bills.
33 Interview: Botha, B. [Adviser, International Affairs, Business South Africa (BSA)]. Interview by author and L. Baccaro. Tape recording, Geveva (Switzerland), 19 June 2002; see also Friedman and Chipkin 2001; Reitzes and Friedman 1996.
34 Interview: Dexter, op. cit.
35 This has been confirmed in our interviews and was illustrated by SANCO's behaviour in the strike, see Papadakis 2006.
36 Buhlungu 2005; Ballard *et al.* 2006; Heller and Ntlokunkulu 2001; interviews: Habib, op. cit.; Ngwane, op. cit.; Mnisi, op. cit.
37 Zuern 2004: 19–20; interviews: Bond, op. cit.; Ngwane, op. cit.; Mayekiso, op. cit.; Mbele, op. cit. The SECC was formed in 2000, initially as a response to the cut-offs of electricity in the East Rand, Vaal and Soweto, subsequent to the privatisation of the distribution network of the national electricity company ESCOM and its decision to adopt a 'cost-recovery' policy. One of its most famous actions has been operation

Khanyisa ('bring the light'), which involved the illegal reconnection of residents' electricity (see Egan and Wafer 2004).
38 Among other things, an agreement reached on the right to strike over retrenchments (Section 189 of the amended LRA) established the right of the workers to strike over the retrenchment of 50 or more employees, which reversed the labour amendment proposal aimed at limiting this right.
39 TAC newsletter, 7 October 2002, emphasis added.
40 *Mother-to-Child Transmission Case*, 2002
41 TAC newsletter, 3 November 2004. According to the Department of Health, by September 2004, only 11,253 patients were put on treatment (see, Progress Report on the Implementation of Comprehensive HIV and AIDS Care, and Management and Treatment Programme, at www.doh.gov.za/docs/reports/2004/hivaids-care/monitorreview. pdf).
42 For instance, TAC's campaign against the pharmaceutical company Pfizer led to the company providing a life-saving opportunistic infection drug, Fluconazole, at no cost to government.
43 See, www.napwa.org.za.
44 'NAPWA hereby takes a position to distance itself from the Treatment Action Campaign and all its activities' (NAPWA 2001).
45 'NAPWA became a perfect and convenient restorer of credibility in the government's continued legitimisation and justification of the Department of Health's outright refusal to provide anti retroviral treatment to millions of people living with HIV and Aids' (Mazibuko 2004).
46 *Mother-to-Child Transmission Case*, 2002: paragraph 82.
47 Interview: Munro (Sister), [AIDS Office Co-Ordinating Secretary, South Africa Catholic Bishop Conference (SACBC); SANAC religious sector]. Interview by author and L. Baccaro. Tape recording, Pretoria (Gauteng), 1 March 2005.
48 Interview: Bundlender, G. [Attorney Advocate of the High Court of South Africa, Member of the Cape Bar, attorney for the TAC and the Grootboom cases]. Interview by author. Tape recording, Cape Town, 23 March 2005.
49 Dryzek (2000) has predicted this risk.

Bibliography

Adler, G. and Webster, E. (1995) 'Challenging transition theory: the labour movement, radical reform, and transition to democracy in South Africa', *Politics and Society*, 23 (1): 75–106.
ANC (African National Congress) (1994) *Reconstruction and Development Programme (RDP)*, Johannesburg: Umanyano Publications.
Baccaro, L. and Papadakis, K. (2004) 'The downside of deliberative public administration', paper presented at the conference on 'Empirical Approaches to Deliberative Politics', European University Institute, Florence, 21–22 May 2004.
Ballard, R., Habib, A., Valodia, I. and Zuern, E. (eds) (2006) *Voices of Protest: Social Movements in Post-Apartheid South Africa*, Pietermaritzburg: UKZN Press.
Baskin, J. (1991) *Striking Back: A History of COSATU*, London: Verso.
Bezuidenhout, A. (2000) 'Towards global social movement unionism? Trade union responses to globalisation in South Africa', Discussion Paper 115, Geneva: International Institute for Labour Studies (IILS).
Bhaduri, A. (2005) 'Macroeconomic policies for higher employment in the era of globalization', Employment Strategy Papers 11, Geneva: International Labour Organisation.
Bond, P. (1997) 'Homegrown structural adjustment: implications for social policy and

social movements', paper presented to the Initiative for Participatory Democracy (unpublished manuscript).

—— (2000) *Cities of Gold, Townships of Coal: Essays on South Africa's New Urban Crisis*, Trenton and Asmara: Africa World Press.

Botha, T. (1992) 'Civic associations as autonomous organs of grassroots' participation', *Theoria*, 79: 57–74.

Buhlungu, S. (2005) *The Anti-Privatisation Forum: A Profile of a Post-Apartheid Social Movement*, Johannesburg: University of the Witwatersrand.

Bundlender, G. (2002) 'A paper dog with real teeth', *Mail and Guardian Newsletters* (Johannesburg), 19 July 2002.

CAF (Charities Aid Foundation) (2000) *Working with the Non-profit Sector in South Africa*, Johannesburg: CAF.

Campbell, H. (1997) 'Challenging the apartheid regime from below: popular strength for democracy in South Africa', *Eastern Africa Social Science Research Review*, 2 (1): 93–128.

CASE (Community Agency of Social Enquiry) and SANGOCO (South African NGO Coalition) (2001) 'Civil society and the state in South Africa: past legacies, present realities, and future prospects', www.case.org.za (accessed October 2001).

Cawthra, H.C., Helman-Smith, A. and Moloi, D. (2001) 'InterFund annual review: the voluntary sector and development in South Africa 1999/2000', *Development Update*, 3 (3): 87–114.

Centre on Housing Rights and Evictions (2005) *Any Room for the Poor? Forced Evictions in Johannesburg* (draft for discussion), Johannesburg: Centre on Housing Rights and Evictions, 17 February 2005, www.cohre.org/store/attachments/COHRE%20Johannesburg%20FFM_high%20res.pdf (accessed June 2007).

COSATU (Congress of South African Trade Unions) (1999) *6th National Congress Declaration*, http:/www.cosatu.org.za (accessed October 2006).

Department of Health (2003) *Operational Plan for Comprehensive HIV and AIDS Care, Management and Treatment for South Africa*, 19 November 2003, www.gov.za/issues/hiv/careplan19nov03.htm (accessed 11 June 2007).

—— (2004) *Monitoring Review. Progress Report on the Implementation of the Comprehensive HIV and AIDS Care, Management and Treatment Programme*, Issue 1 (September 2004), www.doh.gov.za/docs/reports/2004/hivaids-care/monitorreview.pdf (accessed October 2007).

Dewar, N. (1985) 'Municipal government under the new South African Constitution: who gets what, where, who decides?', *Social Dynamics*, 11 (2): 37–48.

Dryzek, J.S. (2000) *Deliberative Democracy and Beyond: Liberals, Critics, Contestations*, Oxford: Oxford University Press.

Egan, A. and Wafer, A. (2004) 'The Soweto Electricity Crisis Committee', A case study for the UKZN project entitled: Globalisation, Marginalisation and New Social Movements in post-Apartheid South Africa: 1–26, www.ukzn.ac.za/ccs/files/Egan%20Wafer%20SECC%20Research%20Report%20Short.pdf (accessed October 2007).

Fine, R. and Van Wyk, G. (1996) 'South Africa: state, labour, and the politics of reconstruction', *Capital and Class*, 58 (Spring): 19–31.

Friedman, S. (2002) *Equity in the Age of Informality: Labour Markets and Redistributive Politics in South Africa*, Johannesburg: Centre for Policy Studies.

Friedman, S. and Chipkin, I. (2001) *A Poor Voice?: The Politics of Inequality in South Africa*, Johannesburg: Centre for Policy Studies.

Friedman, S. and Mottiar, S. (2004) 'A moral to the tale: the treatment action campaign and the politics of HIV/AIDS', Research Report 27, Johannesburg: Centre for Civil Society: 1–32, www.nu.ac.za/ccs/files/Friedman%20Mottier%20TAC%20Research%20Report%20Short.pdf.

Gersharter, D. (2001) 'Sisterhood of a sort: the Women's National Coalition and the role of gender identity in South African civil society', Research Report 82, Johannesburg: Centre for Policy Studies.

Greenberg, S. (2004) 'The landless people's movement and the failure of postapartheid land reform', Research Report 26, Johannesburg: Centre for Civil Society, 1–40.

Habib, A. and Padayachee, V. (2000) 'Economic policy and power relations in South Africa's transition to democracy', *World Development*, 28 (2): 245–262.

Hassim, S. (2000) 'South Africa: a strategic ascent – women's rights', *UNESCO Courier*, 56 (6).

Hearn, J. (1999) 'Foreign aid, democratisation and civil society in Africa: a study of South Africa, Ghana and Uganda', IDS Discussion Paper 368, Johannesburg: Institute for Development Studies, 1–28.

Heller, P. and Ntlokunkulu, L. (2001) *A Civic Movement or a Movement of Civics: The South African National Civic Organisation in the Post-apartheid Period*, Johannesburg: Centre for Policy Studies.

Landsberg, C. (2000) 'Voicing the voiceless: foreign political aid to civil society in South Africa', in M. Ottaway and T. Carothers (eds) *Funding Virtue: Civil Society Aid and Democracy Promotion*, Washington, DC: Carnegie Endowment for International Peace: 105–131.

Lanegran, K. (1995) 'South Africa's civic association movement: ANC's ally or society's "watchdog"? Shifting social movement–political party relations', *African Studies Review*, 38 (2): 101–127.

Marais, H. (1998) *South Africa Limits to Change. The Political Economy of Transition*, London and New York: Zed Books Ltd, Cape Town: University of Cape Town Press.

Mattes, R. and Thiel, H. (1998) 'Consolidation and public opinion in South Africa', *Journal of Democracy*, 9 (1): 95–110.

Mazibuko, L. (2004) 'Scandalous shenanigans', *The Sowetan*, 12 October 2004.

Mbali, M. (2005) 'The treatment action campaign and the history of rights based patient-driven HIV/Aids activism in South Africa', Research Report 29, Johannesburg: Centre for Civil Society, 1–23.

Mother-to-Child Transmission Case (MTC) (2002) Constitutional Court of South Africa: TAC vs. Ministers of Health, Case CCT 8/02, 5 July 2002, www.concourt.gov.za/judgments/2002/tac.pdf (accessed October 2005).

NAPWA (National Association of People Living with AIDS) (2001) *Resolution of the First NAPWA National Congress*, 25–27 May 2001, www.napwa.org.za (accessed November 2005).

National Department of Housing (2000) 'The Housing Code. Part 1. Chapter 2: overall approach to housing in South Africa', www.housing.gov.za/content/housing_code/part1/chapter2.htm (accessed October 2005).

Nattrass, N. and Seekings, J. (2001) 'Democracy and distribution in highly unequal economies: the case of South Africa', *Journal of Modern African Studies*, 39 (3): 471–498.

NEDLAC (National Economic Development and Labour Council) (2004) *Dialogue: the NEDLAC Newsletter*, 8 (2).

Nthambeleni, B. (2003) 'Coordinating civil society: a case study of the South African

National Civic Organisations (SANCO) and the National Association of Residents and Civic Organisations (NARCO)', paper presented at the South African Sociological Association Congress, University of Natal, Durban, 29 June–2 July 2003.

Ntsime, M. (2001) 'Partnership with civil society in the community based public works programme, *Development Update*, 3 (4): 113–126.

Oldfield, S. and Stokke, K. (2004) 'Building unity in diversity: social movement activism in the Western Cape Anti-Eviction Campaign', A case study for the UKZN project entitled: Globalisation, Marginalisation and New Social Movements in post-Apartheid South Africa: 1–35.

Papadakis, K. (2006) 'Civil society, participatory governance and decent work objectives: the case of South Africa', Research Series 112, Geneva: International Institute for Labour Studies (IILS)/International Labour Organisation.

Pieterse, E. (1997) 'South African NGOs and the trials of transition', *Development in Practice*, 7 (2): 157–166.

Rakgoandi, P.S. (1995) 'Community policing and governance', Occasional Paper, Centre for the Study of Violence and Reconciliation, July 1995: 1–8.

Reitzes, M. and Friedman, S. (1996) 'Democratisation or bureaucratisation?: Civil society, the public sphere and the state in post-apartheid South Africa', *Transformation*, 29: 55–73.

SAIRR (South African Institute for Race Relations) (2000) *South Africa Survey 1999/2000*, Johannesburg: SAIRR.

Seekings, J. (1992) 'Civic Organisations in South African townships', *South African Review*, 6: 216–238.

—— (1997) 'SANCO: strategic dilemmas in a democratic South Africa', *Transformation*, 34: 1–30.

South African National Civic Organisation (SANCO) and the National Association of Residents and Civic Organisations (NARCO), Paper presented at the South African Sociological Association Congress, University of Natal, Durban, 29 June–2 July 2003.

South African Reserve Bank (SARB) www.reservebank.co.za (accessed October 2007).

Standing, G., Sender, J. and Weeks, J. (1996) 'Restructuring the labour market: the South African challenge', *An ILO Country Review*, Geneva: ILO.

Swilling, M. (1992) 'Socialism, democracy, and civil society. The case of associational socialism', *Theoria*, 79: 72–82.

Swilling, M. and Russell, B. (2001) 'The South African non-profit sector', (unpublished manuscript) Stellenbosch: Spier Institute, and Johannesburg: Social Surveys (Pty) Ltd.

Torres, R., Hayter, S. and Reinecke, G. (2001) *Studies on the Social Dimensions of Globalization: South Africa*, Geneva: ILO.

Treatment Action Campaign (TAC) (2003) www.tac.org.za/Documents/Other/Mbeki-on-HIVAids-October2003.doc (accessed October 2007).

Treatment Action Campaign (TAC) (2002–2004), various Newsletters, http//:www.tac.org.za (accessed 11 June 2007).

Webster, E. (1996) 'COSATU: old alliances, new strategies', *Southern Africa Report*, 11 (3): 3–8.

Zuern, E. (2004) 'Continuity in contradiction? The prospects for a national civic movement in a democratic state: SANCO and the ANC in post-Apartheid South Africa', Contribution to the project on Globalisation, Marginalisation and New Social Movements in Post-Apartheid South Africa, Durban: University of KwaZulu Natal, September 2004.

Part III

Civil society and governance

Theoretical appraisals

11 Assessing the claims of 'post-parliamentary' governance

Few certainties, much more open questions[1]

Yannis Papadopoulos

Civil-society involvement in policy-making: the expected benefits

The prevailing positive image of civil society today is significantly linked to its beneficial contribution to better policy-making. Along with governmental and administrative units, all sorts of civil-society actors are associated to the formulation or the implementation of collectively binding decisions. Steering through cooperative governance mechanisms involving civil-society agents is praised for its positive effects in terms of policy efficiency and acceptance by target-groups. With cooperative governance, the classic distinction between state and civil society is blurred. Instead of authoritative decision-making, consensual will-formation brought about by common deliberation takes the lead.

This policy style is considered desirable on both functional and normative grounds. It seems to be best suited to deal with problem complexity and social differentiation. As summarised by Fung (2005: 401): 'Fundamentally, deliberative democrats favour governance arrangements in which political decisions are decided according to the exchange of reasons and arguments (broadly conceived and defined) that appeal to shared objectives (e.g. economic growth) or values (e.g. individual liberty or fairness)'. Decisions resulting from deliberation will be more legitimate, because they are supposed to be more informed and rational, to reflect a more equal consideration of interests, and they are less likely to infringe on individual rights. Moreover, deliberation is considered to broaden the interests and perspectives of participants, and the self-reflection induced by public deliberation or the participation that it can require are expected to deepen individual autonomy.

The role of civil society is closely related to the idea of deliberative political decision-making and holds the promise of democracy based on deliberation. It is widely argued that deliberation involving public and non-public actors helps to cope better with problem complexity because it allows to ground decisions on more accurate knowledge. The contribution of civil society quite evidently has the objective of improving output legitimacy. Being a remedy to technical uncertainty, it is expected that taking a wide range of participants will contribute to competent policy-making and is in that respect a necessary ingredient for the *technical* improvement of policy outputs.[2]

Using deliberation between stakeholders, experts and political actors helps to improve the understanding of problems and of alternative solutions, and thus reduces the bounded rationality of individual actors. It also helps to become aware of possible contradictions between objectives one would like to achieve, and thus to clarify the reasons for one's preferences and to order them better (Fearon 1998: 49–52; Manin 1985: 82–84). The belief that actors have learning capacities and are in addition willing to engage into learning processes is central for proponents of deliberative decisional formulas. Not only is deliberation expected to clarify one's preferences but to help acquire information on others' preferences too, and in addition to take account of others' needs and interests (Benhabib 1996: 71–72; Cohen and Rogers 1995: 256; Hunold and Young 1998: 87). Deliberation should also enhance mutual respect, recognition and empathy, and is seen as the appropriate antidote to group selfishness and to social fragmentation. It is a component of contemporary 'management of interdependence' (Mayntz 1997: 272), as it is expected to contribute to less controversial decisions: 'one of the main tasks of deliberation could be to uncover existing normative meta-consensus obscured by the strategic actions of partisans who try to delegitimate the values held by their opponents' (Dryzek and Niemeyer 2006: 639). Therefore, deliberation is considered as a necessary ingredient for the *political* feasibility of policy measures, too.[3]

Hence, engaging civil society into more horizontal policy-making is not so much the outcome of a voluntaristic attempt to democratise decision-making, but rather a piecemeal strategy that primarily results from the pragmatic and instrumental concerns of policy-makers (Bevir 2006). 'Good governance' and 'the deliberative imperative' have become central ingredients of what is advertised as an adequate policy-making style involving civil society in collective deliberation (Blondiaux and Sintomer 2002). The wider involvement of civil society has been a key issue in the White Paper on European Governance (European Commission 2001).

However, does deliberative policy-making in governance networks involving a variety of actors match this idealised, and after all strongly ideological, view? As a matter of fact, one may think that we live in an era where politics is merely about 'problem solving' and not about dealing with conflicts between antagonistic interests, and it is even believed that such conflicts can be managed in a problem-solving spirit (witnessed by practitioners' manuals on mediation procedures, alternative dispute resolution etc.).

Therefore, in order to gain a more balanced view on the potential benefits of civil society, we have to discuss the limits of this type of policy-making, some problems that it can generate, and point out some crucial questions that still remain unanswered about its prerequisites, its operation and its effects. For that purpose it is necessary to link the literature on governance arrangements and on participatory decisional devices to the literature on 'deliberative democracy', which provides criteria enabling us to assess to what extent deliberation fulfils its promises (inclusiveness, quality of discursive interactions, contribution to consensus, etc.). There have indeed been but few exchanges between these two research traditions in spite of some significant overlapping in the issues they deal with. Concerns with issues related to deliberation are more apparent in studies of institutions and practices aspiring to 'deepen the ways in which ordinary people can effectively participate in and influence policies that directly affect their lives' (Fung and Wright 2001: 7).[4]

It is worthwhile to put the myth of civil society under scrutiny, therefore this chapter first discusses the effects of contextual factors on collective deliberation. It points out thereafter a number of problems related to the democratic quality of cooperative policy-making involving civil-society actors and concludes with some suggestions for further empirical research. It should be seen as a plea for more knowledge on forms of policy-making that include civil-society actors, instead of their idealisation that is often found in official discourses.

Ambivalent effects of policy issues, institutions and publicity on collective deliberation

It has been asserted that the nature of policy issues, institutional factors or publicity can positively or negatively affect the deliberative component of policy-making. Let us have a closer look at how each of these parameters is expected to exert its effects.

Issue types

Majone (1994) distinguishes between redistributive and 'efficiency' policies. Redistributive policies operate through the extraction of resources from some segments of the population to re-allocate them to other segments. For such policies, Majone argues, it is illusory to believe that actors will not behave in utilitarian terms, and redistributive conflicts cannot be solved merely through deliberative problem-solving, but rather at best through bargaining or at worst through formal voting procedures (majority rule). One may add to this that policy choices which are a matter of contention because of normative disagreement on ethical values (on the suitability of abortion, euthanasia, genetic engineering etc.) cannot even be made on the basis of bargaining because they have to do with the intractable 'deep core' of individual beliefs. Efficiency policies, by contrast, do not imply a zero-sum game. Rather, they aim to provide solutions that improve the well-being of the whole community, in congruence with the principle of Pareto optimality (e.g. improving public infrastructure in terms of health care, or transportation). Actors will, according to the author, find it much easier to reach an agreement on such policies, and they will be more likely to engage into problem-solving reflections and into mutual deliberation for that purpose. In such a view it is the content of public programmes that determines actors' behaviour.[5]

One should however qualify Majone's essentialist view on an alleged inherent nature of public programmes. The properties of these programmes are defined by the actors who take part in policy debates, and there may be disagreement on them. For instance, actors may tend to render credible the belief that apparently Pareto optimal policies entail costs too (e.g. improving public transportation requires measures inimical to private car owners). Deliberation is here important because it can help to *reframe* issues ('relabeling', 'Umetiket-tierung': Heinelt 2003: 242–243), but only under the condition that actors' preferences are commensurable, i.e. that they can be converted and transposed on a single continuum. In other words, different preferences must be framed in a common language. Redistributive issues (zero-sum game) for instance can be reframed through persuasion processes in terms of a cooperative game: if actors can be persuaded that they are all 'in the same boat', that short-term concessions can be offset by long-term benefits etc. On the one hand, Majone's argument that efficiency policies are propitious for deliberation is thus weakened. On the other hand, however, the argument on the role of deliberation is strengthened: this time as an independent variable, deliberation can lead to a restriction of the universe of redistributive policies, considered by Majone as inimical to problem-solving oriented reflection.

Institutional contexts

B. Jobert (1998: 133–137) distinguishes between the 'forum' and the 'arena' as different loci of policy-making, where actors are animated by different motivations and follow diverse logics of action. In a 'forum', where as a rule bureaucrats and experts are the central actors, reflection and problem-solving guide action and considerations about the technical feasibility of policy measures prevail. In 'arenas', where politicians and perhaps also interest representatives are the main actors, it is strategic action and considerations of political feasibility that prevail. As a result, one can expect deliberation to be more prevalent in 'forums' than in 'arenas'.

This distinction certainly makes sense on the conceptual level and echoes the more generic distinction made by Elster (1997) between forums and markets (with 'epistemic communities' of policy experts being typical of the 'forum' while electoral competition between parties would obey to a market logic). It should nevertheless be refined. Bureaucrats, for instance, pursue their own strategic objectives (e.g. extending their 'territory' or increasing their budget),[6] and major decisions have been analysed as the outcome of bureaucratic competition (Allison 1971). On the other hand, typical 'arenas' such as parliaments can also be open to deliberation, especially when parliamentarians have not fixed preferences, or deal with highly technical issues implying policy choices, the outcomes of which are not easily predictable. Besides empirical research on issues as different as international negotiations, environmental mediation or cultural policy, indicates that bargaining and deliberation may cohabit within the same institution (Gehring 1996; Holzinger 2001; Urfalino 2000). It would, however, be interesting to compare if governance networks including civil-society actors and experts are indeed more 'deliberative' than official representative institutions, because this is part of their normative justification. It is often argued that governance networks are more reflective and more oriented towards the common good because a cooperative logic mitigates the competitive logic therein. What is more, it is also argued that this can offset their defects, such as lack of transparency or selectivity (see Papadopoulos 2003).

Publicity

If institutional design can create more or less favourable conditions to deliberation, the same applies to the role of the public space in governance arrangements. The degree of openness to the public may of course be part of deliberate institutional design, and usually deliberation in governance arrangements occurs behind closed doors. But one should also consider the influence of implicit audiences on participants, i.e. the audiences participants have in mind.

Furthermore, there is some controversy on the effects of publicity (Chambers 2004). On the one hand, it is believed that it has 'civilising' effects. Even for self-interested actors it would be rational to engage into deliberative behaviour under conditions of publicity, because for reasons of self-presentation they will hardly dare advance purely selfish arguments or appear reluctant to learning from others. Risking under public scrutiny prohibitive costs in terms of reputation ('naming and shaming') for egoistic or dogmatic behaviour, actors will hesitate to make pledges that they will not be able to hold, or will find it inappropriate to make threats if they are not satisfied. In sum, publicity would favour a 'logic of appropriateness' where moral considerations are given serious consideration instead of a pure selfish or even cynical 'logic of consequentiality' (March and Olsen 1989). Studies of trust-building stress the virtuous effects on actors' behaviour of 'the moral categories of guilt and shame', no matter if they exert their impact deeply in individuals' psychology or merely at the rhetoric level (Brennan 1998: 216). The 'civilising force of hypocrisy' (Elster 1998: 12) or, rather, the civilising force of the obligation to provide reasons for one's preferences that must be acceptable to the audience (no matter whether actors truly believe in them or not) is considered as an important aspect of deliberative practice, and publicity contributes to this civilising force. Research on the local implementation of policies in France showed, for instance, that opponents who are likely to be discredited in public as 'NIMBYists' (privileging their narrow local interests over the common good) respond by justifying their opposition with more general arguments about procedural problems, the public interest, environmental protection, beauty of the landscape etc. (L. Jobert 1998; Trom 1999).

On the other hand we can expect publicity to have negative effects both on bargaining and on deliberation. This is a justification for committees and similar instances to operate with discretion. Goodin (2006: 241–242), for instance, suggests that it might be wiser to keep radically divisive issues off the political agenda. 'Mobilisation of bias' in order to avoid public discussion is usually perceived as a strategy of the powerful in order to preserve the power balance in favour of the status quo. But it may also well be that the non-thematisation of some issues publicly may help to prevent political life from drifting into a mere power game. If actors are, for instance, 'tightly coupled' (Benz 2000: 113) to their constituencies or reference groups, or if they are closely scrutinised by the media, they may be more reluctant to make compromises (without changing their preferences: bargaining logic), or to demonstrate their willingness to consider some of their adversaries' claims as legitimate (empathy: deliberative logic). For fear of losing face – because they are 'traitors' or 'chicken' – actors may tend to be more prone to demagogic behaviour under conditions of publicity. In our study of transformations of the role of neo-corporatist arrangements in Swiss social policy for instance, most actors (mainly representatives of business and labour union representatives) that we interviewed told us that increased scrutiny by the media (the growth of media coverage was confirmed by quantitative data) rendered mutual concessions more difficult than in the past (Haeusermann *et al.* 2004). In order to address the impact of publicity on actors' behaviour, we also need to know how actors perceive their public(s), which audience (including implicit audiences) is considered by them to be most important, how actors perceive the preferences and the norms of their audiences, and what kind of constraints they consider that audiences pose. We have very little information on these questions.

More generally, governance bodies do not operate in a vacuum. Hence, the influence of contextual conditions on actors' propensity to engage in a deliberative dialogue must be taken into account, too. In particular power relations are a serious limit to the disciplining power of deliberation. Works on deliberation tend to underrate the 'agonistic' (Benhabib 1996: 14) dimension of politics and policy-making. For example, Eder (1995: 19) estimates that the 'exit' option is not easily acceptable by peers in deliberative institutions, yet when representatives of environmental NGOs heard that the Swiss federal government decided to enhance the power of a nuclear plant, they chose to protest by not participating any longer in a mediation forum, the task of which was to facilitate the choice of sites for nuclear waste (Wälti 1995). One can no doubt rely on experiments in social psychology showing that agreement is easier within groups when no third party is involved as an arbiter (Kelman 1992), but in policy-making the political authorities (be they subnational, national or supranational) still play that role, and actors in policy networks operate for their part under the 'shadow of the hierarchy'. Nevertheless, the degree of insulation of cooperative governance bodies vis-à-vis their environment is an empirical question (on constitutional assemblies see Elster 1998a). One needs then to know how participants perceive the resources available to them and the constraints that restrict their options, and how they consider that such constraints and resources influence their own propensity to comply with the conditions of deliberation (moderation, openness to dialogue, empathy etc.). In Swiss energy policy again, promoters of nuclear energy and environmentalists repeatedly attempted to discredit each other's arguments in forums for mediation and to make the authorities side with them (Enderlin Cavigelli 1995: 9–10). Their spirit of conciliation used to fluctuate according to their anticipations of decisions on appeals to the federal court being positive or negative (Wälti 2001). 'Playing' in deliberative forums and counting at the same time on hierarchical intervention is thus a typical mode of 'forum shopping' by collective actors, a mode that can however erode reciprocal trust (Fung and Wright 2001: 34–35). True, less ambitious advocates of deliberation concede that it may be difficult to achieve consensus through deliberative procedures, and argue that it nevertheless allows a narrowing of value differences between the participants ('cultural accommodation': Levine *et al.* 2005: 283–284). This is no doubt useful for 'educative' experiments aiming to form 'better citizens', but less so when the goal is to enhance the legitimacy of collectively binding decisions.

Problems of pluralism and inclusiveness, representation and accountability in cooperative policy-making

It is argued that delegation of policy-making to governance bodies relies primarily on the achievement of a so-called 'output' legitimacy. The latter however is in practice insufficient and fragile because there is no necessary consensus on the outputs to be produced (Thatcher and Stone Sweet 2001: 4), and because outputs are usually accompanied by distributive effects that generate winners and losers (Jabko 2001: 929). Therefore governance bodies should also enjoy 'throughput' (procedural) legitimacy. This requires that cooperative procedures be considered as fair, which implies in turn that they should be broadly pluralist and that they should not be plagued by inequalities. Moreover, their participants should be considered as representative and accountable by their reference groups.

Pluralism and inclusiveness

First, resources should be evenly distributed among participants in cooperative procedures, so that they have equal opportunities to make credible proposals and criticise others' arguments, with communication not being flawed by domination or threats. This should in principle be more or less true for governance networks given that what gathers actors together is their interdependence. Nevertheless, it is doubtful whether actors have equal opportunities to elaborate strong arguments and to have them considered as such by their audience, too.

The capacity to present convincing arguments is unevenly distributed to the prejudice of socially disadvantaged groups (Bourdieu 1991; Sanders 1997: 349; Young 2000: 37–40). One could object that governance networks are composed of public and non-public elites (top bureaucrats, leaderships of associations and experts) that enjoy roughly similar status positions. Thus there should not be any major *internal* inequality problem between actors able to deliberate, and those who are not. However, this remains to be empirically substantiated: research on Swiss 'pre-parliamentary' committees (Germann and Frutiger 1985) showed, for instance, that organisations with fewer resources, such as trade unions, only had a limited number of 'experts' to delegate in these committees. Hence, the same persons had to represent labour interests in several committees, and could not be adequately informed on the many issues featuring on the committee agendas.

In addition, there might be a problem of *external* selectivity: inclusiveness is a necessary attribute of democratic deliberation (Young 1996), yet governance networks and deliberative forums can be exclusive for several reasons. Defining whose claims are legitimate, or who can be considered as a credible 'stakeholder' and should deserve recognition as such, remains controversial. One may also suspect that those having achieved participation in deliberative forums and have increased their influence will thus erect barriers against the participation of newcomers (with much resemblance to the exclusionary logic of the formation of minimum-winning coalitions).[7] Even without adhering to this perhaps overly cynical view, the transaction costs for bargaining and for consensus-building increase with the number of actors having a say, and institutional designers simply must take into account that this complicates the policy-making process. Fishkin (1991) for instance postulates a trade-off between democracy and deliberation, for the latter is only possible in narrow circles of participants.

Further, the deliberative discourse obeys specific rules: rationality, moderation etc. Even if elites or activists have the necessary cultural capital to comply with them, they do not necessarily all *wish* to. Not every group would agree to behave 'responsibly' in deliberative bodies (Fung and Wright 2001: 34). First, a high degree of self-confidence with respect to the distribution of power resources may cause reluctance to behave in a cooperative manner. Deliberation implies a willingness to learn, but as K.W. Deutsch (1963: 11) elegantly puts it, power is 'the ability to talk instead of listen, the ability to afford not to learn'. The question of the (dis)incentives available to those advantaged by the status quo for engaging into deliberative exchange and for putting issues on the deliberative agenda (Ferejohn 2000: 80 and 84) is eluded by most advocates of participatory governance.[8] Despite acknowledging the agonistic dimension of politics, Young (2000: 116), for instance, maintains that more powerful groups have to contextualise their parochial perspectives when they must answer to other less privileged groups; the question however is if they really *have* to engage into such a dialogue.[9] And this is particularly tricky as the integration of actors with a high blackmailing power is necessary to prevent them from adopting non-cooperative behaviour, or from deserting cooperative procedures (rendering them thereby toothless).

As a matter of fact, willingness to learn requires a particular motivational context: uncertainty on preferences, mutual trust, a problem-solving atmosphere etc. (see Checkel 2005: 10). The sharing of common norms can then be a (difficult to achieve) prerequisite for deliberation, rather than a product of it (Mansbridge 1983: 33–34). Some empirical evidence on deliberative institutions during the implementation phase of policies with spatial impacts in Switzerland shows that for such institutions to perform as expected, actors have to demonstrate from the outset their willingness for conflict-resolution, mutual trust is a condition, value disagreements must not be too sharp, and the research confirms that actors must be endowed with relatively equal resources (Wälti 1993: 218).

Deliberation within these institutions is by no means a sufficient condition. One could even go so far as to argue that 'if discussion can effectively reveal private information about people's preferences over policy outcomes, then there is no reason why in particular cases it might not reveal that the extent of conflict is greater than previously believed' (Fearon 1998: 57; see also Ferejohn 2000: 85). Research on the dynamics of deliberation should indeed consider findings such as those of the Palo Alto school (Watzlawick *et al.* 1967), which showed that interaction can decrease but also increase the level of discursive conflict.

Selectivity through the normalising pressures of deliberation can also be seen as an impediment to the representation of *dominated* interests, or at least to an efficient representation that would not lead to a deradicalisation of their claims (Sanders 1997). This is an empirical question too: policy research, for instance, differentiates between, on the one hand, sectors dominated by 'policy communities' and others with looser, more flexible 'issue networks'. The former are composed of a small number of actors sharing similar values and raising obstacles to challengers, while the latter are composed of more numerous and ideologically diverse actors, besides being more open to change and to newcomers. There are first structural barriers to interest associability and representation: broad interests may find it harder to organise themselves than narrow interests (Olson 1965). Moreover, the search for consensus has been criticised (Smith and Wales 2000: 63; Young 2000: 43–44) as an impediment to critical dialogue, and as a result of strategic action and of symbolic manipulation by powerful interests. The social construction of 'moderates' and 'extremes' for instance is a discursive strategy that is part of the symbolic struggles accompanying policy-making (Young 2000: 47). Those stigmatised as extremists are likely to be excluded from cooperative governance. Studying for instance the restructuring of the Canadian welfare regime, Jenson and Phillips (2001: 85–86) pointed to crucial problems raised by 'partnerships', such as alteration of the nature of some third-sector organisations and creation of hierarchies between groups. Those focused on service delivery were placed at the top while those focused on advocacy and social change were considered irrelevant. Such findings tend to show that deliberative policy-making can reshape the power relations within civil society, and not necessarily in a more egalitarian way.

Even under the assumption that deliberation leads to a narrowing of differences among participants' conflicting views, an overall loss of pluralism can be the negative side of cooperative policy-making, and it is not at all certain that such a loss would be offset by managerial-type benefits (conflict resolution). It is likely that 'mutual socialization into a community with common problem definitions and collectively shared approaches to dealing with them' (Jörges and Neyer 1997: 619) will not only be associated with high deliberative quality, but also with 'group-think' that is unfavourable to learning.[10] As a remedy to standardisation, Sanders (1997) proposes to enfranchise voices which are likely to bring out critical 'testimonies' and, according to Sanders, this should be a major goal of democratic reform (see also Young 1996). How cooperative bodies could continue to function after having introduced this kind of narrative repertoire is however debatable. Although it must be acknowledged that the risk of pressure for conformity exists – e.g. in the preference for civility and for 'polite, orderly, dispassionate, gentlemanly' argument (Young 2000: 49) that restricts the discursive repertoire of actors – the necessity to manage and not only to acknowledge plurality is inescapable. Once one has told 'one's own story' (Sanders 1997: 373) the question of how to operate the synthesis between them remains open (see, however, the attempt by Dryzek and Niemeyer 2006). The relationship between the degree of pluralism of cooperative bodies and their contribution to governability should be further explored: is there any 'requisite variety' of social and ideological pluralism that provides legitimacy without undermining governability?

Representation and accountability

It may be argued that inclusiveness can be limited to accountable representatives of a broad spectrum of interests. In addition, one may consider that the role of representatives in general cannot merely be that of reference group 'spokesmen' (as it was criticised by Edmund Burke): representatives should be 'trustees' and not mere 'delegates', to use H. Pitkin's (1967) distinction. The modern conception of representation rules out the imperative mandate in order to allow for 'brainstorming' (Elster 1998) that cannot occur with the Damoclean sword of revocation hanging permanently over delegates. And there is no reason why such a view of representation, although usually applied to parliamentary bodies, would not be valid for group representation in governance networks, too (Mayntz 1999). Another argument supporting this view is that the conception of representatives having to reproduce a 'microcosm' of their environment is illusory in spite of its attractiveness for populist theories of democracy, because the reference groups themselves to which representatives are attached are becoming increasingly heterogeneous (Young 2000: 121ff.; Goodin 2004: 459–461).

Nevertheless, the literature on deliberative forms of governance hardly deals with problems of delegation likely to arise between reference groups and their representatives, and resulting from informational asymmetry, goal displacement etc. It fails to consider that actors in governance networks frequently act as representatives of collective interests and organisations (Schmitter 2005: 431–432). It is useful to recall here research on neo-corporatism that highlights the presence of tensions between the 'logic of influence' prevailing among organisational leaderships and the membership logic (Schmitter and Streeck 1999). Would it be unreasonable, for instance, to hypothesise that network governance in general might fit the pattern of French 'partnerships', which are considered by specialists as the domain of 'established spokespersons of elusive populations' (Gaudin 1995: 92, our translation from French).

Such problems should make us pay particular attention to the accountability issues related to the proliferation of cooperative policy-making mechanisms. Accountability can become problematic, both 'internally' (with respect to the constituencies and reference groups of governance actors) and 'externally' (with respect to policy-takers) (Koenig-Archibugi 2004: 236–237). Mechanisms rendering elites' interactions visible (transparency) are crucial for the accountability of governance processes. They foster deliberation between the power holders *and* the governed, for they oblige the former to give reasons and to provide plausible justifications for their policy choices to the latter. Further, the capacity to hold power-holders accountable should induce the governed to deliberate *among them* too, in order to decide whether power-holders behave or not in a responsive way. In order to ensure accountability, publicity is required: 'the reasons that officials and citizens give to justify political actions, and the information necessary to assess those reasons, should be public' (Gutmann and Thompson 1996: 95). We know, however, that governance networks seldom operate under public scrutiny. It is often argued that this is so because of the imperatives of governability, and interestingly this is related to the fact that publicity can cause prejudice to the quality of deliberation. Not only can publicity favour ideological rigidity as noted before (having similar drawbacks to the imperative mandate), but it can also induce opportunistic behaviour, becoming thus an obstacle to frankness (Gargarella 2000: 200), which is a necessary condition for good-quality deliberation. More generally, too 'tight' a coupling between network members and the constituencies to which they are accountable restricts their deliberative potential, but if such a coupling is too 'loose' this may cause accountability problems. This trade-off should be seriously analysed.

Research on governance might also take inspiration from findings on non-majoritarian institutions, which show that the degree of democratic accountability of independent bodies differs in practice. Similar questions can be raised about governance arrangements: to what extent are authorised bodies such as parliaments able to have an effective oversight over the operations of cooperative governance bodies, constraining them to deliberate under the threat that their decisions will be overruled, and hence forcing them to anticipate their objections ('nested games')? The idea of a 'post-parliamentary governance' (Andersen and Burns 1996) – where parliaments no longer play an influential role in policy-making – should at least be treated as a valuable hypothesis, especially if we consider that the role of democratically elected bodies is weaker at the EU level, and absent in transnational governance (Benz and Papadopoulos 2006). It may, for instance, make a difference if cooperative governance mechanisms are established in the process of law-making (formulating the principles, norms and rules of a policy), or in the process of implementation (taking policy decisions on how to interpret and put into operation what is in the law). In the first case it is more likely that the preferences of elected politicians will be taken into account, because they are the target-group to be convinced. In the second case however it is mainly segments from the administration (many times at the local or regional level) that cooperate and deliberate with civil-society actors, and this happens in remoteness from the politicians that first took the decisions (as we are taught by implementation research).

Finally, even if organisational pluralism is safeguarded, this is not tantamount to democracy. The overall ideal 'frame' of cooperative governance privileges interest and value pluralism over genuinely democratic policy-making. 'Stake-holders' and 'advocacy groups' are co-opted because of the intense preferences they manifest on policy issues, but they are not the citizenry. 'Governance *with some of* the people' writes V. Schmidt (2006: 28–29) cannot make up for 'the lack of government *by* and *of* the people' (emphasis in the original). And one may doubt whether the public at large ('public opinion') – if informed – would value the role of governance networks, especially as deliberation conceived as an integral part of decision-making remains a pure abstraction for most citizens (Hermet 2001: 16).

Acceptance of binding decisions is indeed easier if the costs entailed are after all not unbearable (if issues are not crucial, or if winners and losers are not sepa-rated by abyssal programmatic differences), especially whenever rotation to power can be seen as a realistic prospective, so that majority decisions can be reasonably considered reversible. But it rests on the belief, too, that whatever the costs some decisions may entail for us, they are taken under conditions we con-sider fair. And under the prevalent democratic ideology, the fairness (procedural legitimacy) of deliberative procedures is associated to their openness to actors claiming to be affected by decisions (the 'congruence' principle). We should not then take for granted that the governed would acquiesce – if they become aware of the problem – to decisions largely made in non-transparent procedures that do not correspond to their image of what is legitimate policy-making. Even if some form of unconstrained and reasoned agreement among equals could be achieved within governance networks, in conformity with the requirements of delibera-tion, it may be an agreement that does not provide much more than limited self-referential legitimacy by 'insiders'. This raises not only normative problems of legitimacy, but practical problems of governability, too.

Some prospects for research

In this chapter I sought to point out some problems, limits and open questions related to cooperative governance, which is central in all but the neo-conservative model of civil society.

Cooperative governance is usually considered as 'virtuous' per se, or (less frequently) criticised for masking conflict and domination. I suggested that we need to know more about the perceptions of governance settings by actors involved in them (rather than by theorists or by external observers), because these perceptions guide actors' behaviour in a more or less 'cooperative' fashion. To give an example of the kind of research we are in need of, we hardly know anything about actors' perceptions of the constraints and opportunities generated by publicity or, conversely, secrecy. It is also necessary to have a wider knowledge of the context of cooperative procedures, and of its impact: both ex ante – how it influences the willingness or the ability of actors to behave in a cooperative fashion – and ex post, i.e. what is the fate of the outputs pro-duced by cooperative bodies. A 'pessimistic' hypothesis here might be that gov-ernance bodies hardly have any influence, because they are embedded in an encompassing institutional framework with several 'veto points', performing thus primarily a symbolic function (civil-society involvement as 'window-dressing'). Also we hardly know anything about the links between the composition of governance bodies and the nature of their outputs. Another important matter is how different types of 'outsiders' (collective or individual 'lay' actors) perceive the functioning of governance bodies (provided that they are informed about them!), and how they assess it: this should allow to discuss the accountability of such bodies, which has seldom been put on the research agenda. It is only after having gathered more substantial evidence on these forms of policy-making that one would be able to address in a more informed and balanced way the issue of their contribution to governability and legitimacy. One should indeed know more on their inclusiveness and degree of social and ideological pluralism, on possible representation or accountability problems, on their internal dynamics and ultimately on their real political functions.

However, access to governance bodies, such as committees, roundtables, boards of quangos and public–private partnerships is no easy task for researchers (unlike access, say, to parliamentary institutions). To be sure, access to open deliberative bodies dealing with some policy issues (such as citizens' juries and the like) is easier, and it allowed for a number of experiences of participant observation by researchers, but such bodies are usually disconnected from the decision-making process. Hence the empirical sources available for an assessment of 'post-parliamentary' governance are few. As a first step, the overall policy process these bodies are part of should be reconstructed ('process tracing': George and Bennett 2005). In addition, it is necessary to acquire accurate information on the composition of these bodies, and on links of participants with those to whom they are supposed to be accountable. Regarding deliberations themselves, minutes from meetings are precious, but (if any) they are frequently confidential. Hence the research is likely to rely mostly on in-depth interviews with participants. However, their views should not be taken at face value, and information should be cautiously cross-checked. Someone, for instance, who was not able to convince his/her partners may argue that deliberation did not count, while a 'winner' may tend to conceal under deliberation the power resources he/she was able to make use of, or to neglect the role of reputation of power that makes less powerful actors restrain themselves. Ultimately, not only insiders' views matter, but getting to know outsiders' views on governance bodies is of relevance too. It may in particular reveal problems in delegation and representation (such as conflicts between the leaderships of social organisations represented therein and the rank-and-file), or in the degree of inclusiveness and of pluralism of governance bodies. Such knowledge is necessary to evaluate the 'requisite variety' of the latter that conditions the generation of effective and legitimate outputs.

Ultimately, and more generally, 'post-parliamentary' governance does not only have a participatory and deliberative dimension. We observe today a whole range of shifts in policy-making: internationalisation and the related enhanced role for governments and bureaucratic segments domestically, the decline of neo-corporatist forms of concertation, the advent of the regulatory state, administrative reform (based on new public management recipes, driven by new information technologies etc.), and also 'judicialisation'. These shifts can be contradictory: in some cases – such as those scrutinised in this chapter – the inclusion of civil-society agents is considered necessary, but in others such as 'agencification' it is technocratic policy-making that is privileged, and insulation of the decisional bodies from civil society (and from representative institutions) is deliberately sought. But we have no idea on the relative importance of these changes for the functioning of democratic systems. Therefore we need more systematic empirical research on these subjects too, along with more theoretical refinement to better capture the 'big picture' (if any) of what has been called 'post-parliamentary' governance.

Notes

1 This research was generously supported by the Swiss federal *Secrétariat d'Etat à la recherche*. Previous versions of this text were presented to the Conference 'Empirical approaches to deliberative politics', Florence, European University Institute, 22–23 May 2004, and to the CONNEX – Network of Excellence (RG4, WP1) Workshop: 'Contending civil society frames: policy dilemmas and contradictions', Paris, 9–11 March 2006. I am grateful to Bruno Jobert, Beate Kohler-Koch, John Parkinson and Blaise Larpin for their very helpful comments.
2 Heritier (2003: 113) refers to this aspect as policy effectiveness, i.e. the achievement of the prescribed goals through the selected policy instruments.
3 Heritier (2003: 107) refers to this aspect as the part of political capacity that implies the mobilisation of political support for decisions. She distinguishes her approach on the motives that generate the shift to softer modes of governance from approaches emphasising the role of mimetism and of policy beliefs. The two approaches can be conciliated: for softer modes to be preferred, policy-makers must believe that they are conducive to more political support and more policy effectiveness.
4 These include citizens' juries, deliberative opinion polls, environmental mediation etc.: for an overview see Smith and Wales (2000). Papadopoulos and Warin (2007) discuss the performance of these mechanisms along the aforementioned criteria. See also recently Hendriks (2006).
5 See also Heritier (2003) for a similar argument in line with the 'policies determine politics' hypothesis.
6 See the whole literature on bureaucracy inspired by rational choice approaches.
7 I owe this comparison to Christopher Lord.
8 Cohen and Rogers (2003: 248–249) note perspicaciously: 'actors with sufficient power to advance their aims without deliberating will not bother to deliberate [...] Equally, if parties are not somehow constrained to accept the consequences of deliberation, if "exit options" are not foreclosed, it will be implausible that they will accept the discipline of joint reasoning'.
9 Holzinger (2001a) lists a number of reasons that can make some actors opt for less deliberative alternatives instead of joining mediation procedures, and she maintains (Holzinger 2001a: 93) that 'no negotiation or discursive procedure, regardless of how well it otherwise progresses, can overcome exogenous restrictions and better outside options'. It is not rational for instance for actors to engage into cooperative mechanisms if they do not fear the outcome that will prevail otherwise (Dryzek and Niemeyer 2006: 642).
10 See Sunstein's (2003) concept of 'enclave deliberation'. In terms of policy efficiency

this can yield devastating outcomes when cohesive 'policy communities' are not sensitive to changes in their external environment requiring drastic adjustments (on such an interpretation of the decline of the French steel industry, see Padioleau 1981, written long before the concepts of 'governance networks' or 'deliberative governance' became fashionable).

References

Allison, G. (1971) *Essence of Decision*, Boston: Little Brown.

Andersen, S.S. and Burns, T.R. (1996) 'The European Union and the erosion of parliamentary democracy: a study of post-parliamentary governance', in S.S. Andersen and K.J. Eliassen (eds) *The European Union: How Democratic Is It?*, London: Sage, 226–251.

Benhabib, S. (1996) 'Toward a deliberative model of democratic legitimacy', in S. Benhabib (ed.) *Democracy and Difference: Contesting the Boundaries of the Political*, Princeton: Princeton University Press, 67–94.

Benz, A. (2000) 'Politische Steuerung in lose gekoppelten Mehrebenensystemen', in R. Wehrle and U. Schimank (eds) *Gesellschaftliche Komplexität und kollektive Handlungsfähigkeit*, Frankfurt/Main: Campus, 97–124.

Benz, A. and Papadopoulos, Y. (2006) 'Actors, institutions and democratic governance: Comparing across levels', in A. Benz and Y. Papadopoulos (eds) *Governance and Democracy. Comparing National, European, and International Experiences*, London: Routledge, 273–295.

Bevir, M. (2006) 'Democratic governance: systems and radical perspectives', *Public Administration Review*, 66 (3): 426–436.

Blondiaux, L. and Sintomer, Y. (2002) 'L'impératif délibératif', *Politix*, 57 (15): 17–35.

Bourdieu, P. (1991) *Language and Symbolic Power*, Cambridge: Polity Press.

Brennan, G. (1998) 'Democratic trust: a rational-choice theory view', in V. Braithwaite and M. Levi (eds) *Trust and Governance*, New York: Russell Sage Foundation, 197–217.

Chambers, S. (2004) 'Measuring publicity's effect: reconciling empirical research and normative theory', paper prepared for the Conference on 'Empirical approaches to deliberative politics', European University Institute, Florence, 22–23 May 2004.

Checkel, J.T. (2005) 'It's the process stupid! process tracing in the study of European and international politics', ARENA working paper, October 2005.

Cohen, J. and Rogers, J. (1995) 'Solidarity, democracy, association', in E.O. Wright (ed.) *Associations and Democracy*, London and New York: Verso, 236–267.

—— (2003) 'Power and Reason', in A. Fung and E.O. Wright (eds) *Deepening Democracy*, London and New York: Verso, 237–255.

Deutsch, K.W.D (1963) *The Nerves of Government. Models of Political Communication and Control*, New York: The Free Press.

Dryzek, J.S. and Niemeyer, S. (2006) 'Reconciling pluralism and consensus as political ideals', *American Journal of Political Science*, 50 (3): 634–649.

Eder, K. (1995) 'Das reflexiv-diskursive Modell politischer Institutionen: Analytisch ein Idealtypus – Empirisch ein Mythos?', research project, August 1995.

Elster, J. (1997) 'The market and the forum: three varieties of political theory', in J. Bohmann and W. Rehg (eds) *Deliberative Democracy*, Cambridge: MIT Press, 3–33.

—— (1998) 'Introduction', in J. Elster (ed.) *Deliberative Democracy*, Cambridge: Cambridge University Press, 1–18.

—— (1998a) 'Deliberation and constitution making', in J. Elster (ed.) *Deliberative Democracy*, Cambridge: Cambridge University Press, 97–122.

Enderlin Cavigelli, R. (1995) 'Mediationsverfahren in der schweizerischen Kernenergiepolitik', *Schriften zu Mediationsverfahren im Umweltschutz*, 12, Berlin: Wissenschaftszentrum Berlin für Sozialforschung.

European Commission (2001) 'European governance. A White Paper', Brussels: COM, 428, final 27 July 2001.

Fearon, J.D. (1998) 'Deliberation as discussion', in J. Elster (ed.) *Deliberative Democracy*, Cambridge: Cambridge University Press, 44–68.

Ferejohn, J. (2000) 'Instituting deliberative democracy', in I. Shapiro and S. Macedo (eds) *Designing Democratic Institutions*, New York and London: New York University Press, 75–104.

Fishkin, J.S. (1991) *Democracy and Deliberation*, New Haven: Yale University Press.

Fung, A. (2005) 'Deliberation before the revolution', *Political Theory*, 33 (2): 397–419.

Fung, A. and Wright, Erik O. (2001) 'Deepening democracy: innovations in empowered participatory governance', *Politics and Society*, 29 (1): 5–41.

Gargarella, R. (2000) 'Demanding public deliberation', in E.O. Eriksen and J.E. Fossum (eds) *Democracy in the European Union. Integration Through Deliberation?*, London: Routledge, 189–205.

Gaudin, J.-P. (1995) 'Politiques urbaines et négociations territoriales. Quelle légitimité pour les réseaux de politiques publiques?', *Revue française de science politique*, 45 (1): 31–55.

Gehring, T. (1996) 'Arguing und Bargaining in internationalen Verhandlungen. Ueberlegungen am Beispiel des Ozonschutzregimes', in V. von Prittwitz (ed.) *Verhalten und Argumentieren. Dialog, Interessen und Macht in der Umweltpolitik*, Opladen: Leske+Budrich, 41–68.

George, A.L. and Bennett, A. (2005) *Case Studies and Theory Development in the Social Sciences*, Cambridge: MIT Press.

Germann, R.E. and Frutiger, A. (1985) *Experts et commissions de la Confédération*, Lausanne: Presses polytechniques romandes.

Goodin, R. (2004) 'Representing diversity', *British Journal of Political Science*, 34 (3): 453–468.

—— (2006) 'Talking politics: perils and promise', *European Journal of Political Research*, 45 (2): 235–261.

Gutmann, A. and Thompson D. (1996) *Democracy and Disagreement*, Cambridge: Harvard University Press.

Haeusermann, S., Mach, A. and Papadopoulos, Y. (2004) 'From corporatism to partisan politics: social policy making under strain in Switzerland', *Swiss Political Science Review*, 10 (2): 33–59.

Heinelt, H. (2003) 'Politikfelder: Machen Besonderheiten von Policies einen Unterschied?', in K. Schubert and N.C. Bandelow (eds) *Lehrbuch der Politikfeldanalyse*, Wien-München: Oldenbourg Verlag, 239–256.

Hendriks, C.M. (2006) 'When the forum meets interest politics: strategic uses of public deliberation', *Politics and Society*, 34 (4): 571–602.

Heritier, A. (2003) 'New modes of governance in Europe: increasing political capacity and policy effectiveness?', in T.A. Boerzel and R.A. Cichowski (eds) *The State of the European Union* (Vol. 6: Law, Politics, and Society), Oxford: Oxford University Press, 105–126.

Hermet, G. (2001) *Les populismes dans le monde. Une histoire sociologique XIXe-XXe siècle*, Paris: Fayard.

Holzinger, K. (2001) 'Verhandeln statt Argumentieren oder Verhandeln durch Argumentieren? Eine empirische Analyse auf der Basis der Sprechakttheorie', *Politische Vierteljahresschrift*, 42 (3): 414–446.

—— (2001a) 'Negotiations in public-policy making: exogenous barriers to successful dispute resolution', *Journal of Public Policy*, 21 (1): 71–96.

Hunold, C. and Young, I.M. (1998) 'Justice, democracy, and hazardous sitting', *Political Studies*, 46 (1): 82–95.

Jabko, N. (2001) 'Expertise et politique à l'âge de l'euro: la Banque Centrale européenne sur le terrain de la démocratie', *Revue française de science politique*, 51 (6): 903–931.

Jenson, J. and Phillips, S.D. (2001) 'Redesigning the Canadian citizenship regime: remaking the institutions of representation', in C. Crouch, K. Eder and D. Tambini (eds) *Citizenship, Markets, and the State*, Oxford: Oxford University Press, 69–89.

Jobert, A. (1998) 'L'aménagement en politique. Ou ce que le syndrome NIMBY nous dit de l'intérêt général', *Politix*, 42: 67–92.

Jobert, B. (1998) 'La régulation politique: le point de vue d'un politiste', in J. Commaille and B. Jobert (eds) *Les métamorphoses de la régulation politique*, Paris: Librairie générale de droit et de jurisprudence, 119–144.

Jörges, C. and Neyer, J. (1997) 'Transforming strategic interaction into deliberative problem-solving: European comitology in the foodstuffs sector', *Journal of European Public Policy*, 4 (4): 609–625.

Kelman, S. (1992) 'Adversary and cooperationist institutions for conflict resolution in public policymaking', *Journal of Policy Analysis and Management*, 11 (2): 178–206.

Koenig-Archibugi, M. (2004) 'Transnational Corporations and Public Accountability', *Government and Opposition*, 39 (2): 234–259.

Levine, P., Fung, A. and Gastil, J. (2005) 'Future directions for public deliberation', in J. Gastil and P. Levine (eds) *The Deliberative Democracy Handbook*, San Francisco: John Wiley, 271–288.

Majone, G. (1994) 'Décisions publiques et délibération', *Revue française de Science Politique*, 44 (4): 579–598.

Manin, B. (1985) 'Volonté générale ou délibération? Esquisse d'une théorie de la délibération politique', *Le débat*, 33: 72–93.

Mansbridge, J. (1983) *Beyond Adversary Democracy*, Chicago: Chicago University Press.

March, J.G. and Olsen, J.P. (eds) (1989) *Rediscovering Institutions*, New York: The Free Press.

Mayntz, R. (1997) 'Politische Steuerung: Aufstieg, Niedergang und Transformation einer Theorie', in R. Mayntz (ed.) *Soziale Dynamik und Politische Steuerung. Theoretische und methodologische Überlegungen*, Frankfurt/Main and New York: Campus, 263–292.

—— (1999) 'Organizations, agents and representatives', in M. Egeberg and P. Laegreid (eds) *Organizing Political Institutions*, Oslo: Scandinavian University Press, 81–91.

Olson, M. (1965) *The Logic of Collective Action: Public Goods and the Theory of Groups*, Cambridge: Harvard University Press.

Padioleau, J.G. (1981) *Quand la France s'enferre*, Paris: Presses Universitaires de France.

Papadopoulos, Y. (2003) 'Cooperative forms of governance: problems of democratic accountability in complex environments', *European Journal of Political Research*, 42 (4): 473–501.

Papadopoulos, Y. and Warin, P. (eds) (2007) 'Innovative, participatory, and deliberative procedures in policy-making: democratic and effective?', *special issue of the European Journal of Political Research*, 46 (4): 445–472.

Pitkin, H.F. (1967) *The Concept of Representation*, Berkeley: University of California Press.

Sanders, L. (1997) 'Against Deliberation', *Political Theory*, 25 (3): 347–376.

Schmidt, V. (2006) *Democracy in Europe. The EU and National Polities*, Oxford: Oxford University Press.

Schmitter, P.C. (2005) 'Two cheers for deliberation', *European Political Science*, 4 (4): 430–435.

Schmitter, P.C. and Streeck, W. (1999) 'The organization of business interests. Studying the associative action of business in advanced industrial societies', Discussion paper 99/1, Max-Planck-Institut für Gesellschaftsforschung.

Smith, G. and Wales, C. (2000) 'Citizens' juries and deliberative democracy', *Political Studies*, 48 (1): 51–65.

Sunstein, C. (2003) 'The law of group polarization', in J.S. Fishkin and P. Laslett (eds) *Debating Deliberative Democracy*, Oxford: Blackwell, 80–101.

Thatcher, M. and Stone Sweet, A. (2001) 'Theory and practice of delegation to non-majoritarian institutions', *West European Politics*, 23 (1): 3–22.

Trom, D. (1999) 'De la réfutation de l'effet *Nimby* considérée comme une pratique militante. Notes pour une approche pragmatique de l'activité revendicative', *Revue française de science politique*, 49 (1): 31–50.

Urfalino, P. (2000) 'La délibération et la dimension normative de la décision collective', in J. Commaille (ed.) *La juridicisation du politique. Leçons scientifiques*, Paris: Librairie générale de droit et de jurisprudence, 165–193.

Wälti, S. (1993) 'Neue Problemlösungsstrategien in der nuklearen Entsorgung' *Annuaire suisse de science politique*, 33: 205–224.

—— (1995) 'Mediationserfahrungen in der nuklearen Entsorgungspolitik der Schweiz', *Schriften zu Mediationsverfahren im Umweltschutz* 13, Berlin: Wissenschaftszentrum Berlin für Sozialforschung.

—— (2001) *Le fédéralisme d'exécution sous pression: la mise en œuvre des politiques à incidence spatiale dans le système fédéral Suisse*, Basel: Helbing and Lichtenhahn.

Waelti, S., Kuebler, D. and Papadopoulos, Y. (2004) 'How democratic is 'governance'? Lessons from Swiss drug policy', *Governance*, 17 (1): 83–113.

Watzlawick, P., Bavelas, J.D. and Jackson, D.D. (1967) *Pragmatics of Human Communication*, New York: W.W. Norton and Co.

Young, I.M. (1996) 'Communication and the other: beyond deliberative democracy', in S. Benhabib (ed.) *Democracy and Difference: Contesting the Boundaries of the Political*, Princeton: Princeton University Press, 120–135.

—— (2000) *Inclusion and Democracy*, Oxford: Oxford University Press.

12 It's about participation, stupid

Is it? – civil-society concepts in comparative perspective

Stefanie Edler-Wollstein and Beate Kohler-Koch

Proponents of civil society have difficulties talking to each other because some see it as an empirical reality that is worth exploring with the well-established toolkit of empirical political sociology, whereas others take it as a political concept of society with strong normative overtones. The contributions to this volume concentrate on the concept of civil society, on the role attributed to civil society at different times and in different countries, on the reasons for its surfacing and its multiple forms in political discourse. However, instead of analysing the meanings of civil society per se, the authors endeavour to understand how it is articulated in discourses and used in processes of political reforms in a given historic situation. Civil society is seen both as a myth and a pragmatic remedy presumed to make for a better society. The concept quite obviously has its ups and downs over time and is closely related to the search for legitimate governance. Comparing the different civic frameworks, this concluding chapter tries to shed light on the varied and often contradictory uses of the idea of civil society. By comparing a wide range of countries we try to elucidate similarities and differences that represent different worldviews and are inflicted by different political cultures and forms of government.

On this superordinate level, the differentiated interpretations of civil society call for a heuristic device in order to grasp the complexity of the concept. Therefore, we have developed an analytical framework that highlights core features of civil-society concepts and allows for comparison across time and diverse political and social conditions. We introduce two dimensions: first, we distinguish between two main functions that are attributed to civil society, which is, on the one hand, its role to defend the political rights of citizens and, on the other hand, its function to secure good governance. If we translate this into the well-known terminology of Fritz Scharpf, civil society is deemed to either contribute to input legitimacy or to output legitimacy. It goes without saying that this is an analytical distinction. In real-life situations and in political discourse, the distinction is often blurred and the role assigned to civil society is embracing both functional dimensions. Nevertheless, we argue that the political discourse is mostly enlightened by worldviews which support rather one or the other concept, and we will provide evidence that both in public discourse and in the self-perception of actors, one of the respective concepts prevails. The second dimension is captured by asking who is, or rather is supposed to be, acting as 'change agent'. The concept of 'change agent'[1] is used here in a broad sense, asking who is in the driving seat: is it predominantly the state or civil-society organizations which take the initiative to enable civil society to perform its functional role? Expectations concerning the role of change agents are always inspired by the prevailing image of what civil society is about. Nevertheless, it is an empirical question to whom this role is attributed and what specific context conditions make either the state or civil society a strong player.

Thus, the analytical model, which will be elaborated in detail below, incorporates two dimensions, namely a differentiated view of the main function of civil society, and the respective role performed by the state and by civil-society organizations in bringing civil society to the fore. The combination of these two dimensions allows for a comparative assessment of the cases presented in this volume.

Apart from this heuristic value, the distinction between the two functional approaches makes it plausible why and in what respect civil society is considered to be an asset to democracy. The functional attributions can be linked with normative theories of democracy, with the theoretical discussion on good governance and the advantages and disadvantages of deliberative policy-making. This way, we can demonstrate that 'civil society' in general is seen as a panacea to the democratic deficit, but that the concepts used differ because they are inspired by different theoretical backgrounds. The individual chapters provide ample evidence for the use and misuse of the concept of civil society. When we call it 'misuse', we do not suppose a wrong usage in the sense of the incorrect application of a well-defined term – which civil society is not. Rather, we will demonstrate that the functional role assigned to civil society often is well-intended but ill-conceived and, in the given situation, can not attain the aspired objectives. Furthermore, we will draw the attention of the reader to the many cases of strategic uses of the concept for narrow selfish interests. The discourse on civil society, just as the action of civil-society interest groups, is firmly embedded in political power games in which the reference to civil society is meant to provide symbolic legitimacy.

Civil society as the guardian of political rights

Time and again, civil society is considered a rescue when the legitimacy of a political system is at stake. The most obvious case is the recourse to civil society in opposition to an authoritarian oppressive system. But civil society is also thought of as a remedy to the weakening ties between citizens and the government in established democracies. In regard to the former variant, the issue of political and social legitimacy and representation becomes pronounced when the concept of civil society is constructed as a counter-image to illegitimate rule. The surfacing of civil society follows a normative idea that carries the unifying potential to mobilize social movements, which in turn develop into a political opposition against the authoritarian state, calling into doubt the legitimacy of the existing system. The civil-society discourse is, thus, fuelled by democratic upheavals, which – if successful – pave the way for a democratization process. Civil society was a key concept in the transformation process in the communist states of Eastern Europe, where it embodied citizens' ability to articulate values and induced people to rally behind those who propagated a radical change. With the establishment of representative democracy, however, such a concept of civil society is susceptible to fall into crisis and to be misused. The mythical unity of a society reconciled with itself and organized beyond the reach of (party) political strife, is at odds with the reality of political pluralism and becomes replaced by parties organized along political cleavage lines and competing for power. Attempts to integrate the civil-society organizations which brought about the system change into the newly established government led to their de-legitimization and, in the case of South Africa, to the revival of more radical social movements.

In contrast to the emergence of civil society in authoritarian systems, the return to civil society in functioning democracies is rather instigated by the citizens' disenchantment with existing forms of democracy. Underlying is the idea that civil-society functions as a safeguard of democracy, which comes into action at times of perceived legitimacy crises. If parties and parliaments are perceived as deficient, civil society is called upon to take up the role of compensating those weaknesses. In this affirmative view, civil society is seen as an autochthonous oasis, with responsive citizens contributing to a vibrant social sphere. Civil-society organizations are crystallizing points for political activation. Citizens who are open to be activated share a common notion of what civil society is about, but are not driven by one unifying idea. Civil society is not synonymous with civil-society organizations but with 'citizens-on-call' (Amna 2006: 11), i.e. citizens who are ready to speak up and become engaged for a public cause.

In both cases we witness a recourse to the concept of civil society but, in substance, the appeal is addressing two divergent concepts. In both instances, the respective civil-society concept has the potential to further democracy but becomes dysfunctional under changing conditions. A successful transformation from authoritarian to democratic rule requires a change in concept. Only when the democratization process fosters the differentiation and pluralization of citizens' self-conception, a concept of civil society will emerge that is consistent with the kind of institutionalized competition which is the main precondition for a sustainable democracy. Citizens will renounce the unifying concept of the pre-transition phase and recede to the above mentioned 'citizens-on-call' who can be activated to defend political rights (as they see them). The appeal to civil society as the uniform body of the 'people' may, nevertheless, persist in the rhetoric of populist or nationalist forces. An indication for the use or misuse of the concept is the turn to emotional appeals and an exclusive definition of those who are part of (national) civil society.

The recourse to civil society in response to a political legitimacy crisis may originate from civil society or from the state. As mentioned above, political activists may use civil society as a 'mobilizing action frame' (Glenn, Chapter 2, this volume) to push for system change or civil-society organizations may join forces to infuse an unresponsive representative democracy with grassroots demands. Likewise, state actors may take the initiative to rejuvenate a quiescent civil society. The idea that a democratic state has to take responsibility for the 'civic literacy' (Milner 2002) of the citizens for the sake of sustainable democracy has spread beyond the Scandinavian orbit. The 'teaching function', which in former times Bagehot attributed to parliament, now resides with the executive. Many times a technocratic bureaucracy turns into a benevolent facilitator or even promoter of civic empowerment. 'Participatory engineering' (Zittel 2007) is a new trend that disseminates across the globe. It is the purposeful attempt of political institutions to activate citizens' political participation by either addressing citizens directly or indirectly through associations that represent citizens' interests. Apart from the expected positive effects on governance, participatory engineering is aimed at fostering civil society. It is on the agenda of local and national governments in established democracies but also of the European Union, and it even is on the agenda in authoritarian political systems, such as China.

In the political discourse, all activities which encourage citizens' participation and contribute to the formation and networking of citizens' organizations qualify for democratic improvement. In general, civil society carries a positive connotation and the stronger civil society is in terms of associational life and civil-society engagement in politics, the better for democracy. In the academic discourse the democratic potential of participatory engineering is circumscribed more narrowly. In line with the liberal theory of democracy, extended participation only contributes to democratization when it gives citizens the opportunity to have an effective and equal impact on the political decision-making process (Dahl 2006), whereas from a deliberative democracy perspective, the benchmark of democracy is the openness of public discourse and a communication structure that fuels the exchange of convincing arguments and furthers reciprocity (Habermas 1996).

Civil society furthering good governance and common welfare

The starting point for discussing our second approach is the Scandinavian experience of civil self-organization. The comparative strength of Scandinavian democracy is said to have emerged from a widespread associational life devoted to the idea of an egalitarian citizenship and a close cooperation between an engaged civil society and a benevolent state (Amna 2006: 1). This experience encompasses self-management and the provision of social services in all areas of public life, but also active civil-society organizations making demands on the state to deliver collective goods. Civil society, thus, became part of the corporatist arrangement with the state which supported an ever-growing welfare system.

In this approach, the relation between the state and civil society is mostly seen as a partnership and, consequently, the role of change agent is quite evenly distributed. But even when civil-society actors take the initiative and motivate state actors to respond to their demands, their success comes at the price of a loss of autonomy and strength: the more the state attends to the interests and aims that have been activated by social movements and organizations, the more the associational self-help system is replaced by professional public services. Civil-society organizations may become incorporated but will then be subordinated to the state's public policy, and despite widespread activities they become marginalized because they have lost their function as autonomous political actors. Depending on the specific context, this development can be discerned either in particular policy fields, or it may cover all areas of public interests. This is a story often told and illustrated by telling examples, such as the shifting relations between the temperance movement, once 'the most vocal and mobilising force in the Swedish society' (Rothstein 2006: 2) and the Swedish state. The driving forces of the temperance movement succumbed to the temptation to become a loyal partner to the state and consequently lost 'independence and legitimacy towards their own constituencies' (ibid.). This does not necessarily imply a 'crowding out' of civil-society organizations. Dag Wollebæk and Per Selle point out that in the case of Norway in the time of the expansion of the welfare state these organizations, indeed, 'advocated increased government responsibility within welfare services' but they were neither 'docile servants of the state' nor did they decline in numbers (Chapter 4, this volume, p. 52).

The more recent discourse on good governance also propagates the idea of a close involvement of civil society both in policy formulation and implementation. The promise is to bring policy-making closer to the people and to improve welfare services. The governance discourse, however, takes an instrumental approach. Civil-society organizations emerging from below are perceived to represent a wider diversity of interests than the institutions of representative democracy (WRR 2007: 131), to be closer to stakeholder interests and, therefore, to be better equipped to contribute to efficient problem-solving. Good governance, thus, may be achieved by drawing on the resources of civil society. A productive state–civil society relationship is engineered top-down to work to the benefit of state performance. In this perspective, civil society is seen as an essential provider of output legitimacy. However, a revival of civil society is not always perceived to advance what people consider to be in their interest. This is even more so when voluntary organizations are asked to step in to compensate for a cut-back in public welfare services.

Thus, the functional role assigned to civil society as provider of output legitimacy is as ambivalent as its functional contribution to input legitimacy. Still, today the image of civil society combining self-reliance and a pro-active social force is a cherished concept. It is, however, rather a myth than a remedy to the perceived crisis of the Western welfare state. The governance discourse assigns civil society a more instrumental role. Here, civil-society's function in and contribution to the better performance of democratic governance is under scrutiny, above all when the call for civil society is a response to the dismantling of the welfare state.

200   *S. Edler-Wollstein and B. Kohler-Koch*

Table 12.1 Concepts of civil society in perspective

Change agent	Functional role assigned to civil society	
	Defence of political rights and empowerment of the people	Securing social welfare and good governance
Active civil society	**Source and promoter of democracy** Demanding democracy *Norway 1* Fighting an authoritarian state *Poland, Czechoslovakia, South Africa* Representative of the plurality of individual interests *Norway 3*	**Guarantor of people's social interests** Demanding and providing public services: *Norway 1–2, (partly India)* Grassroots self-help organizations *South Africa*
Active state	**Responsible citizenship** Educated citizens, 'social citizenship': *Norway, Chile* Citizens on call: *EU* Civil society as political ally *India, Italy*	**Partner in good governance** Input provider for better legislation: *EU* Partner in providing public services: *Chile, France, UK* Civilized supportive citizenship: *China*

This analytical framework will be applied to make a systematic comparison of the cases presented in the individual chapters. It is different from the four models presented by Bruno Jobert in Chapter 1. Jobert proposes a typology of civil-society models which give a stylized representation of real historic concepts. Thus the tutelary model corresponds to the phase of the spread of the welfare state in the industrialized countries of the West and in so far as civil society had a say, it was a 'wage earner democracy' (p. 6). The neo-conservative model was conceived as a response to the deficits of the tutelary model giving more power to the market and restricting the role of civil society to the guardian of traditional social values. The Third Way model was designed in opposition to this neo-liberal inspired concept. It aims at constituting civil society beyond the established social partners and values civil-society organizations as social entrepreneurs activating citizens to see to their rights but also to their duties. The integrated civil-society model, in turn, advocates the inclusion of weak interests by strategies of empowerment and the embedding of bargaining and decision-making processes in broader deliberative settings (Chapter 1).

The models proposed by Jobert are meant to give references in order to capture the variety of representations of civil society in civic discourse. They respond to three basic questions, namely 'the role of politics in the constitution of civil society, the modalities of involvement of civil-society organizations in government action, and the conditions of rehabilitation of civil society when it has been disrupted' (p. 4).

Dag Wollebæk and Per Selle, on their part, are interested in different aspects and expectations that are associated with voluntary organizations in civil society and democracy. They argue that civil-society perspectives differ fundamentally on two dimensions; first, concerning the orientation between conflict and consensus and second, between an individual and a collective orientation. Combining the two dimensions, they arrive, consequently, at four approaches which correspond to societal roles ascribed to civil-society organizations. These correspond to different theoretical schools such as pluralism, social capital, communitarianism and public sphere theories, to which they add comparative associationalism and the literature on social movements (p. 49). According to Wollebæk and Selle, within each paradigm, prototypical organizations can be identified. The authors are not interested in a static view on different types of civil-society organizations and do not consider categories of growth and decline, they rather use these different perspectives in order to disclose how organized civil society in Norway has evolved over time. Their empirical findings reveal a movement from conflict and society orientation towards consensus and individual orientation and, accordingly, a transition from one type of civil society towards another (p. 51). In this process, organized civil society in Norway has lost many of the traits that characterized the uniqueness of the Scandinavian model (p. 63). The large member-based organizations that once linked local and national politics, and provided intermediary structures between citizens and the political system have given way to 'freestanding' local associations (p. 61) and efficient advocates of individual citizen's interests. As stated by Wollebæk and Selle, this 'reflects that a tradition which held a dominant position for almost a century is challenged by global trends such as individualization, marketization and a changing conception of time' (p. 65).

Civil-society frameworks in comparison

The contributions to this volume, with the exception of the Norwegian case, document that in the past two decades civil society has become a key concept when democracy is at risk. Under divergent context conditions political forces attached to quite deviant philosophies are conveying the idea of civic involvement as a remedy fostering democratic emancipation and citizens' welfare. Only on closer scrutiny these concepts reveal a highly differentiated image. Obviously, the recourse to civil society is most pronounced in response to political legitimacy crises, but also these differ considerably. The obvious legitimacy deficit of the communist regimes in Eastern Europe or the apartheid regime in South Africa can hardly be equated with the legitimacy deficit attributed to the European Union. As well, the worries concerning the erosion of the democratic infrastructure in Scandinavia are quite distinct from the crisis that was triggered by the breakdown of the Italian political party system. Consequently, it is plausible to assume that the plethora of assessments on civil society, and the political promises that are associated with it, mirror divergent context conditions. This cautions us to take the relevance of the particular contexts into account. The contributions call attention to the variations in the concepts, discourses and strategies of civil society, whereas our analytical approach will help us to find common ground when comparing countries as dissimilar as Norway, Italy, France and the UK, Poland and Czechoslovakia, South Africa, China and Chile.

Civil society fighting for democracy: shifting roles and concepts

Both in Eastern Europe and in South Africa, civil society was attributed a central role in overthrowing an authoritarian rule. However on closer analysis, a striking difference both in the perception of civil society as transformative power and in the later use of the concept becomes obvious.

As described in John Glenn's Chapter 2, in Poland and Czechoslovakia, a civil society consisting of a vast array of associations did not exist. It was the Catholic Church in Poland and the theatres in Czechoslovakia that supplied the base and resources for the social movements and spread a 'collective action frame' (p. 16) for mobilizing the support of previously quiescent groups. This grounds the civil-society concept of the negotiated transformation in Poland, as well as of the mass mobilization in Czechoslovakia, in the actions of those political actors seeking to influence change.

In the South African case, analysed by Konstantinos Papadakis, the overthrow of the illegitimate apartheid regime was accomplished by an alliance of political and civil-society organizations, that is, a wide variety of self-help groups and political activists' movements that survived persecution. They 'shared common agendas and held mutually reinforcing discourses' (p. 152) and 'sought to develop a coordinated mobilization' (p. 153). Their political action frame mainly comprised issues of human rights and anti-discrimination. At the end of apartheid and the establishment of a democratic system, the voice of civil society became institutionalized through its inclusion in participatory governance processes in a range of different policy fields.

In both cases civil society could claim that the turn to democracy was accomplished bottom-up and would not have been successful without the widespread and organized engagement of citizens. The success story, however, turned out to be unsustainable. The concept became politically hijacked and civil society was assigned a functional role that undermined its credibility, calling its legitimacy strongly into question. The reasons behind the crises were completely different, however. In Eastern Europe, while critical for the successful mobilization of movements against the old regime, the civil-society concept was difficult to reconcile with representative democracy. Citizens became disenchanted comparing their engagement for a common cause with the divisive power struggle of party politics. They learned the hard way that 'in parliamentary democracies, the "nation" is not represented by a united "society" but by a range of groups representing different interests' (p. 27). Thus, widespread disenchantment made people receptive to a pervert use of the civil-society concept. Both in Poland and Czechoslovakia, populist and nationalist leaders sought to mobilize political support by conjuring up the mythical unity of a civil society that actually had never existed outside the action frames of mobilization against the communist regimes.

In South Africa, the role of civil society changed in the democratization process from providing grassroots legitimation to the anti-apartheid struggle, to lend political support to a government that had abandoned its commitment to redistribution in favour of a growth oriented market-driven policy agenda. Thus, the formal inclusion in numerous participatory fora de-legitimized civil society. The participating civil-society organizations were seen as mouthpiece of South Africa's single party government, propagating the state's new economic programme instead of defending the former ambitious plans for people-driven redistribution. As a reaction, a number of new social movements, that were excluded from the formal policy-making sphere and mostly acted outside participatory governance structures, came forward. These movements did not arise from the state delegating tasks, but built on their image of self-organization and, therefore, appeared as being independent and trustworthy. Papadakis aptly terms this concept a 'radical civil society' model (p. 151), emphasizing the critical voice of civil society as 'a necessary precondition for the functioning of democracy in the context of South African post-apartheid politics' (p. 151). The very moment, the state took the initiative and tried to organize a selective corporatism, grassroots organizations outside government claimed to be the true representatives of civil society.

Inviting civil society to make for good governance

The contributions to this volume demonstrate the worldwide attractiveness of the civil-society concept. Two chapters stand out because they document that the idea to cope with a looming legitimate crisis by taking rescue to civil society has disseminated even beyond the democratic nation state. The focus is quite clearly on civil-society's contribution to the better performance of democratic governance and the support given to civil society can be assessed as an attempt to change state–society relations. However, as a comparison between the European Union (EU) and China reveals (in all caution when comparing a democracy based to an authoritarian system), they are both examples of participatory engineering aimed at creating civil society top-down. EU institutions are fostering a transnational 'European' civil society whereas the Chinese authorities seek to transform the 'masses' into responsible citizens. Both cases also reveal an ambiguous relation between politics and civil society, suggesting that the attractiveness of the civil-society concept can be a smokescreen obscuring particular interests. The authorities' proclaimed intention to support citizen's engagement by giving them more responsibilities does not always imply the notions of 'good governance', in the sense of strengthening citizens' emancipation and leading to increased social cohesion, but might rather conceal stalwart interests and various hidden agendas.

Helene Michel's Chapter 7 illustrates how the pervasive prevalence of the civil-society discourse has influenced the strong promotion of civil-society participation in the EU, up to the point where the concept has become synonymous with good governance. The White Paper on European governance in 2001 was a key moment in EU policy formalization of the role of civil society, and it has significantly stipulated civil-society involvement in the decision-making process. However, as Michel's contribution shows, this top-down strategy intended to close the democratic gap between European institutions and citizens is full of ambiguities. Faced with a trade-off between input and output legitimacy, i.e. the choice between membership-based associations articulating demands but providing little expert knowledge and expert-based organizations that can deliver the scientific evidence needed, the European Commission has a propensity to opt for the technocratic way. Following the White Paper recommendations on the involvement of a broad range of non-governmental organizations (NGOs), the Directorate General (DG) 'Employment and Social Affairs', for instance, has actively supported the formation of a civil-society consultation. Among others, the European Older People's Platform (AGE) was set up with the financial support by the Commission. Though, in principle, no one objected to the Commission's interest in getting a coordinated view, it was taken as a manipulative use of the concept of civil society and an intentional misreading of civil society's contribution to good, democratic governance. In particular, the European Federation of Retired and Elderly Persons (FERPA), already acknowledged as a social partner by the EU, contested the new concept of older people being represented among others by professionals and business associations.

Even if this criticism may be read as a retort to the creeping marginalization of the social partners, who in the process of increased civil-society involvement lost their privileged access to the European institutions, it raises the issue of the legitimacy of civil-society engineering. The argument is that the EU's 'state-aided' staging of a pluralistic system of interest representation is no remedy to the democratic deficit 'since hardly any of the participating organisations hold a mandate, thus lacking accountability towards their members or supporters' (p. 117).

In a union of 27+ member states and a vast diversity of preferences and demands, the aggregation of interests is decisive but difficult to achieve. It is, therefore, in the technocratic self-interest of EU-institutions to push for networking and cooperation between representative organizations at the EU level. Multi-level representation and multi-level accountability are, however, difficult to achieve. To make matters worse, the proliferation of organized interests seeking access to EU-institutions put civil-society associations under pressure. Faced with tough competition to gain voice and ear-time, the focus is on professionalization and strategic action and not so much on furthering the communicative links between the representatives in Brussels and their home base. Consequently, a wide variety of very active civil-society organizations may contribute to good governance *for* the people but will hardly be a valid indicator for good governance *by* the people.

To draw a parallel between the EU and the Chinese case may seem to be too farfetched since it is commonly argued that the civil-society concept is strongly related to democratic systems. In both cases, however, the political authorities take an interest in the development of civil society at grassroots level that would feed into the multi-level system of governance and in both cases good intentions are no safeguard to trade efficiency for citizens' emancipation.

As elaborated by Thomas Heberer (Chapter 6), both the discourse of civil society and the basic structures of a latent Chinese civil society are gradually evolving, even though it is a state-led, illiberal type of civil society. The pre-requisites for the emergence of associational life are created and controlled by the party-state, including the backing-up of a private economy and a private entrepreneurship. The party-state, in well-defined limits, is also encouraging citizen participation in the public sphere and the introduction of grassroots elections at the local level. Parallel to the political activities, an intellectual discourse on social issues and the future of China's society is developing and, last but not least, public opinion polls prove that a sense of citizenship is evolving.

The notion of civil society in China is opaque. Very present in the official public debate is the capacity attributed to civil society to improve governance and to ease the burden of the state which is overstrained with societal tasks. Thus, primarily for pragmatic reasons, the party-state delegates welfare func-tions by strongly encouraging citizens' engagement in social activities, such as taking care of the socially weak. It is noteworthy that both government officials and the broader public expect civil society to improve administrative perform-ance and public services. The interest in establishing a third sector has to be seen in conjunction with the paternalistic commitment of fostering 'good citizenship'. As Heberer points out, 'in establishing new values, a new public morale and public spirit the party-state assigns to urban neighbourhood communities the pivotal task of creating "new citizens" top-down' (p. 99). The new political objectives go hand-in-hand with a shift in ideological terminology: 'Instead of talking about "masses", the dominant term in the former political concept, it is now propagating the notion of "citizens" which has the connotation of legal and participation rights' (p. 93), and also implies citizens 'taking responsibility and solve some of the social problems by themselves' (p. 101).

Though the terminology sounds relatively close to the Western concept of civil society, the Chinese version is firmly grounded in a community-oriented view, asking citizens to act in the public interest. Furthermore, China is an acti-vating state which does not only facilitate and further civil-society engagement, but tightly controls all legal and financial conditions. Last but not least, the Chinese model is characterized by an ideological self-ascription of the state. It envisages the party-state as a moral agent, improving the 'moral quality of cit-izens and teaching them civic and political skills' (p. 99).

This raises the question about the potential future democratic development in both cases. Will civil-society organizations eventually become emancipated and become a guardian of citizens' sovereign rights? In China, the paradox situation is that the state is actively supporting the formation of civil society but at the same time continues to control and restrict the activities of its citizens. As emphasized by Heberer, at present the existence of an autonomous civil society is not tolerated. However, the changes so far have lead to the emergence of a range of social organizations and movements that are active even in politically sensitive fields, such as the environment or social rights. According to Heberer, at least 'there are types of social actions emerging, which are at first not fully autonomous, but are not congruent with the party-state, either, and which finally may become nuclei of autonomous social fields, beyond state control' (p. 88).

For the EU, a shift in political rhetoric is noteworthy. Whereas under the presidency of Roman Prodi the Commission very actively propagated the involvement of civil society to meet the legitimacy crisis of the EU, the Barroso Commission put efficient performance first. The main argument under his presidency is that the EU has to deliver what people want and to do so efficiently. Good governance is 'governance for the people' and, consequently, emphasis is on 'evidence based decision-making' and the reduction of transaction costs when engaging with civil society. Interest groups are asked to coordinate their point of view and to speak to the Commission with one voice. This approach puts groups representing general interests under particular pressure since they are more loosely structured and lack the resources for efficient coordination. In addition, the more they adjust to the 'logic of influence', i.e. the necessities of surviving in a competitive market of interest representation, the more they will become elitist. The turn to even more professionalization is adding up to all other obstacles to keep in touch with constituencies at grassroots level so that the prospects for the emergence of a European transnational civil society appear somewhat bleak.

Civil society caught in politics

Civil society is held in high esteem just because it is meant to be distant from (party) politics. The idea is that civil society is activated by citizens' dissatisfaction with the political status quo and, in democratic systems, will serve a cathartic function to combat the deficiencies of the existing system of parties and parliament. Putting this idealistic view into a realistic perspective, Alfio Mastropaolo's chapter on the Italian case (Chapter 3) provides a telling story of civil society's instrumentalization and the hazards of a 'continuous amalgamation of civil society and official politics' (p. 41).

More than any other Western Democracy, the Italian political system was shaped by the predominance of political parties, up to a point when the Italian 'partitocrazia' ('partyocracy') became synonymous with an uncompetitive, elitist system of party government. When through the 1970s and 1980s, the continuing alienation of the parties from society brought about a deep crisis of the political system, Italian civil society occupied a legitimate political space. Intellectuals, the media, but also political party activists promoted the discourse on civil society which they pictured as being just the opposite to the power-driven and sclerotic party system: representing values and rights, responsive to bottom-up demands, a living contrast to the scrupulous rent-seeking oligarchy dominating the established parties and the state. The civil-society rhetoric became omnipresent though with quite diverse connotations. For some, it was the embodiment of a democratic force alike to the East European anti-communist movements, whereas for others, it was the alternative to social-pacts and state protectionism opening a window of opportunity for neo-liberal economic policies. Political parties embraced civil society by recruiting movement activists as candidates in elections or – as did the former Communist Party – even reinvented themselves as the representatives of civil society. With the deepening of the legitimacy crisis of the Italian system, the civil-society discourse gained momentum. But it did not constrain the transformation of the party system and the new consolidation of party power. Though the discourse on civil society has been highly instrumentalized, non-governmental organizations managed time and again to stage opposition movements and retain a certain degree of autonomy.

Less visible, but nonetheless important is the expansion of the third sector. Both the state and the church act as facilitator of self-help groups and engage voluntary groups in delivering public services. Citizen participation in the non-profit sector and involvement in deliberative governance should not be disregarded but it only involves that segment of society that is ready anyway to participate in politics.

Summarizing the anti-political uses of Italy's civil society in Alfio Mastropaolo's words, it 'has been primarily a parallel form of politics. It has served as a substitute for official politics and, later, as a substitute for the welfare state. Thus, it has not only lent itself to dubious political manoeuvres, but also to those whose democratic stance is questionable' (p. 45).

The Indian case, examined by Bruno Jobert (Chapter 5), also reveals a political use of civil society and, moreover, a successive changeover from one civil society model to another. Both the discourse and the organization of civil society have responded to political developments, at times being the voice of the opposition to an authoritarian turn in government, at other times articulating legitimate but neglected demands, or aiming at securing good governance. Bruno Jobert's main argument is that the use of the concept is difficult to grasp, unless civil society is seen in juxtaposition to India's political society.

> Civil society embodies a people consisting of citizens; Indian political society is structured around inherited and imagined communities. Hindus want to base the political collective on the Hindu majority's revenge over centuries of foreign domination (including the Mogul Empire). The Scheduled Castes and Other Backward Castes also want to use the law of numbers to repair the injustices of which they have been victims. (...) In Indian

political discourse, homage is ritually paid to the recognition of human rights (...) But this definition of a common base is obscured by the dynamic of collective rights.

(p. 84)

In the early period of independence, associations remained under party and government leadership. It was a truncated civil society, until broad public opposition arose against the imposition of the state of emergency in the 1970s. The civil-society rhetoric was instrumental in denouncing both, the authoritarian practices and the under-performance of the government in regard to economic and social development. The very notion of civil society, however, the question of who was to represent it and its appropriate role in politics differed widely. Consequently, when the opposition forces came to power, their heterogeneity and a paramount interest in stability soon became evident. Projects for the collective organization of the poor were not pursued, rather participatory devices were introduced that were no threat to the supremacy of party government. Nevertheless, from then on, the political discourse on democracy was framed in relation to civil society, and the involvement of civil society in public policy-making was perceived to be crucial to good governance, a view that was largely supported by a prosperous industry of NGOs. Notwithstanding the continued adherence to these new schemes, their success was mitigated by failures in state performance and a continuous attempt to use civil-society participation for inner-administrative power games.

In the Indian political discourse, civil society is considered to be the foundation of democracy, a superior normative force assuring rights and equality. It becomes a central point of reference whenever established politics enter into crisis. Thus far, the discourse echoes more general trends, though one could argue that civil society is more present and held in higher esteem than in other established democracies. Yet, Bruno Jobert cautions the reader: 'The saga of social movements in India has received much attention on the international scene. This should not however cause us to forget the modest role of this civil associational world in the reality of daily life in India' (p. 83). Furthermore, the widespread use of the civil-society rhetoric should not obscure the fundamental differences in the concept and its misuse for political ends. The advocates of a renewal of civil society by the grassroots share with the Hindu activists the belief in the intrinsic virtue of the traditional society that ought to be defended. However, whereas the former see the Indian tradition conducive to the integration in diversity, the latter insist on the reconstruction of the Indian nation around its cultural majority. Hindu nationalists propagate a concept of civil society that is exclusive and militant.

The misuse of the civil-society concept for nationalistic appeals is not unique, as documented by Glenn in the case of Poland. But due to the specific stratification of Indian society in distinct communities, the Indian discourse is susceptive to a factionalist approach. For the same reason, the voices of civil-society activists who call for the protection of individual citizen's rights have remained weak in a political society dominated by the continuous infighting of communities and factions about the distribution of benefits.

Civil society: a partner in improving public services

Quite another strand of the civil-society debate concentrates on the state in action and its attempts to involve civil-society organizations in public policy-making.

The focus is not on civil society's constitution of and contribution to the democratic life of the polity, but rather on the improvement of the 'public good'. The initiative comes from the state, or rather from parts of the bureaucracy and not, as it was partly the case in India, from civil society exerting pressure in favour of a 'civilisation of state institutions' (p. 78). Whereas in the European Union the focus is on 'good governance' in terms of 'better law making', Raul Urzúa and Jacques de Maillard report cases in which the involvement of civil society is meant to compensate for the shortcomings of the state in providing public services. The state is reaching out to engage citizens and encourage them to take more responsibility for their own affairs. Raul Urzúa's study (Chapter 8) provides an example of public–private partnership in public policies in Chile, that aims at providing better public services and, in addition, is meant to contribute to activate and consolidate civil society. Jacques de Maillard's (Chapter 9) presents a comparative analysis of citizen's involvement in the field of public security in France and the United Kingdom, which also mark a change in state–civil society relations. In both cases, the claim associated with civil-society involvement is to bring policy-making closer to the people and to encourage the self-organization of citizens. But in the policy field of security, the delegation of responsibilities is far more circumscribed and, what is interesting to note, it is guided by quite different images of civil society. Thus, in the findings of these two chapters, the importance of the influence of different political cultures becomes quite evident.

In present-day Chile, the request for more direct participation of civil society and the need to change the predominant techno-bureaucratic approach to public policy-making have been voiced in many ways. According to Raul Urzúa, combining civil-society input with public administration is especially difficult in a country such as Chile, where for a number of historical reasons, civil society and social citizenship have been relatively weak, even under democratic rule. The long-term effects of this particular political culture in which the government controls most of the political power, are manifested in Urzúa's case study on two recent government projects aiming at eliminating poverty: while the official discourse might be participatory, the policies were in fact initiated and programmed top-down by techno-bureaucrats, who took the initiative 'in reaction to negative indicators, rather than to public demand' (p. 125). Nevertheless, the resulting policies have established a normative vision that contributed to new ways of modelling civil society. Incorporating a mechanism of top-down implementation and bottom-up response, the policies 'can be considered a case of transit from a state-centralized anti-poverty policy to a new, more decentralized policy in which civil society played an important role' (p. 126).

Although civil society is slowly gaining more recognition, it is not a single concept of civil society that prevails, but several alternative models which give direction. The tutelary modernization model, favouring social partnership, is still preferred by parts of the administration and the trade unions. In contrast, the projects presented by Urzúa have been successful as an empirical experiment of public–private partnership, even though they are rather an exception than the rule. According to Urzúa, the new policies have 'played a role in establishing a beneficial partnership between the state and members of civil society' (p. 127) and they have 'contributed to redefine the role of NGOs, from the defence of the poor under the military regime to the education of social citizens' (ibid.). In this approach, the development of 'social citizenship' is the common point of reference. The readiness of the executive to institutionalize social participation has not met the uniform support of all political quarters but has stimulated the demand for even more participation. Advisory councils composed of experts, elected officials and representatives of a great variety of NGOs have been established. Following Urzúa, there is evidence that this actually has downgraded the role of political parties and opened the door to organized civil society.

The idea of better public services through citizens' participation is also at the heart of the new urban security policies in France and in the UK. Jacques de Maillard's account suggests that although government took the initiative, the role of techno-bureaucrats seems at first sight much less pronounced in France and in the UK, but on closer examination, 'the professionals tend to control the demands of inhabitants top down' (p. 142).

In several Western countries, local safety policies have been marked by a call for more citizens' involvement because the exercise of the traditional monopoly held by elected officials and professionals has been subject to severe criticism. Thus, the attempt to redirect the intervention of state bureaucracies to citizen's self-organization proves once again as an 'almost consensual keyword in the context of the modernisation of political life and public administration' (p. 133). Consequently, alternative strategies have been advocated and tried, introducing new norms, such as involving voluntary organizations in crime-prevention partnerships, and using new policy instruments, such as local fora and consultative procedures. Assessing the nature and scope of these new policy instruments, and how they fit the proclaimed goals, de Maillard finds that in many regards the measures do not live up to the expectations and that both in the UK and in France, the use of participation is much more managerial than political, i.e. it is rather aiming at the improvement of the delivery of security as a public good, than political in the sense of discussing security matters as a collective end.

Apart from this similarity, focusing on the different cultural and political context conditions, de Maillard's hypothesis stands to reason that different traditions and discourses generate different kinds of state–civil society relations. The recourse to civil society differs deeply in the two countries. According to de Maillard, within the cultural and political context of the UK and with the diffusion of the Labour Party's Third Way ideology and rhetoric in the late 1990s, the appeal to 'communities' in the UK is understood as part of a strategy of citizen's 'responsibilization' which is supposed to increase the civic sense of the members of local communities and to improve their quality of life by self-engagement. 'In this process, the government hands over responsibility to private actors, while at the same time supporting them to develop the necessary competence' (p. 143). Despite a concurrent problem definition, namely that security can no longer be the task of the police only, and the proclamation of nearly identical aims, namely increased contributions by society, the policy in France was framed in a different language. The catchwords were 'proximité' and 'co-production', transporting the image of public policies better adjusted to the needs of the citizens. 'Community' is a concept alien to the French public discourses which 'are pervaded by republican symbols, emphasizing the collective basis and the unity of French society' (p. 138).

Consequently, the approach and the reception of activating civil society in France and the UK differed considerably. The result, however, was again quite similar. The political move towards increased civic involvement was not very welcomed by the professionals in charge, and the emphasis on efficiency curtailed the role of civil-society initiatives. Thus, the detailed analysis by de Maillard reveals 'a mitigated image of the so-called return to civil society' (p. 145).

Assessing the benefit of civil-society involvement in government

The now so popular discourse on civil society is nourished by ideas about new modes of governance that are perceived to better fit post-modern democracies. A core hypothesis is that civil-society involvement furthers not just the representation of the wide diversity of societal interests but also deliberation between the variety of actors involved and, thus, will bring about more responsive and efficient government. In Chapter 11, Yannis Papadopoulos takes a critical view. He concentrates on the preconditions and dynamics of deliberative governance, in 'a plea for more knowledge on forms of policy-making that include civil-society actors, instead of their idealisation that is often found in official discourses' (p. 179).

Papadopoulos subscribes to the idea that the idealization of civil society goes along with distrust of institutions and actors of traditional representative democracy. Corresponding with the findings of Hélène Michel in this volume (Chapter 7), he refers to the European Union as an illustration of the depreciation of partisan actors for the benefit of participatory governance through the incorporation of civil-society actors. It is expected from governance mechanisms based on strong civil-society involvement to perform better in terms of quality of deliberation, and as a result in terms of problem-solving capacity, policy efficiency and acceptance by target-groups. Yet, as Papadopoulos' critical analysis of the modes of deliberative governance and the varying context conditions for deliberative democracy reveals, such claims are disputable both on theoretical grounds and on the basis of the available empirical evidence. One of the most obvious inherent paradoxical effects is that the process of deliberation leads, on the one hand, to communication and understanding and, on the other hand, it brings to the surface the more fundamental underlying conflicts. Another intrinsic dilemma bears on the precondition of publicity: democratic legitimacy demands open discourses but contested issues are often negotiated more effectively in terms of reaching a compromise when dealt with off the record.

The beneficial effect of civil-society involvement, therefore, is dubious because it presents various dilemmas and paradoxes and, last but not least, unresolved questions of power. Papadopoulos draws the attention to this latter aspect which is often neglected in the civil-society discourse: the discrepancy of political weight in the representation of civil-society organizations increases with the importance of political fora. The lower the threshold of access, the lower is the impact on decision-making. Whereas online-consultations are open and easily accessible, consultation and decision-making bodies and public–private partnerships in the implementation of policies are difficult to join. Preference for expert knowledge, preconceived agendas and definition of the stakes and last, but not least, differences in resources, epitomize the vitiation of the precondition of equal access. Thus, civil-society involvement in deliberative governance seems aptly described as 'governance *with some of* the people' (V. Schmidt 2006: 28–29, as quoted by Papadopoulos p. 188). Furthermore, Papadopoulos offers a 'pessimistic' hypothesis, saying that it might be 'that governance bodies hardly have any influence, because they are embedded in an encompassing institutional framework with several 'veto points', performing thus primarily a symbolic function' (p. 189). As soon as civil-society involvement is exposed as 'window dressing', the myth of participatory governance will wither away.

Conclusion

In this book, the shift in the meaning and application of civil society has been assessed, from citizen protests to incorporation into public action. Civil-society involvement is sometimes presented as a panacea for a more sensitive reaction to the variety of publics that is more open to the voices of disadvantaged groups. Analysing the conditions of validity of these optimistic hypotheses and comparing the different contexts in which the civil-society concept is used, we have found various inherent predicaments and contradictions. Our analytical model has provided a tool for a comparative analysis demonstrating that the conceptualization of civil society differs profoundly depending on the functional role attributed to it. Furthermore, the criterion of 'change agent' discloses differences in framing state–society relations and political objectives. Nevertheless, the case studies presented in this volume also expose the importance of political, social and cultural differences.

The overall implications of the respective findings are manifold; therefore we will focus our conclusions on a few essential aspects. First, the instrumentalization of civil society is ubiquitous but cannot be simply equated with 'use' and 'misuse' of the concept. As the shifting roles and concepts of civil society in the context of Eastern Europe's and South Africa's democratic revolutions have made us aware, political intentions can readily be activated, submerged or redirected by a certain dynamic in society. Second, it can be consequently argued that use and misuse of civil society is rather linked to the issue of its political entanglement. Taking this as a criterion, we can state that in most cases under discussion in this volume, citizens' emancipation has been at the core of the civil-society concept. Italy and India are exceptions in the sense that citizens' emancipation is also alleged in the civil rhetoric, but the notion has been distorted as civil society has become mired in politics. Third, we have seen that despite the differences due to particular political situations and prevailing ideologies in the various countries, the general discourse has followed more or less a certain chronology. At present, a stage has been reached in which, arguably, strategies of civil-society empowerment and participation are losing their optimistic appeal. This holds true both for the concept of civil society as an agent of democratic transformation and in regard to the proposition that civil society contributes to good governance. But the history can be read in two ways: the examples of the European Union and China underline that the civil-society myth and the promises associated with it are partly ill-conceived and, above all, do not match reality. However, although the results tend to remain way behind the expectations, the appeal to the concept and the new strategies and approaches which came with it, has raised the awareness. Likewise, inviting civil society to improve public services may be interpreted as just another attempt to compensate for poor government performance. But activating citizens top-down opens windows of opportunity to enhance grass-roots participation as the case studies of Chile, France and the UK demonstrate. Thus, last but not least, a minimal general consensus is established on the principle that citizens' voices should be heard, and the call for institutions in which citizens can express their demands is broadly echoed in the extensive discussion on new modes of governance.

Note

1 We use the term in analogy to innovation studies and business administration (Rogers 2003).

References

Amna, E. (2006) 'Still a trustworthy ally? Civil society and the transformation of Scandinavian democracy', *Journal of Civil Society*, 2 (1): 1–20.

Dahl, R. (2006) *On Political Equality*, New Haven: Yale University Press.

Habermas, J. (1996) *Between Facts and Norms. Contributions to a Discourse Theory of Law and Democracy*, Cambridge: Polity Press.

Milner, H. (2002) *Civic Literacy: How Informed Citizens Make Democracy Work*, Hanover: University Press of New England.

Rogers, E.M. (2003) *Diffusion of Innovations* (5th edn), New York: Free Press.

Rothstein, B. (2006) 'Civil society and the state in Sweden: the case of alcohol policy and the temperance movement', unpublished manuscript, Department of Political Science, University of Gothenburg.

WRR Scientific Council for Government Policy (2007) *Rediscovering Europe in the Netherlands*, Amsterdam: Amsterdam University Press.

Zittel, T. (2007) 'Participatory democracy and political participation: can participatory engineering bring citizens back in?', in T. Zittel and D. Fuchs (eds) *Participatory Democracy and Political Participation*, New York: Routledge, 9–28.

Index

For Product Safety Concerns and Information please contact our EU
representative GPSR@taylorandfrancis.com
Taylor & Francis Verlag GmbH, Kaufingerstraße 24, 80331 München, Germany